"The antidote to hubris, to overween-
ing pride, is irony, that capacity to dis-
cover and systematize ideas."

Ralph Ellison

Edited by Mary Cassells

First Printing, 2019

ISBN 9781089633969

Imprint: Independently published

Contact the author: al@thedealhack.com or linkedin.com/in/amcquade

www.thedealhack.com

# THE MOTHER OF ALL HACKS

"They're going to die," explained an engineer to Flight Director Gene Kranz. The flight surgeon clarified the $CO_2$ filter problem. "They're already up to eight on the gauges, anything over 15 and you get impaired judgment, blackouts and the beginning of brain asphyxia." Two hundred thousand miles away, Apollo 13 was limping back to Earth after an oxygen tank exploded, crippling the craft. Having sent the immortal message, "Houston, we've had a problem here," the three astronauts on board survived the blast, but they were forced to power down the command module and move into the two-person lunar module for the journey home. The crew had limited power, extreme loss of cabin heat, and a shortage of drinking water. As if the situation wasn't precarious enough, the carbon dioxide removal system was now about to fail in the lunar module and kill all three astronauts on board.

"What about the scrubbers on the command module?" asked Kranz.

"They take square cartridges. The ones on the Lunar Module are round," replied the engineer.

"Then I suggest you gentlemen invent a way to put a square peg into a round hole. Rapidly," replied Kranz.

Working against the clock, one of the most famous "hacks" in history began. A team of engineers took on the challenge. With copies of the available materials they worked through the night to design an adapter for the $CO_2$ cartridges. Using only what the astronauts had on board, including hoses from spacesuits, tube socks, and duct tape, the improvised filter was successful, and the crew returned safely to Earth on April 17, 1970, six days after launch.

Putting together and running the "hack" was a key reason for the success of the return mission. NASA, at the time, had a famously bureaucratic system of decision making, a system that had resulted in two filters with the same job, on the same mission, but one was square, and one was round. NASA was so bureaucratic it prompted the famous Saturn V rocket scientist Wernher von Braun to say, "Our two greatest problems are gravity and paperwork. We can lick gravity, but sometimes the paperwork is overwhelming."[1]

With the lives of three crewmembers at stake, and the clock ticking, the traditional bureaucratic approach would not work, and so the rules were changed and a hack was created with a sense of urgency to solve the problem.

Transforming sales performance has a similar slow and bureaucratic feel, where change seems so hard it gets kicked into the long grass of a distant future. Or worse, change efforts that last for months, or even years, fail to deliver the expected improvements in sales performance. It's time to rethink the traditional cumbersome approach to sales performance optimization and implement the Deal Hack, *with maximum results in a minimum amount of time.*

# CONTENTS

# FIGURES AND MODELS

# INTRODUCTION

"... hacking just means building something quickly or testing the boundaries of what can be done."

Mark Zuckerberg


"*C*an we not just short circuit the sales training process and use the tools and techniques directly in the deals?*" asked Brian Sharp, my client. Brian was Global VP of Commercial Management at Sealed Air Corporation, a multi-billion-dollar multinational in the throes of transforming their sales force. Brian was frustrated that, once again, they had rolled out a sales training initiative but the sales people were still not using the required process, tools and techniques. Intellectually they knew how to use the tools, but they were not doing so in practice. Despite significant investments in sales training and coaching by the business, there was a significant gap between what the sales teams were trained to do and what they were actually doing. As a result, sales performance was moving in the wrong direction. *"Yes,"* I replied to Brian, *"We can hack the process."*

After 20 years of leading and consulting in sales enablement for a number of global organizations, I have seen more than most what works and what doesn't work when it comes to organizational sales effectiveness and sales transformation. I recently asked an old friend who has a similar amount of experience in sales training and coaching for major companies, *"Do you not mind that the sales people you're training and coaching will not change and will not improve?"* *"It's all part of the job,"* he replied in a matter of fact way. The most shocking thing about this conversation is the acceptance that failure in sales transformation is almost inevitable. We all know what we should do in a sales process, but for some inexplicable reason we do something else, and this failure exists at all levels in sales organizations. This was the failure that Brian Sharp had witnessed in his sales organization and, through frustration, wanted to develop another path beyond sales training and coaching, the primary tools in the sales organizational development toolkit. Since that conversation with Brian, I've been running Deal Hacks for over six years now, across a number of sales organizations. In that time, I've perfected the Deal Hack process and scaled Deal Hacks through sales organizations. I've written this book to share my findings and demonstrate what deal hacks are, how they can be implemented and used alongside sales training and coaching to maximize organizational sales performance and transformation.

The film 'Alien' was conceptually described, to would-be investors, as "Jaws in Space." That was because there were two key concepts that came together to make the film. Firstly, a there was suspense concept like that found in the film 'Jaws' and secondly there was the concept of it being in outer space. Deal Hacks are not held in outer space, and only occasionally can be described as a 'horror', but we can use the same technique to describe them conceptually: "Team based deal reviews in a workshop." The first concept is that deals are reviewed, but this is done in a team-based workshop environment rather than the traditional one to one environment. They are not training because training focuses on skills gaps and Deal Hacks focus on improving the deals. Deal Hacks are similar to coaching, but they are specifically 'Deal Coaching' in a group setting. Traditional coaching focuses on developing the coachee. Improving the deal outcome is the most important outcome of a Deal Hack. Improving deal outcomes has a more direct and immediate impact on sales results. Importantly, it is this focus on winning results that creates the engine of change which pulls change through the organization. It's easier to see the immediate and direct impact on their deals, something that is harder with more abstract alternatives like sales training and traditional coaching. Through Deal Hack reporting we're able to give the sales leadership insights into the health of their deals across the whole sales organization. This helps them to make better decisions when it comes to leading and managing sales performance and resources. As we'll see in part one, our understanding of where our performance gaps are, or where they are not, is often significantly wide of the mark. This means that many sales performance interventions are solving the wrong problems, and that is a major reason that many sales transformation programs are ineffective. They have a fundamental flaw running through them. Deal Hacks don't suffer from this problem, and they can make diagnosis more accurate for training and coaching interventions that sit alongside.

Deal Hacks narrow the gap between what we intellectually know we should do to win sales, and what we actually do in practice. But there's one more thing. When designing sales negotiation training for LinkedIn, the Director of Sales, LinkedIn Learning Solutions, Ami Borsetti, said to me, "Al, we don't have the time to do all that design and development; we need results now. We're building the plane as we're flying it!" This describes the typical business environment today that we're all experiencing. The urgency and the desire to improve sales more quickly, and for the sales populations to adapt more rapidly to market changes. Companies don't have months to spend designing and launching sales training programs anymore. By this time the opportunity has been lost. To give you an idea of how quickly Deal Hacks can diagnose and fix sales performance gaps, I recently held a Deal Hack with a team of inside software sales people. We worked on four deals and improved the deals while sharing best practices and insights across the team. From the results of the Deal Hack the team agreed they all had gaps in value creation in the sales process. The next week we held a training workshop to fill these gaps based on the deals we'd hacked. The time from diagnosis to fix was *one week*, and we directly improved four deals in the process. No skills gap analysis, no vendor/program selection, and no scoping. No sales people saying they were too busy or didn't need the training. The same company rolled out value based sales training the year before. One of the metrics used to measure success was how many of the sales people were creating a value based business case for their prospects. One year after the sales training only five of the one hundred deals forecast had a value based business case. Time to roll out the training again? No. We implemented Deal Hacks and in the next quarter there were 50 value based business cases, moving the value selling metric by 10 times. The results of the training alone were considered a failure, but implementing Deal Hacks turned the program into a success. The sales training focused on how the sales people should sell, while the Deal Hacks focused on challenging and supporting the sales people to help them change how they sold. The two are completely different problems to solve as we'll see. Changing sales performance through Deal Hacks is performed in-field, it aligns with how sales people think, and how they work. Training does not do that. The result of the combined approach is an immediate and direct impact on sales, which is instantly measurable, and aligns with today's fast-paced business environment. From these successes, momentum is created, people buy-in and sales performance is transformed.

This book shows what Deal Hacks are, why they are needed, why they work, how they fit alongside traditional training and coaching, and how they can be implemented easily and successfully in a complex business-to-business sales organization. I've created a simple five step process called HACKS to guide you through the book:

Figure 1 - Deal Hacks Framework

This is a sequential journey that culminates in improved sales performance and sales results by setting up a program of 'Deal Hacks.' Like any significant journey, there are necessary stops along the way. Each of the five parts in this book build on each other. In Part One we look at the blind spots sales people and sales leaders have that can shut down our ability to adapt and change how we sell. We look at the problem of diminishing returns and understand the limitations of focusing too much on how people sell by simply using more sales training and coaching to improve sales performance, and not effectively working on the separate issue of changing behaviors. In Part Two we look into the brain of the individual to understand how to design performance interventions that work with the sales brain and not against it, which facilitates change. In Part Three we look at how to create a growth mind-set culture in sales organizations that increases performance instead of shutting it down. In Part Four we look at what Deal Hacks are and how they take learning outside of the classroom and put it back into the workflow, creating the engine of change. In Part Five we look at how to set up a Deal Hack program and scale Deal Hacks across complex business to business sales organizations. Tempting though it is, jumping to the 'solution' in Part Four, will leave you lost and confused. Please don't allow your Social Brain to make the decision to short-circuit the process. We need you to switch on your Intellectual Brain to make the best decision, because as you'll see in Part Two, Social Brain thinking is one of the root causes of low sales performance.

# PART ONE

# HIGHLIGHT THE BLIND SPOTS

D espite the highest levels of support and resources in history, more and more salespeople today are missing their sales targets. It appears the more support we put into our sales teams, the less performance we get out; a diminishing return we'll call the *Sales Performance Paradox*. In the first part of the book we aim to understand the extent of this problem and propose a solution. Part One comprises three chapters:

I.  **Chapter One** shows that sales organizations and sales people, more than other professions, are unaware of and failing to adopt proven techniques known to improve productivity and effectiveness. In short they are failing to adapt and failing to change.

II.  **Chapter Two** shows this is because sales leaders and sales people are particularly prone to a set of cognitive biases that create blind spots, reducing awareness of their performance capabilities and skills gaps.

III.   **Chapter Three** reveals how blind spots can be reduced and the cognitive biases that cause them can be minimized by improving self-awareness, through a growth mind-set. Self-aware sales leaders and sales people with a growth mind-set take advantage of the support they are given, can adapt and change, minimizing the *Sales Performance Paradox.*

# CHAPTER 1
# DIMINISHING
# RETURNS

*"Ideas are a dime a dozen. People who implement them are price-less."*

*Mary Kay Ash*

I n 1963, after 25 years in direct selling, Mary Kay Ash quit her job as National Training Director at World Gift. Once again, a man whom she had trained was promoted above her and given twice her salary. After resigning, Ash decided to write a business book to help overcome the negative effects of her experience. Sitting at the kitchen table, she made two lists on a notepad - one contained the good things she had seen in sales organizations, the other, the things she would improve. When she reflected upon the contents of this manifesto, she challenged herself to put it into action and fulfil her dreams of running her own company. Ash then used the manifesto to launch her company, Mary Kay Cosmetics, going on to become one of the best business leaders of all time. In 2003 she was voted the greatest female entrepreneur by Baylor University.[2] According to *Direct Selling News*, Mary Kay was the sixth largest direct selling company in the world in 2015, with a wholesale volume of US$3.7 billion,[3] with 3.5 million sales consultants.[4]

Ash instinctively knew what it took to make a successful salesperson and to make a great sales organization. She was ahead of her time, identifying a number of ways to create competitive advantage by adapting her sales force and doing things differently. For example, far earlier than other business leaders, Ash identified emotional intelligence to be a key determinant of sales success. The standard profile for sales success at the time was a man whose primary communication mode was transmit, rather than listen, and their expertise was measured by the ability to a close a deal. Ash famously smashed this stereotype by specifically recruiting women instead of men. The predominantly female sales force that Ash created was perhaps the most significant driver of success for her business. *"Ideas are a dime a dozen. People who implement them are priceless,"* said Ash at the time, and this is the key. Ash not only saw the opportunity to innovate, she *also* implemented it.

Most sales organizations today are less male dominated than when Ash set up her company in the early 1960s, but my own anecdotal experience suggests that sales teams today remain significantly more male than female. Sales consultant Steve Martin studied the similarities and differences between men and women in sales and has also seen this phenomenon, "Over the past decade I have noticed a significant decrease in the percentage of women in business-to-business sales within the companies I consult with. While some vertical industries such as the pharmaceutical and healthcare industries employ a higher proportion of women, the percentage of women in other vertical industries such as high-technology has fallen dramatically. In fact, I would estimate the sales force composition to be over 85 percent male in seven of the last ten technology companies I have worked with."[5]

Dana Kanze has found, similarly, that although women found 38 percent of US companies, they only get two percent of the venture funding[6]. Kanze has shed light on why these biases exist, how they can be identified and how they can be overcome. But despite these insights, and despite Ash highlighting gender bias as a negative contributor toward sales success back in the early 1960s, organizations remain a long way from turning gender bias from a disadvantage into a competitive advantage, in the way that Ash did. The negative consequences of failing to capitalize on the complete pool of available talent in sales is reduced sales figures, slower deal cycles and lost margin. Unless you've just arrived in a time machine from the mid part of the 20$^{th}$ century, you should already know this. So the real question we should be asking ourselves is why are we not converting this type of proven insight into competitive advantage? Let me be really clear. This book is *not* about the different performance capabilities of male and female sales people, although that would make for a compelling read. The example of Ash breaking with the traditional gender bias and identifying a new and innovative approach to sales performance is just one of many sales innovations that she and others have proved successful in the field. This book seeks to explain why such innovations do not gain acceptance and traction in sales organizations today, even though they have been proven and, like the gender bias example, often march out of step with mainstream business culture. We look at the gap between where sales organizations are and where they could be, the missed opportunities that exist in the sales profession because we seem incapable of adopting such insights. This failure to adopt proven successful strategies is what we call the Sales Performance Paradox.

The Sales Performance Paradox runs much wider and deeper than just this example of gender bias. There are countless more examples we will see, but let us return to Ash who understood how to innovate and adapt her sales organization to create competitive advantage beyond gender. Ash challenged other sacred cows of selling that still exist today, in particular the requirement to have a successful past track record of selling to be recruited. It's easy to understand why people think that experience in selling will help predict future sales success, the link between experience and success is baked into our collective consciousness. Indeed, Malcolm Gladwell put some pseudo-science behind this notion in his book *Outliers, "Researchers have settled on what they believe is the magic number for true expertise: ten thousand hours."*[7] After ten thousand hours you can consider yourself a master of whatever you've been doing. Ten thousand hours is about ten years, which means that Ash would have qualified in sales mastery by some distance. Have you achieved sales mastery? How many salespeople have achieved mastery in your sales organization? How many companies can say that collectively their sales population has achieved sales mastery? If you measure mastery by Gladwell's ten thousand hours rule, then quite a few will have worn out their shoe leather on the long and windy path of sales, clocking up the ten thousand hours of mastery. Is it that simple? Sadly the weight of scientific evidence, when it comes to sales, is contrary to the 10,000-hour rule[8]. An empirical study of lawyers learning to be negotiators saw no correlation between a negotiator's effectiveness and their years in practice[9]. The 10,000-hours concept originated in a 1993 paper written by Anders Ericsson, a Professor at the University of Colorado, called 'The Role of Deliberate Practice in the Acquisition of Expert Performance.' *"The 10,000-hour rule was invented by Malcolm Gladwell who stated that researchers have settled on what they believe is the magic number for true expertise: 10,000 hours. Gladwell cited our research on expert musicians as a stimulus for his provocative generalization to a magical number,"* Ericsson said, casting doubt on the 10,000-hour rule[10].

These doubts align with the anecdotal experience of many sales enablement professionals that longevity in the role is not an identifier of sales mastery, but it can paradoxically become a barrier to learning and growth. Not unsurprisingly the length of tenure was not on Ash's list of "good things" she'd seen in companies. Ash went exactly the opposite way and hired people with *no sales experience.[11]* A clean slate onto which she could write her formula for success. The removal of the 10,000 hours shackles is good news for us all in sales because it indicates that we can onboard new sales people relatively quickly and effectively. It is not necessary to always fish in the same talent pools, which is an issue some industries and sales forces continue to wrestle with. Perhaps best of all, it shows that we don't have to be held hostage by salespeople with long tenure who threaten to leave; a trend that is surprisingly common in successful companies who inadvertently create entitled salespeople.

Ash challenged the status quo of selling in the 1960s and created competitive advantage for her company in the process. It seems, however, like others who followed with successful innovations, these lessons have still to be learned by sales organizations today. The gap between what we should do in sales, and what we actually do, is the reason for this book. The implications of this are stark. Let's take a quick pulse check of the sales profession today:

- 59% of salespeople are hitting target[12]
- 65 to 70% of salespeople consistently exhibit average performance [12]
- 55% of people engaged in selling are in the wrong profession [13]

- 53.4% of the time salespeople are wrong about the predicted outcome of a deal. [14]
- 80 percent of new products and services fail within six months. [15]
- 88% of CEOs say their organization's sales performance is 'very poor' to 'average. [16]

My anecdotal experience, in addition to this data, indicates that there are pockets of sales success out there, but there remains massive room for improvement overall. We all intuitively know this to be the case. If you're in the sales profession then you know things are getting harder. If you're not in sales, you may have the feeling that the sales force in your organization is not performing as well as it could be. The above data suggests that you're not alone. There is a recognizable and predictable pattern across industries and geographies, and the pattern is that despite the highest levels of support in history, salespeople are finding it increasingly hard to hit sales targets. Twenty billion dollars is being spent every year on sales training in the United States alone.[17] Research by Accenture shows that Chief Sales Officers (CSOs) have increased annual training spending considerably since 2012. Nearly 45 percent are now spending between $2,501 and $5,000 per year on each sales representative.[18] Despite the uplift in training spending, CSOs are surprisingly unclear what measurable improvements result from this investment. The obvious question must be, "*If we're spending so much on supporting our salespeople, why is there such a global performance gap?*" This diminishing return we call *The Sales Performance Paradox*. Let's reframe the statistics above to demonstrate how far we are from achieving sales success:

- 59% of airline pilots land on the targeted runway
- 65 to 70% of surgeons exhibit average performance
- 55% of people engaged in nursing are in the wrong profession

- 53.4% of the time doctors are wrong about the predicted outcome of a treatment
- 80 percent of new cars don't start.
- 88% of head teachers say their school's performance is 'very poor' to 'average.'

I'm sure you wouldn't get onto that airplane, and nor would you set foot in that operating theatre. You wouldn't send your children to that school. These fictitious figures uncover the unique way in which sales performance is treated compared to the performance of other professionals of commensurate stature. The contention of this book is that those of us who work in or around sales have become desensitized to the systematic volume of acceptable failure in the sales profession. We accept that failure is a natural consequence of the sales environment due to the risks and uncertainties involved. Sales departments stand alone in their capacity to suffer 40 to 50 percent failure rates on defined key performance indicators (KPIs). In all other departments, a 40 to 50 percent failure would be considered a spectacular fail, warranting heads on sticks in the company foyer. No other population in commercial companies would be allowed to tolerate these levels of failure. *"The accounts are only 60% correct, so we only paid 60% of our taxes. The government won't mind, it's tough to measure these things. I left messages for John, but he didn't call me back with the figures I needed."* It is unlikely in other areas of corporate life that such levels of failure would be tolerated as openly and as frequently. There is a significant opportunity cost to the underperforming status quo that has developed in sales, and a massive opportunity exists if we can fix the problem, or even just reduce the problem by a fraction.

Should we compare selling to other professions at all? Selling is different, after all. Or at least I'm told so, on a frequent basis, by salespeople and non-salespeople alike. It can be conceded that closing a sale is never a 100 percent certainty, but that is exactly why we have pipelines with a multiple of prospects. If the closure rate is 1:4 for a salesperson and their target is $100k, they need a pipeline of at least $400k that is replenished as deals come out of the pipeline. Known as "The Law of Replacement" you must constantly be pushing new opportunities into your pipeline to replace the opportunities that will naturally fall out. And, you must do so at a rate that matches or exceeds your closing ratio. So when we see annual targets not being met, it is not because of the uncertainties of selling as a profession. We know that not every deal will close, and we should know our closure rate, so we should know if we're going to hit the sales target or not, well in advance of the end of the month, quarter or year. The uncertainty of landing deals, per se, does therefore not explain why so many salespeople are not hitting their sales targets. It's just a smokescreen.

If we look at the professions preceding, they have institutions and regulatory bodies that apply a minimum of two levels of regulatory challenge to their membership. The first level of challenge is the barrier to entry. *"If you don't have the credentials, you're not getting in."* Typically, you won't be allowed to operate on a person or fly a passenger aircraft unless you have the qualifications to do so. The second level of challenge is that these professions work to the processes, procedures, and safeguards laid down in their respective fields. I think you know where I'm going. There are typically no barriers to entry for sales people. No gold-plated sales qualifications required. No required letters after your name. There are also no agreed and defined universal sales processes to work to that have been created by an external regulator with an adequate level of perceived authority. According to the Australian Institute of Management, approximately 32% of salespeople have a sales qualification.[19] This is significantly higher than in my personal experience, but again imagine if 32% of teachers, lawyers, airline pilots, and doctors were qualified. According to Hubspot, 15% of salespeople seek out their own training and coaching, which confirms professional development is a minor concern to at least 85% of salespeople.[20] Selling is a profession with no checks and no balances. It's a bit of a free-for-all out there in the sales world.

This may start to explain why the brand of the sales profession is suffering as much as the sales figures. There are generally two opposing views of selling. The first is very positive. Benjamin Franklin's name can often be seen on lists of the 'Greatest Sales People.' As a child, his family was poor, and he sold printed pamphlets in the streets to survive. His sales ability saw him rise through the political and social strata until he became one of the founding fathers of the United States. This is a very positive rags-to-riches story. It was his innate sales skills that enabled this to happen. In this example, selling is seen as noble and sales skills readily transferable to other positive areas of life. Other people have undertaken this arduous journey and are admired for doing so. Kenny Troutt, the founder of Excel Communications and worth £1.5 billion, paid his way through college by selling life insurance. John Paul DeJoria worth £2.9 billion created John Paul Mitchell Systems and sold the shampoo door-to-door while living in his car. Ralph Lauren worth $6.8 billion was once a sales clerk at Brooks Brothers. The list goes on. These people are considered natural salespeople and have used their sales skills to become successful, build fortunes, and cross class boundaries.

But there is another side to selling. In the book, *To Sell Is Human,* Daniel Pink describes the common view of perhaps more average salespeople[21]. 'Pushy' was the primary word used to describe salespeople. Pushiness is how bad salespeople are characterized, and importantly the word pushy reveals two insights:

1) Pushiness implies the buyer is being pushed into some-

thing they don't want to do.

2) Pushiness originates from the self-interest of the seller pushing their agenda over and above the agenda of the buyer.

I've repeated Pink's experiment. But instead of interviewing non-salespeople, I repeated the experiment with salespeople. The question asked of over 600 salespeople was, "What single words come to mind when you think of "sales?".

Figure 2 - How sales people describe the sales profession

The results are remarkably similar to the results of Pink's research. It would appear that salespeople have no loftier view of their own profession than non-salespeople do. Interestingly, when asked if that applied to themselves, the answer was negative. It only applies to the other salespeople. Pink's finding is really important because it goes straight to the heart of the issue and identifies the single biggest reason for the negative view of selling. Put simply, people don't like being pushed to do something they do not want to do, by a person whose overriding involvement is self-interest.

We recruit salespeople with a strong self-interest into sales positions, in an attempt to harness this characteristic for our own gain. Ironically, it is this propensity toward pushiness and self-interest that is harming the sales profession as a whole. According to Forrester, *"Executive buyers tell us that only 20% of the salespeople they meet with are successful in achieving their expectations and creating value. As a consequence, 1 million US B2B salespeople will lose their jobs to self-service e-commerce by the year 2020.*[22]" The self-interest, in the long term at least, is counter productive. This view is backed up by the Corporative Executive Board (CEB) who have found that, "On average, customers are 57 percent of the way through a typical purchase process before proactively reaching out to a supplier's sales rep for their direct input on whatever it is that they're doing." [23] These statistics are telling us that customers no longer see salespeople as an asset when making a purchasing decision. The gap between how salespeople sell and how customers want to buy has never been wider. And it's getting wider.

There is a high price to pay for this customer disengagement. Customers are investing in procurement to manage their suppliers through the buying process, something that salespeople once had a monopoly over. These purchasing professionals have the analytical skills and tools to calculate, communicate and capture value for their own organizations. They have adapted, changed and taken advantage of the latest knowledge. The outcome of which is good for the buying organizations as they are increasing the amount of value they can capture from suppliers in the buying process. The consequence for sellers is that they are increasingly losing significant margin in the deals. Differentiators that have taken significant resources to develop by the sellers are not being capitalized upon at the point of sale. Frustrations build in the selling company. Non-salespeople are frustrated at the lack of sales performance and point the finger at the sales teams.

Salespeople are frustrated because the power seems to rest with the buyers and nobody else seems to understand this. Differentiators appear good on paper, but do not provide the differentiation needed to beat the competition and achieve the list price at the negotiating table. Sometimes it seems that the buyers are having the party and the sellers are crying into their beers. *"There is going to be a big shakeout in sales,"* says Eric Esfahanian, a Senior Vice President at sales-data analytics firm Gryphon Networks. *"The bottom 10% or 20% of business-to-business salespeople, especially those who are selling a simple product with a short sales cycles, are going to lose out to B2B e-commerce."*[24] Esfahanian's words are being played out as companies swap sales roles for more scalable and cost-effective online alternatives. As technology, and, in particular, artificial intelligence and augmented reality advance, this trend will only increase. Who is at fault for this tectonic shift in the fortunes of the sales profession? Is it the fault of the salespeople? Should they be holding more meetings and asking better questions? Is it the fault of the sales leaders? Should they be out with their salespeople instead of hiding behind spreadsheets? Is it the fault of companies for being out of touch, setting targets too high, and getting the products and pricing wrong? Is it simply the train of inevitability approaching?

Some sales jobs will indeed be lost to e-commerce. More will be lost to artificial intelligence and these are inevitable. However, there is nothing inevitable about the decline of the sales profession that we see. Customers will always need to make purchase decisions, and there will always be an opportunity to help them do so. Whether or not the sales profession can adapt and become the 'go to' person for helping buyers to make better purchase decisions remains to be seen. It is that adaptation that is the central question. How can sales organizations adapt to change because there's a significant body of evidence to suggest that sales organizations are systematically incapable of doing so. The customer of the early part of the 20th century is very different from the customer of the early part of the 21st century. Despite customers changing beyond all recognition, the sales profession is mind bogglingly slow to adapt, and in some cases not adapting to change at all. We saw at the start of this chapter the foresight of Mary Ash to recruit women into her sales force in the 1960s. However, despite demonstrating how successful this strategy can be, men still predominate in sales. This is one example of many, and we will see more examples as we move through the book. But why does the sales profession find it so hard to adapt and change?

In order to change, people must learn new skills, and the skills salespeople need to learn are knowledge-based skills. Peter Drucker popularized the phrase 'Knowledge Worker' in his book, The Effective Executive when differentiating between knowledge workers and manual workers. Manual workers, according to Drucker, work with their hands and produce goods or services. Knowledge workers work with their heads, not hands, and produce ideas, knowledge, and information. In a U.S. study[25] to assess whether computers could replace people for routine and non-routine forms of work, salespeople were classified as knowledge workers, but came under the lower level category of "complex communication" and not the highest category of "expert thinking."

1) **Expert thinking** includes solving problems outside of rules-based solutions, with computers assisting but not substituting. As well as high-level research and creative work, this might also include the mechanic who can identify a solution to a problem that computer-based diagnostics could not.

2) **Complex communication** includes interacting with other people to acquire or convey information and persuading others of their implications, with computers assisting but unlikely to replace – examples might include

some managers, teachers, and salespeople.

There is clearly a broad spectrum of different kinds of sales-people, but there is a common move across most business-to-business (B2B) sales organizations towards solution selling. Companies are increasingly investing in product and service innovation to defend against the forces of commoditization. Such companies are collectively experiencing a reduction in time from product launch to market maturity. They not only need salespeople who can capture the increased value of this innovation, but can adapt and capture that value more quickly. It is surely the case that B2B sales populations need to be in the category of *'expert thinker.'* After all, *'high-level research'* is required to understand prospects' businesses and differentiate from the competition. *'Creative work'* is required to map the changing innovations of the solution to the changing customer needs. Persuasion is needed to align the team of buyers behind the solution.

The juxtaposition of communicator and expert thinker is a clear marker of the evolving change that is happening in the sales profession. 20 years ago a sales population that fitted the 'communicator' banding could thrive. Communicating features, advantages, and benefits was a core sales skill. This is because of the asynchronous nature of the communications in the typical sales relationships at the time. Sellers had knowledge that the buyer needed to make a purchase decision, and sellers managed the flow of that information. Sellers would use that information as leverage to get what they needed to maximize the size of the sale and to close the sale. Sellers would give information in return for information that lead to a sale. The problem for modern salespeople is that they no longer have exclusivity over the types of information they once had. This means they no longer have that leverage. Unsurprisingly customers are going to other less biased and less demanding sources for that information, for which they provide nothing in return. So today, having a sales population of communicators that do not have the skills of expert thinkers is the kiss of death to any sales organization. Salespeople need to be expert thinkers because they need to add value to the sales process beyond communicating, and that is typically through analyzing, modeling, and creating solutions. All of these are expert thinking skills and tasks.

You may be thinking, "*Of course we want our salespeople to be expert thinkers, why wouldn't we?*" Indeed, the question is not why wouldn't we? The real question is, do we? Do we actively recruit, nurture, support and reward expert thinking in our salespeople? There are a couple of ways to identify expert thinkers. The first is that they can identify how they are thinking. They have the ability to recognize and influence their own ways of thinking. Monitoring your own thinking is what psychologists call metacognition (*meta* being Greek for "about"). We'll see in the next chapter that salespeople can be particularly *unaware* of their thinking and particularly prone to blind spots. The second way to identify an expert thinker is by seeing if they regularly update and improve their thinking. Expert thinkers are not born fully formed into mobile encyclopedic brains, they develop. Like athletes, there's a requirement for training and developing. This story from *Made to Stick* by Chip Heath and Dan Heath helps to shine a light on the issue of developing our thinking:

Teacher of mathematics, Dean Sherman is asked rhetorically by his students, "*When will we ever need to actually use algebra?*" Sherman replied, "*Never, you will never use this. People don't lift weights so that they will be prepared should, one day, someone knock them over on the street and lay a barbell across their chest. You lift weights so that you can knock over a defensive lineman, or carry your groceries or lift your grandchildren without being sore the next day. You do math exercises so that you can improve your ability to think logically so that you can be a better lawyer, doctor, architect, prison warden or parent. MATH IS MENTAL WEIGHT TRAINING. It is a means to an end (for most people), not an end in itself.*[26]

Dean Sherman makes it abundantly clear that succeeding intellectually requires that we engage in the process of our own personal growth. If we had sales populations of expert thinkers, there would be evidence of them engaging in their personal growth or, as Sherman calls it, their mental weight training. So where is the evidence? For most professionals, the evidence of their learning on the job is classed as Continuous Professional Development (CPD). They undertake CPD to develop their expertise and ensure they remain at a minimum level of competence commensurate with their professional requirements. CPD has the benefit of exercising the brain. It also has the benefit of updating on changes and developments in a profession. How are the sales brains of our sales populations when it comes to CPD? Getting ripped abdominals through a torturous discipline of mental weight training? Or atrophying like a small lonely walnut through lack of use? How do sales populations compare when it comes to undertaking CPD and exercising the 'old gray matter'? Our research shows that when you ask sales people if they professionally update themselves, 100% will say they do. But when we drill down a little further and ask what sales books they have read or courses they have attended, a disappointing 8.3% of salespeople can answer satisfactorily. Less than ten percent of sales people are regularly exercising their sales brain by updating their sales knowledge for six hours a year. From this we can draw two conclusions. Firstly, most sales people think they are professionally developing, but they are not. There is a delusion that we will examine closely in *chapter two*. Secondly, nine out of ten salespeople are not undertaking any continuous professional development at all. Sales people are not the expert thinkers we had hoped for. Nine out of ten sales brains are in a state of atrophy, getting weaker over time. As customer purchasing power is strengthening due to increased awareness, and as the competition is getting stronger, it seems the majority of salespeople are sleepwalking in the opposite direction.

How do sales compare with other professionals? How much CPD do our professional cousins do? Here's the official minimum requirement for CPD for similar professions at the time of writing:

- CIM – Marketers 35 hours/year
- ACCA - Accountants 40 hours/year
- SRA - Lawyers 16 hours/year
- RICS - Surveyors 20 hours/year

If salespeople were students in Dean Sherman's mathematics class, they'd be getting the *'must try harder'* report from him compared to their fellow students. Why is this the case? Surely if salespeople are expert thinkers, they should be exercising their brains? According to a Gallup poll, 59.4% of professional people exercise their bodies for at least 30 minutes, three or more days per week.[27] While I have no data to show how many salespeople exercise regularly, it's not a dangerous mental leap to propose that salespeople are more likely to be found building their biceps down at the gym, than training their temporal lobes in a good book.

Salespeople are typically ambitious, competitive, and are driven to succeed. Why then do they not continuously develop professionally? Why are they letting their sales brains atrophy? One answer is that not all of the Marketers, Accountants, Lawyers, and Surveyors who do their CPD, do so attentively and studiously, and for the love of learning. Many undertake CPD because it is directly linked to their professional status and therefore linked to their ability to work.

Salespeople have no such formalized and agreed body to undertake and enforce professional development through accreditation. This puts the accountability for undertaking and recording CPD with the employer organization rather than the sales populations themselves. Intel Corporation, with whom I consulted for a number of years, have the best CPD system that I have seen. CPD is measured, and it is part of their performance management system. But companies like Intel are very much the exception and not the rule. Most companies push the accountability down the chain to the salespeople themselves, which is precisely why we get the massively underwhelming professional development results we do.

What happens if we move to the top of organizations? Do we encounter an oasis of sales experience, capability and learning? It would appear not. When it comes to wearing out shoe leather on the path of sales experience, only 33% of company board members and 38% of CEOs have sales-related experience[28]. Do they make up for this with sales related learning? Typically, the entrance ticket to a board position is the MBA. Does the MBA provide the sales learning to accelerate sales success? It would appear not. Finance, marketing, operations, and strategy are all there, but sales skills are almost completely absent. According to the publication *The Economist,* at the time of writing the number one MBA globally is the University of Chicago Booth School of Business MBA. There is no mention of 'sales' or 'selling' at all in the curriculum[29]. Walter Friedman, a lecturer at Harvard Business School, wrote in his book 'Birth of a Salesman' that *"...Business schools do not offer courses in salesmanship. The topic remains, just as it was in the 1910s more suitable for popular how-to books and memoirs of successful salespeople than for academic classes."*[30] There's more than a whiff of snobbery coming from the academic institutions that Friedman is referring to. Despite the relevance of sales skills to business success, selling is surprisingly not a part of MBA programs. When it comes to challenging and supporting the sales team, it must be an opportunity cost when two-thirds of the best people in the company cannot get involved tactically in sales because of a lack of capability. A lack of understanding of sales can also have a negative strategic impact. Jim Collins, in his book *How the Mighty Fall*, describes the stages of decline for great companies. Stage Two he describes as the 'undisciplined pursuit of more.' *"Although complacency and resistance to change remain dangers to any successful enterprise, overreaching better captures how the mighty fall."* How can you have a disciplined approach to growth if you do not understand how your key growth assets work? Stage three according to Collins is 'Denial of Risk and Peril.' *"As companies move into Stage 3, internal warning signs begin to mount, yet external results remain strong enough to "explain away" disturbing data or to suggest that the difficulties are "temporary" or "cyclic" or "not that bad," and "nothing is fundamentally wrong."* What could be more like denial than abdicating responsibility for sales completely to the VP of Sales? If you've ever said, or have ever heard that, *"The sales target is down to the sales force, and they alone will live and die by their numbers,"* or words to that effect, that is a form of denial. If the people on the board don't understand sales, then it becomes easy for poor sales practices to be explained away, for example, *"We lost the deal because the competition threw money at it and undercut us."* Or, *"We lost the deal because the buyer and the seller are friends on the golf course."* These types of excuses should not be taken at face value. Board members should be able to challenge and find the real reasons for lost opportunities so they can act accordingly. *"People on the board must never accept something that they don't understand. This applies to established members as much as new members. If something is not clear, the board must ask the question even if it seems a stupid one. They must have the confidence to admit that they don't understand."* Anthony Habgood Chairman of RELX Group.[31] No one would argue that improving the sales capability of the board and getting the board members involved in key deals is a good thing, but how can we make this actually happen? What's their jump on point? What's going to drive them to prioritize and do this? *Deal Hacks* can give senior people, who are not normally involved in sales, the jump on point they need, the clear role and mandate to add value to the sales process, building up their sales expertise over time. Bringing board members into the sales process will add capability, expertise, and support to a sales organization. What about others across the wider organization, can they help improve sales performance too? In a survey by Salesforce.com 20% of the sales teams were considered to be 'high performing' because they had significantly increased year-on-year revenue growth. Of this 20% segment of high-performing sales teams, 83% said their company is aligned on the importance of cross-team collaboration, and such collaboration has increased sales productivity by more than 25% with commensurate increases in pipeline.[32] This indicates strongly that cross-functional team collaboration within the sales organization is a cornerstone of successful selling today. When describing the best way to approach value creation in complex sales, the acclaimed author Peter Cheverton said, *"Please don't leave it to the sales force. Here, we see the need for a truly cross-functional team, wedding sales with marketing, R&D with manufacturing, and senior management with those that carry out the work at ground level."* [33]

These insights highlight the imperative of building a cross-functional virtual team to work alongside the salesperson in today's selling environment. Team selling is, once again, something that has been proved successful and that we all agree upon intellectually, but its absence in many sales organizations is becoming increasingly conspicuous. In 1999 Neil Rackham proposed that sellers should try to match the investment made by the buyer team in a sale.[34] At the time, this was an extremely important insight that allowed sales organizations to see the benefits of moving away from transactional selling. Rackham wrote in 1999, *"Sales forces are caught in the middle. On the one side, their customers have changed dramatically in terms of how they purchase and what they expect. On the other side, their own corporations have shifted, going through downsizing, restructuring, and cost-cutting... CEOs and sales vice presidents we have worked with have felt an increasing frustration as existing models and methods have proved unable to cope with this changed world."* [35] In 1999 people used landline phones to dial into their 'internet service provider' to physically get onto the internet. Mobile phones were phones, and not much else. Google was in beta testing mode and, with Mark Zuckerberg in short trousers in the eighth grade, the world would have to wait five more years before the launch of thefacebook.com. CEOs were frustrated at that time about the lack of sales force adaptability to customer change. With 88% of CEOs saying their organization's sales performance is 'very poor' to 'average' today, it appears they're no less frustrated today. [36]

Rackham's observation about matching the customer investment is as important now as it was then. Customers are putting buying teams together to maximize the value that they can create and capture in the buying process. Like any team, however, there are always gaps and the build to be made on Rackham's work is that we need to also complement the customer buying team. If we know where they have knowledge gaps, skills gaps or resource gaps we can plug them with resources from the seller side. This will make sellers more attractive to the buyers who will invite them to engage earlier in the buying process. On the selling side, all parties tend to agree that it would be beneficial to do this, and agree that we should match and complement the buyer investment, but cross-functional team selling does not seem to be happening. Are we any nearer than we were in 1999? According to Brian Sharp, Global Commercial Strategy and Execution Leader at Sonoco, the gap is widening: *"There are significant differences in the investments made between buyers and sellers. Our research shows that in deals over $1m, 60% of buyers spend over 30 days* *preparing for large supplier engagements, whereas sellers invest under six days. The number of stakeholders in the buying team for this deal size is a minimum of nine whereas in the sales team it can be as low as three people. Just as important, buyers also start the process of preparation for supplier engagements further out, buy in some cases half a year.*

When Rackham said we need to match the buyer-side investment, we tend to think of the investment being people and money. When it comes to account management, Sharp highlights the importance of timing. When do we start preparing for sales engagements? Many times I've been called in for a 'Deal Hack' and the response is, *"That's all well and good Al, but we have to submit our proposal on Monday. We don't have time to do all this! Why weren't you here six months ago?"* They're right, we should have started six months ago, but that takes investment, process and discipline. Not the magic wand they were looking for.

It appears we're a long way from matching the buying team, maybe even further than back in 1999 because the buyers are adapting and changing more quickly. If you work as a salesperson in a sales organization, you know this to be implicitly true. The salespeople I talk to feel out-gunned and significantly out-resourced. We've known for a long time that sales populations should:

1. Add value in the sales process
2. Match and complement the buying team investment
3. Build a cross-functional selling team supporting the seller

It might be happening in pockets, but in most of the sales organizations that I observe, this is a pipe dream. The question to be answered, and the question on which this book is based, is *why can't the sales profession change and adapt?* Why when we know to do these things do we not do them? Rackham's work on creating customer value was published in 1989, in his book *Major Account Sales Strategy*[37]. Rackham's book on matching the customer investment and cross-functional selling was published in 1999[38]. This information has been in the public domain since the 1980s and 1990s. If we know that we should make such changes, why don't we? Why is it that so many sales organizations and salespeople have missed the opportunity that has been so clearly signposted? It's not just this signpost. Companies are driving on autopilot past many others. In 2011 the CEB released *The Challenger Sale,* which resonated very well with sales leaders and sales support professionals alike. The CEB has done some great research and drawn conclusions that got everybody nodding collectively like sales training classes where they teach the Pencom nod (an old sales technique where the seller nods to encourage agreement from the buyer)[39]. One of the most compelling insights, as stated earlier, was that customers are already 57% through the purchase process before they approach a supplier. This articulated and gave credence to what had been long suspected, that customers are increasingly failing to see value in salespeople. We're some ten years on from that. Challenger Sale techniques are freely available for anyone to buy. How many salespeople are using them? Is the trend of customers avoiding salespeople reversing? The CEB was right about the need for increased challenge, but in order to challenge the customer, we need first to challenge the sales organizations to change at an altogether different level.

The gap between where we are, and where we could be, the missed opportunities that exist in the sales profession, is what we will call the Sales Performance Paradox. To overcome the Sales Performance Paradox we're going to build on the work of people like Rackham who has, perhaps more than anyone, reduced the ambiguities of selling and made selling into an acquirable skill. Rather than re-explain the skills of selling, in a slightly different guise like many books on sales performance, we're going to focus on the very different problem of getting salespeople, and cross-functional selling teams, using the sales skills we know we should use, but don't.

Now that we have our problem statement out on the table, let's focus our energies on the fix. The fix follows the HACKS process, the first stage of which is 'Highlight the blind spots'. Salespeople need to be self-aware in order to improve and as we'll see in the next chapter, as a profession, our collective lack of awareness has generated a significant number of systemic blind spots. Blind spots, not just at the individual level, but under closer examination we will also see organizational blind spots that cause a failure to deliver the performance improvements and sales growth so often promised and so badly required. We will see how Deal Hacks can help to uncover these individual and organizational blind spots by challenging and supporting live deals inside the workflow. The balance of challenge and support within live deals is the key to increasing self-awareness, and the key to reducing the individual and organizational blind spots that are blocking optimal sales performance.

Figure 3 - Deal HACKS Framework

# CHAPTER 2
# BLIND SPOTS

*"If you're really incompetent, you can't know you're incompetent."*

Laurence J. Peter author of *The Peter Principle*.

On April 19, 1995, a five-foot-six, 270-pound bank robber stormed a bank in Pittsburgh brandishing a gun. In broad daylight, the security cameras captured clear images of his face. Making no attempt to hide his facial features, he pointed his gun at the bank clerks demanding money. With clear photo evidence, the police broadcast the robbery on the local 11 o'clock news. After tip offs from informants who recognized the robber, within an hour after the broadcast the police were knocking on a suspect's door. The suspect was a confused and surprised McArthur Wheeler.

Wheeler's manner was incredulous when being interviewed by the arresting officers. *"But I wore the lemon juice,"* he remonstrated. Commander Ronald Freeman was chuckling when describing the situation to journalists, "Someone had told him that if you put lemon juice on your face it makes you invisible to the surveillance camera! He was shocked when we showed him the surveillance pictures."

By interviewing Wheeler, Sgt. Wally Long pieced together the careful planning that Wheeler had undertaken. As part of the preparation, Wheeler had tested the lemon juice theory by taking a selfie with a Polaroid camera. In the tests and to his delight, he didn't appear in the Polaroid selfie. "He said he lemon juice was burning his eyes, and he was having trouble seeing and had to squint." Sgt. Long said, concluding that Wheeler's selfie experiment had most likely failed, but had still convinced him that rubbing his face with lemon juice rendered him invisible to the CCTV surveillance cameras. Due to compelling CCTV images, Wheeler was convicted in federal court of the robbery.[40]

The next year this astonishingly witless robbery appeared in the 1996 *World Almanac* where the story was picked up by David Dunning, a Cornell psychology professor. The story inspired Dunning and his colleague Justin Kruger to investigate a phenomenon that has become known as the Dunning-Kruger effect. Dunning and Kruger found that people who score low on a performance test tend to overestimate their performance relative to others. For example, if a person scores badly on a mathematics test, they would typically overestimate their mathematics capability compared to others. Conversely, those with high mathematics scores would tend to underestimate their capability.[41] In the words of the actor John Cleese, "*To know whether or not you're good at something takes exactly the same skills as actually being good at it in the first place. So if you're no good at something, you lack skills to know that you're no good at something. But if you're good at something you have the skills to actually know if you're good.*"[42] Their theory was confirmed by C.L. Downing who found that people with below-average IQs tend to overestimate their IQ, while those with an above-average IQ tend to underestimate theirs.[43]

The arises because of a lack of self-awareness. And, a lack of self-awareness that *others* can see is a blind spot. McArthur Wheeler provides us with a story that allows us to laugh at his blind spot, his belief that lemon juice made him invisible to the surveillance cameras. We know something he didn't. He had something fairly substantial in his blind spot. But there's a serious point. We all have blind spots and, like McArthur Wheeler, they don't do us any favors. On an individual basis they stop us getting the promotions we want, the relationships we want and the status we want. Collectively, at the company level, they stop companies from growing and maximizing their competitive advantage.

The list of corporate blind spots is lengthy. Kodak, once one of the world's biggest brands, is one of the best-known examples of a corporate blind spot. A young Kodak engineer, Steve Sasson, invented and patented the technology behind the digital camera for Kodak in 1974. Given that, today, almost everyone carries on their person two digital cameras on their single mobile devices, this invention and patent should have been one of the most lucrative technology patents in human history. But instead of popping the champagne and rushing this technology to market, it was not until 1995 some 21 years later, that Kodak released their first digital camera. They did not take digital cameras seriously until 2001. Completely missing the chance to lead the field they had invented and patented. Instead Kodak's market monopoly of film was usurped and they filed for bankruptcy in 2012.[44] Back in 1984 Forbes released an article, *Has the World Passed Kodak By?* The article laid bare their blind spot publicly for all to see.[45] We all intuitively know that blind spots are bad for us, but the Kodak story illustrates perfectly the worst thing about blind spots; we're blind to them. Sometimes, we're willfully blind to them. Had Kodak, listened to the Forbes article, and others around them, they would have had ample opportunity to lead the emerging field that they had uncovered. But what did they do? Not seeing their blind spot, they issued a series of rebuttals in the press and blamed factors beyond their control. [46] Kodak were literally blind to the opportunity that they had created.

What about in the sales profession? Do we too have blind spots? I'm now going to help you to see a blind spot that you or your sales colleagues may have. This blind spot exists in most sales people and sales leaders I encounter. I reveal the blind spot using a simple test with the delegates in my workshops. Nine common sales practices are listed, and the question is posed, "When were these first taught to salespeople?"

1. Closing skills
2. Specialization as a hunter or a farmer
3. Transactional vs. consultative selling
4. Features, advantages, and benefits
5. Objection handling
6. Open and closed questions
7. The first defined sales process
8. Listening skills
9. Order takers v active salespeople

Which one of these do you think is the oldest? Which one the newest? Don't know? Most salespeople and sales leaders don't know. I'm often asked what number two is, but generally, people guess that these concepts were introduced in the last 20 to 30 years. However, that's just a guess. And not a good guess. Here are the correct answers:

1. Hunters were first separated from farmers in the insurance industry between 1850 and 1900

2. The first sales process was defined in 1898. Called AIDA it was developed by E. St. Elmo Lewis and is still very much in use today.
3. The *Psychology of a Sale* was written in 1914 by Charles Forbes-Lindsay documented the defined skills for insurance salesmen including:
    I. Objection handling skills
    II. Closing skills
    III. Open and closed questioning skills
    IV. Features, advantages & benefits skills
4. Sales roles were differentiated between order takers and active salespeople in the 1961 essay, "The Mystique of Super-Salesmanship", by Robert McMurray. Here he defined the roles regarding a spectrum from order takers to field salespeople.
5. Transactional v Consultative selling was defined in 1985 by McMurray in, "The Determinants of Salesperson Performance" by Gilbert Churchill, et al.
6. Listening and customer focus were defined as key sales skills in 1987 by Neil Rackham in *Making Major Sales.*

The delegates are always surprised that so many of the techniques they currently use were developed over 100 years ago. Features, advantages and benefits (FAB), objection handling, closing skills, and open and closed questions were being taught in sales training sessions in 1914. If you're in a sales training session and they are teaching the features, advantages and benefits of the product, then you're experiencing exactly the same training as sales people from one hundred years ago.

It's a blind spot for sales people to not know this, but so what? Who cares when these were first taught after all they work, don't they? Brian Fetherstonhaugh, Chairman, and CEO of OgilvyOne Worldwide, helps to explain the significance of this; *"In the old world so many (sales) people grew up with driving customers through the sales funnel. The sales funnel was invented in 1898, so it's enjoyed a very good run! But this notion of the marketer or seller driving people through the selling funnel is just not relevant anymore."* [47] It's not relevant anymore because that's not how people buy anymore. The fact that most sales people and sales leaders are oblivious to the relationship between how they sell and how their customers buy is a massive problem because it's limiting sales performance. Dunning and Kruger made the link between a lack of knowledge and a lack of awareness, ultimately leading to a lack of performance. The less knowledge you have, the less aware you are that you don't have the requisite knowledge. That's what makes this blind spot so important. Not knowing the original application of these sales skill means that you're less likely to how they apply to customers today. I can walk into almost any store today and buy something using my wristwatch, or I can place orders anywhere in the world from my phone. How we buy today was not even imagined when most of these techniques were devised. Yet I see sales people unquestioningly using sales techniques from the Victorian age to help professional and educated buyers to buy today. Is it possible that the way you and I buy has fundamentally changed, but the professional and educated people we sell to are happy to buy in a way that has not changed in 100 years? We need to get to the level of knowledge where we can challenge the validity of the sales skills we use, because some of these skills can help and some can be detrimental to a sale. For example, Neil Rackham demonstrated the negative consequences of training commercial salespeople to close large deals in 1995. You didn't read that last sentence incorrectly. Back in 1995, Rackham really did prove that traditional closing techniques could be detrimental in large sales with sophisticated or repeat buyers.[48] Such traditional closing techniques are still being requested and still being taught, as I found recently in a story which is the corporate equivalent of McArthur Wheeler and a really good example of why we need to know about legacy sales techniques. I was asked to meet with a Director of Commercial Operations for a $30-billion pharmaceutical company who wanted a sales training program to replace their in-house sales program. The existing sales program was an unauthorized copy of Huthwaite's SPIN Selling program. It was not working because they had missed off the N part of SPIN. They had copied the SPIN program, which was illegal, but not only that, they had copied it incorrectly - and that was why it wasn't working. Top of the list of requested improvements to remedy their situation was more "closing". More closes were demanded, and harder closes, too. Ironically the man who wrote SPIN selling was Neil Rackham who had proved that closing techniques could be detrimental in large sales with sophisticated or repeat buyers - just like in their situation.[49] My attempts over several months to help them so see their blind spot did nothing to diminish the desire for 'closing' the sale to be the focus of the program and the key competency. This confused and outdated approach was not what their sales population needed at all. It was detrimental to their sales efforts as the environment was high value and repeat sales. The company share price declined over that whole year due, in part, to low sales. I declined to work with them, but there's always someone who will deliver this type of old-school sales training because it is still in demand and for sales training companies it is easy money for the consultants. The fact that those supporting and driving sales performance routinely ask for the same legacy training from a bygone era is surprising and particularly problematic for companies that want to grow. The lesson here is that those in sales and those who support sales performance need to have an intimate and up to date working knowledge of legacy and modern sales practices, and their effects on their customers and sales process. Those who don't can have a profoundly negative impact on sales performance through this 'lemon juice' like blind spot. And the really big problem, as Dunning Kruger predict, is that the people who know the least about sales techniques are exactly the ones who tend to think that they know the most. I've lost count of the number of people I've met who learn a specific sales technique and then enthusiastically port it over into another company and another market. In fact, there's something almost religious about their beliefs for the success of their method of selling, and this over confidence closes them off to alternatives. Alternatives that could do a better job. What they don't realize is that someone in their previous company looked at the way their customers buy and designed a sales process and methodology to fit this. That was why it was successful. It's just a matter of luck when moving the same sales methodology to another market. It may work and it may not, that's the gamble. The best way to create a sales process and methodology is to look at how your customers buy and create a sales process that drives their buying process. But that takes effort and a really good knowledge of sales processes and associated tools. It's easy to see why some people just 'borrow' what they already know. It saves time, money, and it feels right. Or, like the pharmaceutical company, it could end up costing them in the long run. That's the gamble which is made all the riskier by not knowing sufficiently about the sales techniques and processes being asked for and being used.

Now the heavily loaded question. How would you describe your knowledge of selling? On a scale from 1 to 10. One is poor, and 10 is world class. Do you have the number in your mind? And yes, there is a question behind the question: *"How good are we at estimating our knowledge of selling and sales capability?"* in other words *"What's our level of self-awareness concerning our own sales knowledge and capability?"* This is metacognition and it is the key skill to overcome the Dunning Kruger effect and our blind spots. Metacognition is the ability to monitor and measure our own thinking. It is a tough skill to master, but it brings big rewards. Being able to monitor your thinking effectively enables you to assess your own performance more effectively and reduce potentially harmful blind spots. You may think you can already do this. Some people can do this better than others, but in all of us, there are cognitive biases that help to build our blind spots. Cognitive biases are systematic errors in the way that we process information and they recur predictably in particular circumstances. These cognitive biases get in the way of us being accurate about our capabilities, our knowledge and our performance. It turns out that some of these cognitive biases are particularly strong in sales people.

In sales workshops I ask the question, *"If the average in the room is 5, how good are you at selling from 1 (poor) – 10 (world class)?"* This survey has been run with thousands of salespeople from different countries in different industries. There's never been anyone from any sales population score themselves at less than a five. Not one person, ever. I don't know how good you are with statistics, but it can't be possible for everyone to be better than everyone else. This 'optimism' cognitive bias means at least half of the sales people in the survey are overoptimistic about their capability, which manifests as an illusion of superiority over their colleagues.

There is a very good reason that people are typically more optimistic than pessimistic. According to Tali Sharot, director of the Affective Brain Lab and faculty member of the department of Experimental Psychology at University College London, *"Optimism may be so essential to our survival that it is hardwired into the brain."*[50] Sharot describes how being over-optimistic about oneself can be seen in everything from smoking and diet to marriage. Smokers think that the other smokers will die. People eat unhealthy food regularly because someone else will get heart disease, and even people who marry for the second time believe it is once again 'forever.' But my research shows that when it comes to salespeople, the optimism reaches an altogether higher level. Which in some respects is good, because if there's one behavior that we want salespeople to have in spades, it is optimism. So this is not completely bad news. We want salespeople who are optimistic about their products, optimistic about their customers and the market. However, when it comes to self-awareness we also want salespeople to be aware of their capability and, specifically, aware of their capability gaps. If they are more aware of their capability gaps, they are more likely to do something about it, and sales performance should improve as a result. This is where boundless and unchallenged optimism can get in the way. If salespeople are unaware of their capability gaps, not only are they less likely to do anything about them independently, but they are also less likely to take advantage of any support being offered. When I ask salespeople if they need training, they invariably answer, "*Yes.*" So on the surface, there's engagement. But when I drill down a further layer and ask what they mean, the answer changes: "*The training will benefit the others, the underperformers, and the new guys. I'll take just the bits that I need.*" This example of the optimism bias is the person overestimating their qualities and abilities, relative to others, and masks significant blind spots.[51] From this, we can see why some salespeople are not engaged in the support that is provided for them, for example, training and coaching. They feel that the support is not relevant to them. Some may go further and feel that it is insulting to them and their situation because they simply don't need to improve. That's a surprisingly common blind spot in sales populations.

We run a similar survey with the same salespeople after the workshop. We ask the question: "*From 1 (poor) to 10 (world class) how good are you at using these new techniques?*" This is performed after they are aware of their optimism bias. Even then, and even with new skills just learned, skills that they have never performed in the real world, the salespeople are equally over-optimistic about their capability. Again, everyone is above the average of five. This confirms that when challenging a sales population on their sales capability, at least half will be over-optimistic about their capability. And that is the case even if they are aware that their responses are over-optimistic! My field observations of salespeople with prospects and customers backs this up. As part of the diagnostics and before the field visits, I ask the salespeople to predict their score of the competencies to be measured in the meeting. I also ask sales managers and sales leaders to predict the scores for their teams. Let me give an example to illustrate this. Let's say the sales leaders want the sales teams to perform a certain sales skill, for example, hold an in-depth review of the prospect's situation at the start of the sales process. The sales managers and sales leaders are asked to predict the capability levels of their salespeople at doing this in the meetings. Each salesperson is asked to predict their score before a meeting, too. An observer then accompanies the salesperson and scores what they observe. After a representative sample of salespeople has been observed, I compare the predictions with actual observation. What I consistently find is that salespeople typically overestimate their capability by approximately 25% in even the most basic sales competencies. Sales managers typically overestimate the sales capability of their sales populations by approximately 20% above that of the sales population's estimations. Remember that the sales populations are overestimating their capability by 25%, and so the sales managers are overestimating capability by 45%.

Sales leaders typically overestimate the capability of their sales teams by 3% above the sales managers. So the sales leaders are nearly 50% adrift in predicting the capability of their salespeople on core competencies. As Darwin observed in *The Descent of Man*, "*Ignorance more frequently begets confidence than does knowledge: it is those who know little, not those who know much, who so positively assert....*" The learning is clear:

1) Sales leaders, sales managers, and salespeople all over-estimate the capability of salespeople in customer facing sales opportunities

2) To get an accurate picture of capability, someone outside of the sales team should be used to observe behavior to eliminate the biases that cause these blind spots.

It's not just capability where we see cognitive biases creating blind spots and having negative consequences for sales populations. I see big blind spots when it comes to the levels of understanding in complex deals. When I ask salespeople from the same sales team, who sell to identical customers, if they understand their customers' buying process, I get 100% positive responses. *"Yes, we know the customers' buying process."* But when I ask the same people to describe in detail the customer buying process, there are a lot of blank faces in the room. *"What do you mean by buying process?"* The realization that they did not really know their customer's buying process hits them when they are asked to draw it and present it in the workshop to others. I also see this phenomenon with complex accounts. *"How knowledgeable are you of the account you're working with?"* The responses range between 80 and 100% of the required knowledge, often prefaced by, *"You can never know 100%"*. When we ask them to describe the account and challenge them, they realize they do not know as much as they thought, often not even knowing basic information. This cognitive bias is called 'the illusion of explanatory depth,' and it is the tendency to overestimate how well we understand something.[52] This can partly be explained by the fact that people have knowledge at one level of explanation, which causes them to mistakenly believe that they have knowledge at another level. We see this in Deal Hacks when we document and analyze the customer journey. The cross-functional 'Hack Team' are collectively able to describe the customer journey and the customer buying process, in far greater depth and detail than the salesperson alone. Because of the dedicated focus and resource, Deal Hacks can go to a much deeper level of customer knowledge than most salespeople are accustomed to going. It's only once the salespeople can visually see on the wall and experience the gaps that show up in the sessions, that they see what they are missing, and their awareness of their own gaps in customer knowledge improves. These gaps are made visible by the Deal Hack Visual Toolkit where the deal is visually drawn on the walls of the Deal Hack, visible for all to see and staring the sales person in the face. The gaps are also made visible by others in the Deal Hack challenging at an altogether different level, as you will see in the coming chapters.

In the book *Extraordinary Minds,* Howard Gardner the developmental psychologist, concludes that exceptional individuals have, *"A special talent for identifying their own strengths and weaknesses."* How many of our sales teams have this special talent? Of the 'special' talents that sales people have, identifying their weaknesses and gaps is clearly not one of them. This makes it hard for those challenging and supporting salespeople to find the 'reality' of a given situation. When we ask a straight question, we expect a straight answer. For example, *"Do you perform ROI calculations with your prospects?"* If the real answer is 'no,' we should get the response 'no.' But in the world of sales enablement we often get a 'yes,' which is technically a lie. But think about the last time you went to the doctor, and she asked you how much you exercised and how much you drank. What are the chances that you estimated both accurately? Survey measures of alcohol consumption are acknowledged to underestimate consumption. Comparisons of such survey measures with government data on alcohol sales suggests that survey estimates of consumption represent between 55% and 60% of the true figure.[53] It appears we humans, generally, find estimating and communicating our behaviors a challenge. Similarly, when it comes to estimating the facts about our wider lives, we also seem to struggle.

A Mori survey in the UK asked the question, *"For every 100 people in England and Wales, how many of them are Muslim?"* The average answer from this survey, which was supposed to be representative of the total population, was 24. British people, therefore, think that 24 out of every 100 people in the UK are Muslim. Official figures reveal the figure to be about five.[54] It appears there's a big gap between what we estimate about ourselves and our environment, and what others objectively observe and empirically measure. So when we ask salespeople, sales managers, leaders and sales support professionals about levels of sales performance we expect an accurate answer. Perhaps the biggest surprise is that we're surprised when we find the answers we're given are significantly wide of the mark.

Deal Hacks create a level of transparency in deals that helps to close these gaps. At the start of every Deal Hack, the deal coach asks the sales person these questions:

1. What is the deal name and how much is it worth to you?
2. How comfortable (happy, neutral, sad) are you in these four areas of the deal:
   a. Decision makers
   b. Decision criteria
   c. Decision process
   d. Deal value
3. What is the forecasted closing date?

The output of the conversation is captured, and after the Deal Hack converted into a red, amber and green (RAG) traffic light system that shows how the sales people feel about their deals:

| | Why Us? | | Why Now? | | |
|---|---|---|---|---|---|
| | Decision Makers | Decision Criteria | Value | Decision Process | Forecast |
| Deal 1 | Green | Amber | Amber | Amber | Q3 |
| Deal 2 | Green | Amber | Amber | Red | Q3 |
| Deal | Green | Green | Green | Green | Q3 |
| Deal 4 | Amber | Green | Amber | Amber | Q3 |

If we think outside of Deal Hacks for a moment, this is typically the deal information that is broadcast upwards in the sales organization for forecasting purposes. But Deal Hacks go a stage further. After the Deal Hack, the deal coach also provides their assessment of the same deals, based on the same criteria, like this:

| Deal Coach | Why Us? | | Why Now? | | |
|---|---|---|---|---|---|
| | Decision Makers | Decision Criteria | Value | Decision Process | Forecast Probability |
| Deal 1 | Red | Red | Red | Amber | Low |
| Deal 2 | Amber | Red | Red | Amber | Medium |
| Deal 3 | Green | | Green | Green | High |
| Deal 4 | Amber | Red | Red | Amber | Low |

Put side by side, we can see at a glance where the blind spots are. Such reporting is a good cure for blind spots at both the individual and company level. There is the information and feedback the sales person needs to identify and close the blind spots in the deal. There is also information and feedback on their performance, so they can close personal skills gaps too. This is possible because the more objective deal coach strips out the cognitive biases to reveal the blind spots. When you've held a number of Deal Hacks, it will become apparent that memoirist Anais Nin was on the button when she said, "We don't see things as they are, we see them as **we** are." In my experience sales people don't see deals as they are, they see the deals as they want them to be. That is why the deal coach assessments are invariably less optimistic than those of the sales people. When both views of the deals are provided to

49

sales leaders, the leaders are in a better position to see what deals are likely to close, what deals they need to focus on and resource to hit target, and the competency areas where their teams are falling short, which is the path to future success.

When you're taught to navigate using a map, you quickly learn the most important thing to know is your present location. If you don't know where you are, you can't plan a route to where you want to be. Because of significant blind spots, most sales organizations on a journey of growth are struggling locating accurately their current location, their current reality. This makes finding the destination of increased sales performance and growth almost impossible. If we are to maximize sales performance and growth, we need to know exactly what has to be improved. It sounds so obvious, but relying on our own view of our sales performance is misleading because of cognitive biases hard wired obstinately into our brains. The bad news is that we have cognitive biases that limit our self-awareness and subsequently our decision making capability. The good news is that we can do something about it, and Deal Hacks are designed to reduce the effects of cognitive biases in the sales process. The second thing you need to know when navigating using a map is where you're going to. What's the destination? Most sales organizations have a financial goal to reach, but is that the destination we're looking for? I prefer to think of the financial wins as the fruits of getting to the destination. So what is the destination then? If the starting point is knowing capability and capability gaps, the destination is a self-aware sales team who can control the cognitive biases that reduce sales performance. A team who can autonomously see their performance gaps, rise to challenges, take on critical feedback and adapt to market changes. Something Carol Dweck calls a 'Growth Mind-set'.

# CHAPTER 3
# MIND-SET

*"If you want to build a ship, don't drum up your men to collect wood and give orders and distribute the work. Instead, teach them to yearn for the vast and endless sea."*

**De Saint-Exupéry**

*'W*ell done! You're so smart Jonny! You got 8 out of 10 in the test!"* said the teacher to little eleven-year-old Jonny after the IQ test. *'Well done! Jenny, you must have worked really hard, you got eight out of ten in the test!" said the* teacher to little eleven-year-old Jenny after the IQ test. Jonny and Jenny were two of several hundred children aged between ten and eleven, who had become the unwitting participants in a scientific experiment that would turn the world of education and parenting upside down. In 1998 psychologist Carol Dweck and her colleague Claudia Mueller wanted to understand the effect of feedback on the academic performance of students. The children selected for the test had the same IQ levels, and they were randomly divided into two groups, E and I, and all given the same IQ test. Group E was praised for their effort by telling them how hard

they must have worked. Group I was praised for their intelligence by telling them they were smart. The academic performance of both groups was then monitored.

Over time, group I children who were congratulated for their intelligence, shied away from challenging assignments by pressing for easier assignments. Group E children, congratulated for their effort, in contrast, wanted more challenging assignments. When challenging assignments were given to both groups, those praised for being intelligent became discouraged, losing confidence in their own ability. Their scores, even on easier assignments, deteriorated compared with their own previous results on equivalent assignments. Conversely, students in Group E, who were praised for their effort, did not lose confidence when tackling harder assignments, and their performance improved markedly on the easier problems that followed. Ninety percent of Group E wanted challenging new assignments that they could learn from. There was one more finding in the study that was perhaps more alarming. The teachers told the students, *"You know, we're going to go to other schools, and I bet the kids in those schools would like to know about the assignments."* The students were given a page to provide their thoughts about the assignments. On the page was a space for them to put their score. Almost 40 percent of Group I, who had been praised for their intelligence, lied about their scores by inflating them.[55] Dweck describes two types of mind-set that people can have. We're using the term mind-set to mean the propensity to make decisions in a predictable and particular way. Mind-set is ongoing, what you might also call a decision making habit or behavior.

A 'Fixed Mind-set' happens when people believe that the results they achieve are attributed to their natural talents and abilities. In such circumstances, when mistakes occur they attribute these mistakes to a lack of their own ability. This negatively affects their personal status, which creates a powerful emotional defensive reaction that guides their decision making. The types of decisions they make are to avoid situations where they may make mistakes, or where their mistakes might be highlighted, especially by others. They make the decision to avoid challenging situations that could result in mistakes. They make the decision to avoid constructive feedback from others that could highlight mistakes. The way that Group I were treated by their teachers triggered this type of fixed mind-set decision making.

Dweck contrasts the fixed mind-set with a 'Growth Mind-set'. A growth mind-set is where people believe that the results they achieve are attributed to their hard work. In such circumstances, mistakes that happen do not produce a defensive response to protect their personal status because they know that by working hard they can learn from, and overcome mistakes to achieve their goals. People in a growth mind-set will therefore make decisions to embrace challenges, and welcome constructive feedback, because these increase the likelihood of achieving their goals. The combination of challenging events and feedback creates better results. They know this and make decisions that actively seek them out. The way that Group E were treated by their teachers triggered growth mind-set decision making, and this is why Group E achieved better results than Group I.

This study of primary school children is remarkable on a number of levels. Firstly, the study identifies, and clearly differentiates, between two different mind-sets, the fixed mind-set and the growth mind-set. This had not been done before. Secondly, the study shows that a person's mind-set and decision making habits can change, and be changed. People are not necessarily fixed in a fixed mind-set. Thirdly, the study shows that a person's mind-set can be affected by their environment and their experiences, and these can drive either fixed or growth mind-set decision making. According to Dr. Sherrie

Campbell, the key message from the mind-set study is that, *"To develop a growth mind-set, we must train ourselves not to view "deficit" as a deficiency in our ability, but rather, as a deficiency in our own learning or experience. Since, we are all capable of learning and experiencing, these two constructs can be easily fulfilled."*[56] Campbell eloquently de-personalizes deficiencies in our capability, *'It's not you, it's your learning or experience'*. We'll see in the next section how and why we're programmed to take such deficiencies personally and keep them tucked away in our blind spot rather than see them as opportunities to grow.

Using the mind-set lens to examine the world of sales, we clearly want sales teams with growth mind-sets who make decisions to embrace challenges and seek feedback on their performance to adapt and achieve their goals. In fact, that's a case of stating the obvious. Of course we want this, why wouldn't we? That's what we want, but what do we have? Do we actually have sales people with growth mind-sets? Is the sales profession known for being a showcase for growth mind-set decision making? We saw in Chapter 1 that overall sales capability is reducing despite increases in resources and performance support. We saw that sales people are not proactively learning and are often not taking advantage of performance support initiatives. We saw legacy sales techniques being used despite better alternatives being available. It's not a dangerous leap to hypothesize that a fixed mind-set could be causing this. In Chapter 2, we saw that sales people and their leaders are frequently blind to their skills gaps, and overestimate their capability, leading us towards the conclusion that we have sales populations who struggle with performance feedback and so are prone to making fixed mind-set decisions. This manifests itself both at the individual and leadership levels. According to global commercial heavyweight Brian Fetherstonhaugh, Chairman, and CEO of OgilvyOne Worldwide. *"Selling has changed because buying has fundamentally changed."*[57] Being the Chairman and CEO of one of the largest marketing communications companies in the world, Fetherstonhaugh knows a thing or two about the shift in buyer behavior and the impact on selling. Fetherstonhaugh points to a chain of causation between what's happening to buyers and the effect on sales populations and the need for salespeople to be able to adapt to this change. This is why sales people need to have a growth mind-set, so they can readily adapt to these significant changes in the market. To be successful individuals, sales people should be able to adapt and change to the changing environment around them. To be successful sales organizations, sales leaders should be able to steer their sales teams through the environmental changes, turning external threats into opportunities. Fixed mind-set people really struggle with such adaptation. Fixed mind-set sales leaders really struggle to identify change opportunities and steer their teams to take advantage of these changes, such as market changes. We saw the example of Kodak that illustrated this. The effect is a limitation on growth and a failure to build competitive advantage, or what we have been calling the Sales Performance Paradox.

What about your organization? On a scale of one to ten, one being a fixed mind-set and ten being a growth mind-set, where are your sales teams? You'll not be surprised to know that the Dunning Kruger effect and the optimism bias co-habit comfortably under this particular rock. When asked this question, sales people typically describe themselves as having a growth mind-set. No surprise there. But when we compare this to a test designed to assess their mind-sets, and compensate for their biases, we find they are more prone to a fixed mind-set. This adds a layer of complexity onto the situation, because we're not just dealing with a population who have a fixed mind-set, that would be problematic enough. We're dealing with a population who are particularly blind to their fixed mind-sets. And, as if that were not bad enough, sales people are masters at covering their fixed mind-sets, after all, they

55

are employed for being socially adept individuals who can filter their responses for customers. Let me explain. When I ask salespeople if they need training, they invariably answer, "*Yes*." So on the surface, we have a growth mind-set response. We'd expect that person to be engaged in the sales training. But when I drill down a further layer and ask what they are particularly looking forward to, the answer changes to the less filtered: "*The training will benefit the others, the under-performers, and the new guys. I'll take just the bits that I need.*" This view, behind the filter, betrays evidence of a fixed mind-set because they are ruling out the majority of self-development opportunities in advance. So here's the conundrum. We have a population who need to make growth mind-set decisions because of the changes in their profession and the market, but when we test them we find fixed mind-set decision making. To complicate the situation, they are blind to this fact, but really good at covering it up. In terms of problems to solve, you have to admit we've picked a good one! Fortunately, Dweck gave us a number of insights about mind-set that are relevant to sales organizations and sales enablement functions, that help us to structure our journey in this book. Dweck told us that mind-sets can be changed, the question for us is how do we do that in sales? How do we move sales teams from making fixed to growth mind-set decisions? Put simply, I've developed a simple five step process, around which this book is organized, which can be used as an organizational development framework to develop a growth mind-set culture in complex sales organizations:

Figure 4 - Deal Hacks Framework

The first step on the journey is to have a mechanism for highlighting the blind spots that are a cause of the fixed mind-set behaviors. We've already seen how Deal Hacks can do this at both the individual and organizational levels. In Part Two we go on to look at how people make decisions to see why sales people are particularly prone to social brain thinking, which is a key component of fixed mind-set behaviors. From this, we develop strategies to avoid social brain thinking and re-actions. Dweck showed us that mind-sets are affected by the environment, so in Part Three, we look at the organizational impact on sales cultures. In Part Four we look at how, by keeping learning in the workflow, we can drive a growth mind-set sales culture and grow sales as a result. Finally, in Part Five, we return to the organizational development perspective to look at how reporting and feedback structures can keep the growth mind-set culture on track for the long term.

# PART ONE SUMMARY

We have hit a diminishing return, in many sales forces, where a significant number of salespeople are not achieving their performance goals despite having more available resources and more support than ever before. Something we call the sales performance paradox.

Due to cognitive biases, many sales people and sales leaders are unaware of their capability levels. This lack of awareness creates an over confidence that results in blind spots. Unable to see the need to improve, a block on learning is created which reduces the ability to adapt to change at a time when it is badly needed.

Unidentified and unchallenged, the blind spots develop into a fixed mind-set that anchors to the status quo, avoids challenge and change. As markets and customers change, sales teams can therefore be slow to adapt which reduces competitive advantage and the ability to grow a business.

Mind-sets can be changed, and a growth mind-set is what sales people need to succeed. The first step to creating growth mind-sets in a sales environment is to **highlight the blind spots** and raise the awareness of the real reasons that sales results are being held back. Deal Hacks do this by having an independent team of people challenging and supporting live deals.

# PART TWO

# AVOID SOCIAL BRAIN THINKING AND REACTIONS

S ales organizations have hit a diminishing return where many salespeople are not achieving their goals despite having more resources and support than ever before. Due to cognitive biases, many sales people and sales leaders are, however, blind to the lack of capability that is causing this failure. One of the blind spots is using a type of thinking in the sales process that cuts corners and reduces the value created in the deal, what we'll call Social Brain thinking. Part two gives us a working model of the brain so that we can identify that type of thinking and build strategies to avoid it.

Chapters four to six cover:

4) **Inner Conflict** – why do we make poor decisions?
5) **Why Good Decisions Are Hard** – do you have the ability to do the right thing?
6) **Social Drivers** – how can we influence the decisions we make?

# CHAPTER 4
# INNER CONFLICT

*"In each of us, two natures are at war – the good and the evil. All our lives the fight goes on between them and one of them must conquer. But in our own hands lies the power to choose – what we want most to be we are."*

Robert Louis Stevenson

T here was a massive explosion. Co-workers went to see what had happened to Phineas Gage, the foreman of a railway construction gang. They had been preparing the railway bed for the Rutland and Burlington Rail Road near Cavendish, Vermont in 1849. He had been working with explosives, tamping the explosives with an iron bar. The explosion had driven the 3 feet 7 inches long, 13 1/2 pounds tamping iron straight through his skull and out the other side. Entering in his cheekbone, it exited the top of his head and landed 20 yards behind him, gruesomely covered in bits of Gage's brain. After being knocked to the ground, it is believed that Gage only temporarily lost consciousness, even though most of the front left side of his brain was destroyed. Given up for dead, he was, nonetheless, taken to a local hospital where a young Dr. John Harlow attended him. Unexpectedly Gage made a dramatic recovery and returned home from hospital just ten weeks later.

Phineas Gage is probably the most famous person to have survived severe damage to the brain. He is also the first patient from whom we learned something about the relationship between personality and the function of the front parts of the brain. Some months after the accident, probably in about the middle of 1849, Gage felt strong enough to resume work. However, because his personality had changed so much, the contractors who had employed him would not give him his place again. Before the accident, he had been their most capable and efficient foreman, one with a well-balanced mind, and who was looked on as a shrewd, smart business man. After the accident, however, he was described by his physician John Harlow as, *"Fitful, irreverent, and grossly profane, showing little deference for his fellows. He was also impatient and obstinate, yet capricious and vacillating, unable to settle on any of the plans he devised for future action. His friends said he was no longer Gage."*[58] The story of Phineas Gage has helped us understand that humans have two minds because that day, Gage literally lost one of his.

When it comes to feeling conflicted, most people are familiar with the concept that we have two minds that act differently and can oppose each other. Left brain and right brain thinking is a popular example of this. The timeless conflict between 'head' and 'heart' in art and literature is another example. The feeling of conflict derives from the choice of which decision to make. Shakespeare's play Romeo and Juliet is perhaps one of the most famous of this type in literature. Romeo and Juliet are conflicted because they are in love (heart) but are from feuding families and know that they are not allowed to be together (head). The decision for the star crossed lovers is should they be together (follow their hearts) or should they obey their parents (follow their heads). The story builds around this internal conflict and ultimately they decide (spoiler alert) to follow their hearts, which is the emotional pull of the story. If they had followed their heads the story would not have been so compelling. The inner conflict comes not just from balancing the different decision options, but also from our desire to make the best decision. The more important the decision, the bigger the potential conflict. Growth and fixed mind-sets are another example of dual brain thinking. Should I take the feedback from my colleague and thank her for it (growth mind-set), or shall I avoid the feedback because I disagree with her (fixed mind-set)? These may not seem like conscious decisions, but they are decisions that we make. To know how to manage our mind-set we need to understand how and why we make decisions in the way we do. Once we understand how we make decisions we stand a chance of being able to influence the mind-sets of our sales populations, so let's take a deep dive into decision making.

The fact that we possess two kinds of thinking has been around four thousands of years, but few people have any real idea what the two brains are, how they differ, the roles that they have and how to constructively manage the tension between them.[59] The story of Phineas Gage helped build the theory of dual brain thinking, but it is only recently, thanks to advances in brain imaging technology in the field of neuroscience, that the understanding of how we make decisions is becoming clearer. According to Hilary Scarlett there are gains to be made by learning from this emerging field, *"Neuroscience helps us understand ourselves and others better. For some leaders I work with, just having this new perspective on change and deeper understanding of people has been enough to make a significant difference to their ability and confidence to lead others through change."*[60] The insights from brain imaging are creating new branches of neuroscience and psychology that are providing us with useful and practical improvements in the areas of decision making, business, economics, learning and mental health. Behavioral economics is one such new discipline that is having an enormous impact on business. It is the study of cognitive, social, and emotional influences on people's observable economic decision making. Behavioral economics research uses psychological experimentation to develop theories about human decision making and has identified a range of biases that affect decision making. The field is changing the way economists think about people's perceptions of value and expressed preferences. Behavioral economics has been applied to various domains, including finance, health, energy, public choice, and consumer marketing.[61] Behavioral economics is, however, not yet making traction in sales due to the fixed mind-set behaviors we uncovered in Part One (pages 25-26). Sales people drive decision-making in their prospects. Yet, in my experience, most have not even heard of the fields of decision-making science that are springing up around them, let alone taken advantage of the performance enhancing insights they bring. This book builds on the work of scientists and psychologists who gather under the banner of behavioral economics and aims to contribute towards closing that gap. There are two benefits to doing so.

1)   If salespeople can understand how their customers make decisions, they are more likely to be able to add value to that decision process, be included in the process and influence it.
2)   If sales leaders and sales enablement professionals can understand how salespeople make decisions, they will be able to provide leadership and support that aligns with the needs of the sales teams, and ultimately influence their sales teams to perform better.

If we can understand how decisions are made, we can influence them, we can harness them and improve them. There's no more valuable prize in the commercial world where the decision to buy, or the decision to buy-in, are the hallmarks of success. It's not quite mind reading, but it's as close as we can currently get. Under the banner of behavioral economics, psychologists Keith Stanovich and Richard West, first used the generic terms System 1 and System 2 to describe the two different types of thinking that we experience. They divided them into two distinct groups like this:

| System 1 - The Social Brain | System 2 - The Intellectual Brain |
|---|---|
| Evolved early | Evolved late |
| Similar to animal cognition | Distinctively human |
| Emotional | Non emotional |
| Fast processing | Slow processing |
| High capacity | Capacity limited |
| Subconscious | Conscious |
| Biased responses | Normative responses |
| Contextual | Abstract |
| Automatic | Controlled |
| Experience-based decision making | Consequential decision making |

Figure 5 - System 1 and 2 Thinking

The two systems that Stanovic and West described are two brains. Physically separate, they work independently, but they are connected and communicate closely with each other. In this book, we adopt the model of the brain used by Stanovic and West because it is readily understandable and is used by most behavioral economists today. We'll make one slight change, and call them the Social Brain (system 1) and the Intellectual Brain (system 2). The reasons for this will become apparent as we move through the book.

Let's explore the characteristics of both brains to help differentiate between the two types of thinking. Knowing which type of thinking you're using is essential for understanding how to improve decision making. Let's start with the So-cial Brain. You've experienced your Social Brain when driving yourself to work, but you can't remember the journey. Some-one drove you to work that day, and that was your Social Brain, what Phil Barden describes as your 'autopilot.'[62] The Social Brain probably chose the shampoo that you put into your shopping basket and almost certainly chose the seat you occupied in the canteen at lunchtime. The Social Brain took complete control when a work colleague challenged your ac-countability for a lost deal. Your Social Brain caused you to get nervous and forget your train of thought when presenting to the room of potential clients. It chose the TV program you watched and the drink that helped you get over the stress of the incident with your work colleague. You probably think you made all of those decisions yourself, but you didn't. They were made below the level of consciousness, the conscious-ness which is your internal voice reading these words. These decisions were made by your Social Brain. The types of deci-sion that the conscious 'you' makes are more complex. They take a lot more thought and effort.

The Intellectual Brain is what you consider to be you. The internal voice in your head, your personality, the conscious you. It makes the decisions that involve complex planning, decisions that affect the future, and decisions that have a number of factors to be weighed up. When your boss asked you for the statistical analysis of the market, it was your Intel-lectual Brain that wrote the report. When you chose which college to go to and which house to move into, that was your Intellectual Brain making complex and focused decisions. When you felt dog tired after writing that 50-page tender pro-posal, that was your Intellectual Brain feeling tired because it had worked so hard. It's important to know that the Intellec-tual Brain tires very easily. The Intellectual Brain is the part of the brain that Gage lost when the iron bar was propelled through his skull. He could function surprisingly normally just using his 'Social Brain,' but in the words of his physician John Harlow, *"He had become a child intellectually but with the animal passions of a strong man."*[63]

The Intellectual Brain is located in the outer layers of your brain, towards the skull, which means information arrives there via the Social Brain. All information that comes into the conscious Intellectual Brain has had to come through the unconscious Social Brain first.[64] We tend to think information comes straight into our Intellectual Brain to make logical decisions first, but that information, including what you're reading now, has already been processed by the Social Brain first. The notion that we can freely choose between different possible courses of action is fundamental to our sense of self. However, it has been found that this subjective experience of freedom is no more than an illusion and that our actions are initiated by unconscious mental processes long before we become aware of our intention to act.[65] In an experiment in 1983 by Benjamin Libet, a pioneering scientist in the field of human consciousness, electrical brain activity was recorded while subjects were asked to press a button when they felt the urge to do so. Remarkably, the conscious decision to press the button was preceded by a few hundred milliseconds by a part of the Social Brain involved in motor preparation. [66] The implication is that the Social Brain had already unconsciously decided to act before the person became aware of it.[67] More recent studies have confirmed that the decisions can be made several seconds in advance of arriving in the conscious mind and the person being aware of making the decision.[68] *"We think our decisions are conscious, but these data show that consciousness is just the tip of the iceberg,"* says John-Dylan Haynes, a neuroscientist at the Max Planck Institute for Human Cognitive and Brain Sciences in Leipzig, Germany, who has studied this phenomenon.[69] It's not just when decisions are made but how. If you felt slightly uneasy at any point during that last paragraph, that was your Social Brain communicating with you. This is important because the Social Brain communicates through feelings and emotions, it cannot use language. It sees the world very differently to the more rational and logical Intellectual Brain. Professor Steven Peters articulates the relationship between the two brains imaginatively describing the Social Brain as the chimp: *"The Chimp is an emotional machine that thinks independently from us. It is not good or bad, it is just a Chimp."*[70] Because the Social Brain processes information emotionally before handing it to you, you'll sometimes feel in conflict with yourself. Sometimes you make logical and reasonable decisions that you don't live up to. You wanted to go to the gym this morning but didn't manage to find the time. You wanted to eat more healthily but ate the chocolate bar instead. You wanted to have a relaxing family day but unexpectedly shouted at the children. According to Peters, *"It is not you doing these things, it is your Chimp that is hijacking you."* When we think of something like 'mind-set,' Peters helps us to see that actually, the Social Brain has a mind-set all of its own. As you can imagine, the mind-set of a chimp is more likely to be a fixed mind-set than a growth mind-set. There's very little logic to a fixed mind-set; it's an emotional place, it's the Social Brain pushing its agenda of maximizing energy expenditure, reducing risk and exploiting status and reward. Mark Manson amusingly describes those who over identify with Social Brain decision making, *"Everything is justified for no other reason than they felt it. "Oh, I broke your windshield, but I was really mad; I couldn't help it." Or "I dropped out of school and moved to Alaska just because it felt right." Decision-making based on emotional intuition, without the aid of reason to keep it in line, pretty much always sucks. You know who bases their entire lives on their emotions? Three-year-old kids. And dogs. You know what else three-year-olds and dogs do? Shit on the carpet. An obsession and overinvestment in emotion fails us for the simple reason that emotions never last. Whatever makes us happy today will no longer make us happy tomorrow."*[71]

The insight for those of us involved in selling, is that when we interact with other people, we need to know that we're dealing with two personalities or, more accurately, two brains. We all have a Social Brain and an Intellectual Brain, and the two brains work very differently. Customers have two brains and so will make emotional and logical buying decisions. Sales people have two brains and so will make emotional and logical selling decisions. Sales leaders have two brains and so will make emotional and logical leadership decisions. Sometimes emotional and logical decisions align, but more often they don't. If you've seen Star Trek, the Intellectual Brain is Spock, and the Social Brain is Captain Kirk. The Star Trek stories are entertaining because of the tension between Kirk the emotional and passionate human and Spock the intellectually cold Vulcan. What Neuroscientists have found is that we're made of both Captain Kirk and Spock, but Captain Kirk gets to see all information before handing it over to Spock. He is, after all the Captain. The story would not perhaps have worked so well if Spock was the captain and in charge. Or maybe it would? We're going to look in depth at these two decision making modes and find ways to harness effective decision making in sales. But before we do, let's take a moment to understand why we have this flawed decision making apparatus in the first place. Knowing this context helps the overall topic make much more sense. To understand why we are what/who we are, we need to look back at how our brains developed historically.

Compared to other animals our brain is approximately seven times too large for the size of our body.[72] This is the main reason why as a species we're so brainy, despite what Dunning and Kruger might say about many of their test subjects. What do we mean by brainy? Like computers, our brainpower can be measured, and we can do this in two ways:

1) **Processing power** – how fast the brain can process data (sensory information)
2) **Storage capacity** – how much data (memories) the brain can store and retrieve

Let's test how brainy you are. Which is the brainier of your two brains? The Social Brain or the Intellectual Brain? Is there a clue in the name? Is it that obvious? When it comes to processing power, how fast the brain can process data, you may be surprised to know that the Social Brain has more power than the Intellectual Brain. How much more processing power? Twice as much? Five times as much? Ten times as much? It's a good question with extremely important implications. Scientists have found that the Social Brain can process around 11 million bytes of data per second from all of the senses, whereas the Intellectual Brain can process only around 50 bytes of data per second. That's not a typing error; there is a staggering difference in processing capacity between the two. The 50 bits of data per second is calculated using a typical reading rate of 300 words per minute, which works out to about five words per second. Assuming an average of five characters per word and roughly two bits per character yields the rate of 50 bits per second.[73] Put another way, If the Intellectual Brain is a distance you drive to work and back, the Social Brain is a trip to the moon and back. Performed three times. It is like comparing a brand new high spec computer with a crummy old calculator that has leaking batteries. In terms of processing power, they are not even close. This differential is referred to by Daniel Kahneman, the father of Behavioral Economics, as thinking fast (Social Brain) and thinking slow (Intellectual Brain) because the Social Brain is considerably faster[74]. It's faster because it's structure developed earlier in evolutionary terms and has had more time to tune and improve its performance. The Social Brain processes data much faster because it uses automatic processes called 'heuristics.' Heuristics are a sort of shortcut, proposing intuitive answers to problems as they arise. Because of its processing power and the fact that it processes all information first, the Social Brain also has the motive, opportunity, and means to actively influence and even override any decisions made by the Intellectual Brain. If the Intellectual Brain had to process all decisions made by the Social Brain it would be so overloaded that we would not be able to get out of bed in the mornings. If Gage had lost his Social Brain in the mining accident, he would have died instantly, and the mess would have taken a lot longer to clear up.

The Social Brain is much faster than the Intellectual Brain, but that speed comes at a cost. The heuristics used to help process the enormous amount of data are shortcuts, and like with all shortcuts things get missed. Here's an example of how heuristics work and how shortcuts can impact on decision making. Take a moment to look at the picture below:

Figure 6 - Optical Illusion

Which is the darker square? The square with the word 'Deal'

or the square with the word 'Hack'? You may be surprised to know that they are exactly the same color. Please feel free to test this image with a light meter or eyedropper tool from a graphics package. Why do we see two different colors? According to Edward H. Adelson, Professor of Vision Science at MIT in 1995 who made the original illusion, *"The visual system is not very good at being a physical light meter, because that is not its purpose. The important task is to break the image information down into meaningful components, and thereby perceive the nature of the objects in view."*[75] The Social Brain is essentially predicting the color of the squares based on the context, which feels right, but is, in fact, an error. Even when you become 'intellectually aware' of the visual illusion, it's impossible to consciously reverse the effects of the heuristic. That's because heuristics are hard wired into the Social Brain. Here's the image without the shadow, which reveals the true colors:

Figure 7 - Optical Illusion Revealed

The illusion is compelling in terms of seeing that our Intellectual Brains can be fooled easily by the heuristics in the Social

Brain, but what is the relevance to selling? Let's see how heuristics can have a direct impact on the value created in a sale. Answer the question: if a bat and a ball together cost $1.10, and the bat costs $1 more than the ball, how much does the ball cost? If you're thinking that the answer is ten cents, then you're using Social Brain heuristics to judge the calculation. Your answer may feel right, and most people also do this, but ten cents is in fact an incorrect answer. What's happening is that the problem looks easy to solve, so the Social Brain says, *"Don't worry, this is easy, step aside 'Intellectual Brain,' I'll deal with this."* It then plucks an answer from experience. The Social Brain substitutes the relative *'More than'* statement in the problem (the bat costs $1.00 *more than* the ball) with the absolute statement (the bat costs $1.00). This makes the problem easier to solve. If a ball and bat together cost $1.10 and the bat costs $1.00, then the ball does indeed cost ten cents. But that's not the question you were asked. The Social Brain is incapable of complex mathematics because complex mathematics was not required to survive in the pre-historic jungle. Complex mathematics is a function of the Intellectual Brain. So when the Social Brain can't pull the answer from memory, it all goes horribly wrong. To solve the problem, we need to switch from using the 'Social Brain,' which feels easy, to the more expensive 'Intellectual Brain,' which feels 'harder,' as you'll now experience. Please concentrate, which means switch on your intellectual brain. The correct answer to this problem is that the ball costs five cents and the bat costs (being a dollar more) $1.05 which does, in fact, make a total of $1.10.

This is important for salespeople to know because customers are making value-based decision to buy their products and services all the time. They are using a mixture of Social Brain gut feel (the ball costs 10 cents) and Intellectual Brain thinking (the ball costs 5 cents). Deciding that the ball costs 10 cents is the easy decision to make, it feels nice to make the decision that way, but it is factually inaccurate. If that were a purchase decision, the incorrect calculation would reduce value in the sale. It would be a sub-optimal choice for the buying team and their company because the decision is based on incorrect economic input. It's easy for complex business-to-business purchase decisions to be made using Social Brain thinking, but Intellectual Brain thinking makes the decision more accurate. In business today, value can be added to the buying process by helping people to make better decisions by identifying the use of Social Brain thinking and making sure robust and accurate value based decisions are made.

The ability of the Intellectual Brain to do the hard mental work required for a robust purchase decision, like the hard mental work necessary for the calculation above, is limited by how the brain was originally designed. Approximately 1.5 million years ago, there was an important decision to be made by Mother Nature. Should the limited energy resources (food) available to early humans be used to power the development of the brain, or power the development of muscle mass? With limited metabolic energy available this was a necessary trade-off. If we compare ourselves to our cousins, the Great Apes, proportionately more energy was diverted toward muscle development in Great Apes, and proportionately more energy was diverted to brain development in humans. At three times the muscle mass of a human, but with a smaller brain, this is why a Great Ape can pull your arms out of the sockets, but can't play you at chess or discuss the light texture of a Victoria sponge cake. The diet that the Great Apes enjoy is insufficient to power a brain like that of a human, at the same time as powering their considerable muscle mass. During human evolution, when energy was a scarce resource, proportionately more energy was diverted toward developing the brain in humans, and this is why we will always beat a Great Ape in a general knowledge quiz at the pub, but probably lose an arm in an arm wrestle. With one gram of brain requiring more energy than one gram of body mass, the investment of constructing and running the brain in energy terms is significant. As an organ, the brain comprises 2% of human body weight, yet it receives 15-20% of cardiac output and energy.[76] The Social Brain is acutely aware of the value of energy and makes decision choices that prioritize energy efficiency. Suzana Herculano-Houzel describes how the brain evolved with energy limitations in mind; *"The human advantage lies, first, in the fact that we are primates, and, as such, owners of a brain that is built according to very economical scaling rules that make a large number of neurons fit into a relatively small volume, compared to other mammals."*[77] We may currently be in a time of over resourcing when it comes to available food energy, but the Social Brain is unaware that the world has changed and that food energy is now perhaps too abundant. You can't tell the Social Brain that food is now abundant because, like the visual illusion, it's hard wired that way. The Social Brain still does everything it can to conserve what it sees as a scarce resource critical to survival. The hungriest area of the brain is, ironically, the Intellectual Brain. Having developed very rapidly and later in evolutionary terms than the Social Brain, the Intellectual Brain is considerably less efficient when it comes to energy usage.

Our brains are built and run with limited energy mind. We know this because we feel a slight discomfort when effort is required. The avoidance of this discomfort is one reason that we have so many energy saving devices around the home. It's the reason that most people use their Social Brain thinking, or their gut feel, to make a purchase decision, even complex purchase decisions. It feels right, so it must be right. Right? Wrong. There's a chance it could be right, but equally, there's a chance it could be wrong. Is it worth leaving the success of purchase decisions to luck? The Social Brain uses shortcuts to make decisions faster which is fine if you're not sure that the spider on your shoulder is a plastic joke spider or a deadly red back. So let's continue to use Social Brain thinking to do the spider dance, just in case. But in business-to-business buying and selling decisions, businesses are interested in a lot more than speed. They're interested in maximizing the input data so they can reduce uncertainty and risk to make the best possible buying decision. The heuristics used in the Social Brain cut corners by working with less data, which feels better mentally because it saves energy, but it also increases uncertainty and risk in the decision. Because of this, heuristics can cause systematic errors to occur in complex decision making.[78] The impact of making sub-optimal purchase decisions is a risk for all organizations. Purely in transactional terms, the cost of increased pricing linked to poor procurement practices is around 5.4% of total revenue obtained.[79] The impact goes beyond pricing, a survey by the International Association of Contract and Commercial Managers (IACCM) indicated that the average cost of poor contracting is 9.2% of an organization's annual income - and even higher for large capital projects, up to 15% of the contract value. A study by the European Commission discovered that 65% of major projects 'fail' or severely underperform, with the average cost overrun of 80%.[80] The impact of making sub-optimal selling decisions can be seen in Chapter One and is the source of the Sales Performance Paradox. Once we recognize the implication of Social Brain thinking in complex decision making, we can counteract it. President Obama could see that using behavioral economics to control heuristics could add value to government. In 2015 Obama released this Executive Order, *"A growing body of evidence demonstrates that behavioral science insights - research findings from fields such as behavioral economics and psychology about how people make decisions and act on them -- can be used to design government policies to better serve the American people. Executive departments and agencies are encouraged to recruit behavioral science experts to join the federal government as necessary to achieve the goals of this directive."*[81] Could there be a similar opportunity for salespeople to add value to the customer buying process by helping the customer to make better purchase decisions? Could there be an opportunity for sales leaders to support their sales teams to make better selling decisions?

To make better buying and selling decisions, and overcome the systematic errors of Social Brain thinking, customers need to process more information about the sale and not less. In the book *Nudge,* Thaler and Sunstein identify that, *"Experience, good information, and prompt feedback are key factors that enable people to make good decisions."*[82] Processing 'good information' requires Intellectual Brain thinking. However, because our brains default to the quicker and easier heuristics of the 'Social Brain,' B2B sales people and customers are predisposed to making sub-optimal buying and selling decisions. Could salespeople, therefore, do the heavy lifting for the customer and act as their 'Intellectual Brain Partner' in the buying process? Could sales people provide the experience, good information, prompt feedback, and the 'Intellectual Brain Power' that is required to make a better purchase decision? Could this then bring salespeople earlier and more intimately into the buying process once again? The takeaway from this chapter is yes, there is a massive opportunity to create competitive differentiation and improve sales effectiveness by helping to manage Social Brain thinking in the buying process of our customers. But to do that, we first need to learn to manage social brain thinking in our sales people and sales leaders. It would be impossible to take on the role of Intellectual Brain partners for customers with a sales force pre-disposed to Social Brain thinking. And therein lies the challenge for sales enablement. How do we get our sales teams to become the bastion of Intellectual Brain thinking? Do we train our sales people about the way they and customers process information in their brains? Will this close the gap? Based on past experience, this won't make the slightest difference because the learning won't be applied. And that is the underlying problem. Given the choice, sales people (being human) will most often choose a less effective way and easier way of selling over a more effective but more challenging way of selling because of the energy saving shortcuts built into their Social Brains. You could give a salesforce the best sales process in the world and 90% of them would never actually use it. To solve this problem we need to understand why, given the choice, a sales person would consistently choose a less effective way of selling over a more effective way. Something that makes no intellectual or logical sense. Why would anyone do that? In the next chapter we find out why this happens and why Deal Hacks can help to turn this situation around.

# CHAPTER 5

# WHY GOOD DECISIONS ARE HARD

*"Through discipline comes freedom."*

**Aristotle**


I n the 1960s young children at Bing Nursery School were part of an experiment to help understand the strength of their willpower. Walter Mischel and his team gave the children a choice between one reward (for example, a marshmallow) that they could have immediately, and a larger reward (an additional marshmallow) for which they would have to wait, alone, for up to 20 minutes. The type of reward was selected by the children. Some were offered marshmallows, others cookies, mints or pretzels, but the test has become known as the marshmallow test. The children sat alone at a table facing the marshmallow. Next to the marshmallow was a bell they could ring at any time to call back the researcher and eat the one marshmallow. Alternatively, they could wait for the researcher to return and, if they hadn't left their chair or started to eat the marshmallow, they could have two marshmallows.

The famous 'Marshmallow Test' was a test of how the children handled the inner conflict between their two decision making systems, or what might also be described as measuring the children's willpower to delay their gratification. In the book, 'The Marshmallow Test' Mischel himself said of the events, *"Everybody is eager to know how willpower works, and everybody would like to have more of it, and with less effort, for themselves, their children, and their relatives puffing on cigarettes. The ability to delay gratification and resist temptations has been a fundamental challenge since the dawn of civilization. It is central to the Genesis story of Adam and Eve's temptation in the Garden of Eden."*[83] Mischel and his team found that the children fell into two distinct cohorts, those who could wait and get the bigger prize and those who couldn't wait. Those that could delay eating the marshmallow to get the second one used delaying strategies to achieve this. Some turned away and looked at the wall, some sang a song, but ultimately this cohort managed to delay their gratification, and win the small prize.

Mischel and his team found that there was a strong correlation between the ability to delay gratification in the test, and their success in later life. Not just academic success, but success across a wide range of factors. The researchers followed the children through their lives, sending them questionnaires on various topics over the subsequent years. The results were nothing short of astonishing. *"The more seconds they waited at age four or five, the higher their college-admission SAT scores and the better they're rated social and cognitive functioning in adolescence."*[84] *"At age 27– 32, those who had waited longer during the Marshmallow Test in preschool had a lower body mass index, a better sense of self-worth and pursued their goals more effectively."*[85] By passing the marshmallow test, the children had proved that they could master their inner conflict and their Social Brain thinking. Are you the sort of person who can master your Social Brain thinking? Would you be able to master your inner conflict and pass the marshmallow test? More importantly, to achieve sales growth, would the salespeople in your organization be able to pass the marshmallow test?

What if there was something more than a marshmallow at stake? What if you had a life-threatening illness, and your Doctor told you that changing your lifestyle would save your life. What if you were conflicted because you knew that keeping your existing life style would kill you within two years. What would you do? Would you change and live longer or stay the same and die sooner? How would you cope with this inner conflict? Would you pass a marshmallow test when your life rested on it? When it comes to the imbalance of power between the Social Brain and the 'Intellectual Brain,' Dr. Edward Miller, the Dean of the medical school and CEO of the hospital at Johns Hopkins University has some sobering news. At the IBM Global Innovation Outlook event Dr. Miller said, *"If you look at people after coronary-artery bypass grafting two years later, 90% of them have not changed their lifestyle. And that's been studied over and over and over again. And so we're missing some link in there. Even though they know they have a very bad disease and they know they should change their lifestyle, for whatever reason, they can't."*[86] Everybody I ask tells me that they would change their lifestyle rather than die. 100% of people in my workshops say they would change and would succeed in doing so. However, the research gives a different reality. Faced with the choice of changing or dying, only 10% of individuals manage to change their lifestyle. 90% of people die early as a result. Why is this the case? Why would you not change if it meant you would die? It makes no logical sense. And that's exactly the point. It's not the logical part of the brain, the Intellectual Brain, that is the decision-maker here. The marshmallow test experiment is really important for us to understand, because it provides a really clear insight into how people manage the conflict between the Intellectual Brain and the Social Brain. The longer the children could wait in the marshmallow test, the better control they had over their Social Brain. Only 10% of adults can override their Social Brain consistently, even when their lives depend on it. This is why delayed gratification was described by Daniel Goleman as 'The Master Aptitude'[87] because the ability to control your impulses, behaviors, and emotions is connected directly to success on so many levels, especially in sales.

Do sales people in your sales organization have the Master Aptitude? In Chapter Two it was highlighted that Neil Rackham had pioneered 'adding value' into the sales process back in the 1980s and 1990s. The common finding from many sales training companies, where salespeople are trained to add value for customers in the sales process, is that the behaviors are applied at first after training, but not by everybody in the whole sales force. There are pockets of people who adapt, but overall the majority fail to adapt and so don't add as much value as they potentially could. Additionally, this capability reduces over time, as people go back to the old way of doing things, the easy way. I can give countless examples where I've see this. Here's just one recent example from a company I worked with that had rolled out value based sales training through a well known sales training consulting company in the USA. One of the metrics used to measure the success of the program was how many of the sales people were creating a value based business case for their prospects, which was part of the sales process. One year after the sales training only five percent of the deals forecast in any quarter had a value based business case. Only five percent of the deals were being sold in the way the sales people had been trained, and how the company wanted them to sell. It was desirable to sell this way because 90% of deals with business cases typically closed, so creating a business case dramatically improved the likelihood of winning a deal. The company had a team of people whose job it was to actually write the business cases on behalf of the sales teams, so there was a significant amount of support available to do this. Why would the sales people not use this valuable resource? To the sales leaders it made no logical sense. But it does make sense if you look at it through the lens of the Social Brain. Adding the creation of a business case into a sales process takes time and Intellectual Brain thinking. It is far easier just to leave it out of the process and save time. The salespeople were using Social Brain thinking to save time by cutting corners. We saw earlier why the buyer would adopt Social Brain thinking in the buying process, because it is easier and feels better. The same is true in this example where the salespeople also defaulted to Social Brain thinking to shorten the sales process, for exactly the same reasons. But not playing the required playbook was having a detrimental effect on sales, so they implemented Deal Hacks. In the quarter following the implementation of Deal Hacks, the number of business cases rose from 5% to 50% of the deals. The previous training program was considered to be a failure, but implementing Deal Hacks turned the initial program into a success. The original training focused on how the sales people should create, use and sell business cases in the sales process. The Deal Hacks focused on challenging and supporting the sales people to help them change inside the workflow, in real live deals. The two are completely different problems to solve.

This lack of business case creation is an example of the sales people using Social Brain thinking at a given stage in the sales process. But the sales process is in fact a series of marshmallow tests for salespeople, where they get to choose how to sell. On the one hand, there's the hard Intellectual Brain way of doing things, and there's the Social Brain easier way of doing things. Let's look at four common examples of where Social Brain thinking causes short cuts to be made in the sales process reducing value and reducing sales effectiveness:

1) **Decision Makers:** We know that in complex deals

we need to align a coalition of decision makers in the customer organization. There's the Social Brain way to crack this one, the easy way, where we deal with one or maybe two people. For example, we only interact with the people who are introduced to us by the customer. Then there's the Intellectual Brain hard way to crack this one, where we build a clear picture of all the people who have an influence over the customer buying process and develop aligned coalitions in both the buying and selling organizations. We build coaches, the champion and the economic buyer as well as a wider network of influencers. We know this second approach is more effective, but it is harder. It takes a proactive approach and requires the building of complex information, analysis and strategizing associated with Intellectual Brain thinking. We know from experience that most buyers overstate their power in a purchasing decision. Challenging the prospect on their level of purchasing authority can be seen as a threat to the social status of the person providing the answer, something the Social Brain will avoid. If the person we ask is not a champion or the economic buyer, that means we need to build a relationship with someone else, which takes time and effort, something the Social Brain will want to avoid. Having one person making all the decisions brings a level of certainty to the situation. The thought that a group of people we don't know are involved in the decision makes things less certain. The Social Brain craves certainty and wants to avoid losses, so will convince itself that the decision making team is as simple as possible. This is why so many accounts we look at in Deal Hacks have a single point of contact.

2)    **Decision Criteria:** why should the customer choose us? The Social Brain way is to allow the customer to determine differential value by comparing the features and benefits in the proposal to other competitive proposals.

Then there's the Intellectual Brain hard way of determining the decision criteria of the combined stakeholder coalition, then calculating and communicating clear and visible differential value in the context of the other propositions being considered.

3) **Deal Value:** Where and how much value does the proposal add to the whole buying team and the wider organization? The Social Brain approach is to examine the immediate customer context, matching features to benefits and then providing a price. Then there's the Intellectual Brain, harder way, of building a visually clear and communicable picture of value across the whole buying organization. This includes how the solution impacts the strategic goals of the business as well as the goals of whole buying team. The Intellectual Brain approach is to calculate the "innovation adoption and validate this with the buying team. When I ask sales people in workshops if they perform ROI calculations for their proposals, the response rate is rarely above 0. The problem is that Social Brains finds value based selling just that bit too hard.

4) **Decision Process:** How will the prospect organization make the purchase decision? The Social Brain way of understanding the decision process is to ask as few questions as possible because it wants the sale to happen as soon as possible. Understanding the full process invariably adds process steps that make the process longer, potentially delaying the order and making the closing of the order less certain. The Intellectual Brain knows the importance of knowing this information and does not stick it's head in the sand.

These are just examples, but they are examples that cover the four key elements of any deal that we measure in Deal Hacks, the Four Ds:

**Why buy now?** 1) Decision Process  2) Decision Value

**Why choose us?** 3) Decision Makers 4) Decision Criteria

Get any one of those wrong and the deal is at high risk of being lost. The important takeaway for B2B selling is that there's always an easy way and a hard way to sell to customers. These are the continual and ever-present marshmallow tests that salespeople face, on a daily, or even hourly basis. Are the salespeople in your organization winning that internal battle to sell comprehensively, or losing it? How are you measuring your answer to that question? Can you definitively prove one way or the other, as we can when Deal Hacks have been implemented? I'm on the same page as Dr. Edward Miller on this one. When I start doing Deal Hacks in a sales organization, less than 10% of the deals are being run according to the set sales process. In fact 10% would be a good score, it's usually less.

Nobel prize-winning economist and Turing Award winner, Herbert Simon, described Social Brain thinking as 'satisficing.' He said, *"Evidently, organisms adapt well enough to 'satisfice'; they do not, in general, 'optimize'. A 'satisficing' path, a path that will permit satisfaction at some specified level of all its needs."*[88] Satisficing is a portmanteau of the words 'satisfy' and 'suffice'. Simon's work is extremely influential in the world of Artificial Intelligence, because he helped to decode how people make decisions in a way that can be applied to machines. Simons identified that there are two components to any decision, not one as many people assume. The first component is to 'satisfy' the need. All well-trained salespeople know this, and that's the satisfy part of 'satisficing'. But there is a second and arguably more important component of decision making, and that is to bring the decision making process to an end. We all seek closure because of the human need for reliability and certainty. If we do not achieve closure we find ourselves in a

less certain situation, which uses up more cognitive resources, because it requires more thinking. This is evolution-
arily less desirable, because our brains were designed for a
time when energy (food) was a scarce resource. Because of
this, there is a strong desire to bring any decision to a close as
quickly as possible. Shortening the decision process will in itself affect the decision outcome. For example, when there is a
high need for closure, perhaps due to time constraints, individuals are more likely to use simple cognitive structures to
process the information more quickly, and close the decision.[89] While we all think that professional people take the
time to make thorough and well thought out decisions, the
time and resources available to make those decisions is always limited. Making good decisions involves research,
analysis, consultation and debating. All of these things take
time and effort, which steers the brain towards the more simple decision making heuristics of the Social Brain because
they will 'suffice'. That's the second part of 'satisficing', the decision will suffice given the limited resources we want to ex-
pend on it. This affects customers who, when under pressure
to make a purchase decision, will make a sub-optimal economic decision by using Social Brain heuristics, or shortcuts.
This is why high-pressure selling works (at least once). This
can also affect the seller who will make sub-optimal decisions
by similarly defaulting to Social Brain decision making heuristics. For example, think of a salesperson at the end of the
quarter making a routine decision about how to process a new
prospect through the sales process: *"Shall I take the time to
undertake a business case? No, the customer said they really liked
our product and just needed a price. It's practically in the bag and I
need it to close sooner. That will just delay so I'll save time and send
out a standard proposal for them...."* That saves time in the sales
process, and it moves it through the initial stages of the sales
pipeline, which looks good on a report and feels good emotionally. But how can they differentiate, influence and negotiate now? It's a matter of luck if that proposal comes in. Profes-

sional buyers know this and use simple techniques, often focused on reducing time, certainty or status, to switch on the sales person's Social Brain so that their Intellectual Brain shuts down. These include keeping the sales person waiting in reception, being aggressive, not responding, waiting till the end of the month/quarter and focusing on price. It doesn't take much to tip a sales person into Social Brain thinking where logic leaves the room and decision making shortcuts can be taken advantage of. Professional buyers know how to turn on Social Brain thinking in the sales people they buy from so they can capture more value from them. But they also use oversight and processes to turn off Social Brain buying within their own organizations and defend value. Deal Hacks bring an equivalent level of objective oversight and process into the sales organization. We need to do this because the selling decisions we make feel so right!! And they might be right, but they might be wrong and our minds are not geared to spotting our own short comings and blind spots. The objective oversight in the Deal Hacks highlights Social Brain thinking biases and challenges the decisions to optimize the deal outcome by creating value, reducing risk and defending value, in the same way our professional buying counterparts already do.

When it came to making lifestyle changes, only 10% of people in the study managed the changes when their lives depended upon it. 90% of people died within two years because they were unable to change. We have little evidence to suggest that more than 10% of salespeople can change from the traditional Social Brain way of selling that is so pervasive. It certainly gives credence to the statistic that 70% of sales performance interventions fail[90]. It also ties up with the significant amount of documented and anecdotal experience of transformational change projects that change happens in small pockets, but overall the sales population fails to change. If sales people are not able to identify and control their own Social Brain decision making, they will not be able to learn how to support the customer with their Intellectual Brain decision making in the buying process. For salespeople to do this they would have to be capable of identifying and using Intellectual Brain decision making themselves consistently, and that would put them in the top 10% of the human population who can consistently control their Social Brain thinking, as we saw from Dr. Edward Miller's observations. But everything we have seen so far puts them at the other end of the spectrum. The consistent over-estimation of their own capability and the lack of ability to see their own performance gaps and the short circuiting of the sales process, points to a profession that is anchored in Social Brain thinking and prone to decision making errors, particularly in complex and information rich environments. That is why, like our professional buying counterparts, we need objective oversight and processes to protect against Social Brain thinking inside the sales process. In other words we need Deal Hacks, a mechanism for moving towards Intellectual Brain thinking in the sales process. We know it's hard for people to do this on their own, so Deal Hacks provide the consistent challenge and support they need, inside the workflow, and inside the deals when they need it, to develop Intellectual Brain thinking strategies and improve decision making.

To see how Deal Hacks help to build those strategies, we need to look in detail at what drives Social Brain thinking and reactions in the first place. What we'll see is that the legacy methods we're employing to improve and enable sales capability can actually cause the Social Brain thinking we're trying to move away from.

# CHAPTER 6
# SOCIAL DECISION DRIVERS

*"While we tend to think it is our capacity for abstract reasoning that is responsible for Homo sapiens' dominating the planet, there is increasing evidence that our dominance as a species may be attributable to our ability to think socially".*

**Matthew Lieberman.**

L ying inside the dark, cylindrical tube was a young woman waiting for the experiment to begin. The tube was a Functional magnetic resonance imaging scanner (fMRI) measuring brain activity by detecting changes associated with blood flow. She had been told that two others would be simultaneously having their brains scanned while they played a video game with her over the Internet called 'cyber ball.' The scientists told her they were interested in how brains coordinate with one another to perform simple tasks like ball tossing. After a few minutes of playing, the two other participants stopped throwing the ball to the young woman. But they continued to throw the ball to each other, effectively excluding her from the game. What the young woman didn't know, was that there were no other subjects in the experiment. She was playing with pre-programmed avatars, programmed to stop throwing her the ball after a short period.

The leader of the experiment, Matthew Lieberman, was not measuring coordination as he had said. He was in fact measuring the effects of being socially rejected. After the experiment, the participants were taken to a room to answer questions about their experience. Lieberman explains how they reacted: *"Frequently these individuals would spontaneously start talking to us about what had just happened to them. They were genuinely angry or sad about what they had gone through. This was unusual for a fMRI study because most tasks didn't generate personal emotional reactions."*[91] When Lieberman and his team examined the data, they compared the images of emotional pain to images of physical pain. The images should have been very different, but they were strikingly similar. What Lieberman and his team had found, was that social pain is identical to physical pain. The neural circuits used for physical pain are exactly the same circuits used for emotional pain. The implication is that for humans, social threats are as important as physical threats. Lieberman sums it up nicely, *"Humans need to feel social separation as painful. It keeps infants and caregivers close together. That may have been the reason evolution gave us social pain, but now we are stuck with it our entire lives, and it colors almost every social experience we have".*[92]

Lieberman proved that the Social Brain is hard-wired to be 'Social' and that emotionally driven social connections are more important to humans than almost anything. We are driven by deep motivations to stay connected with friends and family. This has a significant impact on our behavior and starts to explain why we don't always make the logical decisions we aspire to. In fact, when somebody you know makes a decision that seems illogical, try to look at the decision through the Social Brain lens, and it starts to make more sense.

Being able to decode the world through the lens of the Social Brain will help us harness the power it has. In the world of selling, this means making it work for us rather than work against us. To do this, we need to be clear on what the Social Brain values, or what it wants.

By studying the brain in fMRI scanners, we can see that our brains are structured around the core survival function of whether something is good for us, or bad for us. Will something help us? This will bring about the desire to find more of it. Or will something hurt us? This will bring about the desire to avoid it.[93] Over time we've developed an underlying binary mechanism for organizing what we encounter in everyday life. Everything significant we come across is categorized as either 0) a danger or 1) a reward. *The core organizing principle of self-adaptation which underlies all aspects of brain and body activity and behavior is to minimize danger and maximize reward.*[94] This binary mechanism, developed in the Social Brain of prehistoric humans, is a way to minimize threats of danger and to maximize opportunities, increasing our chances of survival. The 'Threat Response' was developed by the brain to produce a physical reaction to stimuli that could do us harm, such as predators, poisonous insects, and poisonous plants; the things we needed to be aware of and to avoid. The 'Reward response' was developed to encourage us to take advantage of stimuli that were good for us like food, drink, comfort, sex, relationships, etc. Things that maximize our chances of survival. The English philosopher Jeremy Bentham shows that this is not a new concept when he described it in 1789, *"Nature has placed mankind under the government of two sovereign masters, pain and pleasure. It is for them alone to point out what we ought to do, as well as to determine what we shall do."*[95]

This survival mechanism is a continuous process that is handled by the Social Brain and below the level of consciousness. This means that you consciously know little or nothing about it, but it's importance cannot be underestimated. Think of placing a large plastic spider on someone's shoulder. Without the Social Brain doing the spider dance for us, we would have died out as a species long ago. If the Social Brain decides that something will help us, that will manifest to the Intellectual Brain as feelings of reward, through a big shot of the neurotransmitter dopamine, creating the feeling of happiness and satisfaction.[96] If the Social Brain decides that something will hurt us, that will manifest as feelings of threat. In the threat response, a cocktail of adrenalin and cortisol gets released, which increases heart rate, blood pressure and blood sugar to boost energy for the impending conflict. Threat feelings include anxiety, discomfort, sadness, and fear. If serious enough it can evoke the freeze, fight or flight survival mechanism.[97] We've all been there. We've all experienced the dizzy heights of happiness when we get something we really want. We've all experienced the gut-wrenching feeling of panic when we lose something we really value, something called loss aversion. Sales people are familiar with this, using such techniques to sell to customers such as pain and gain, opportunities and threats, wins and losses, etc.

We're all experts in threats and rewards, even if we're not always conscious of it. When it comes to learning new sales skills, are the skills seen as a threat or as a reward? Let's decode that using the threat/reward filter. The first question on the Social Brain's mind is, *"Will the new sales skills help me? Or will they hurt me?"* Intellectually we know that training will ultimately help. Even if the subject is already familiar to the learner, there are possibilities to deepen that knowledge, update on the latest thinking and learn from colleagues and their experiences. When I ask this question of sales people, most say that improving their sales skills will help them. Indeed, good sales performance optimization programs sell the benefits of change to the participants. Here are some typical example benefits:

1) This is an investment in you
2) You will win more deals
3) You will achieve higher closure rates
4) You will be able to negotiate greater margins

What salesperson wouldn't want this? Logically this invest-ment will make you better at your job, and you'll earn more money as a result for many years to come. Yay! But not every-one buys into taking sales performance interventions as we saw in part one. Why is this the case when the benefits are so clear and self-evident? We're taught by the father of econom-ics, Adam Smith, that people buy into something when ra-tionally it is in their self-interest to do so, for example, when benefits outweigh costs. Smith famously said, *"It is not from the benevolence of the butcher, the brewer, or the baker, that we ex-pect our dinner, but from their regard to their own interest. We ad-dress ourselves, not to their humanity but to their self-love, and never talk to them of our necessities but of their advantages."[98]* This is a rational approach to decision making where the Intellectual Brain is working alone. Do we make rational eco-nomic decisions? We now know that the Intellectual Brain is influenced and can be easily overridden by the Social Brain. The benefits of attending sales training listed above appeal to the logic orientated Intellectual Brain that understands ab-stract concepts and is conscious of the future. So it's a yes from the Intellectual Brain. It may be the case that these bene-fits do not appeal to the Social Brain. We will see in a moment. We're using sales performance interventions as an example, but it's not just buying into sales performance interventions where we see the phenomenon of people making counter-intuitive value decisions. There's a resounding agreement from salespeople in workshops when I ask the question, *"Have you ever been involved in a deal where the logic for the customer to buy is watertight. The product satisfies the needs of all stake-holders far better than the competition. The price is in budget. The customer would have to be barking mad not to buy. And they don't?"* There are reasons that despite a watertight economic value proposition, people don't buy. A significant reason is that the Intellectual Brain decision making and the Social Brain decision making have not been identified, aligned and systematically dealt with. In sales, we have the tools and understanding to put together the case for economic value, for example, creating a "innovation adoption calculation or even something as simple as listing the benefits of a deal. In other words, we're fabulous at talking logically to the Intellectual Brain. And intuitively we sell to the Social Brain, for example we often say, 'People buy people'. Natural sales people are said to do this very well, and it is often described as the 'art' of selling. But do we have a systematic way of selling to the Social Brain in the same way we do to the Intellectual Brain? In other words do we have a way of systematically scaling and enabling what natural sales people do? I think this is why there are tens of thousands of books on how to sell because, unlike the science part of selling, there is ambiguity and the 'art' is subjective and hard to pin down. Until now, that is. With advances in neuroscience we can now understand how the Social Brain makes decisions and this can help us to build a framework and process to measure and scale the art of selling in the same way we do with the science of selling. Let's start by asking why the Social Brain became 'Social' in the first place?

Humans are intensely social compared to other animals. Foals can stand up and walk independently not long after birth, ducks can swim, and chickens can peck for food soon after hatching. These behaviors in their young are driven by environmental factors and are requirements for their survival. Human babies are, however, particularly needy compared to other young. The gestation period for humans should be 18 months. But as any mother will attest, with brain size in mind, this would make an already difficult process impossible.[99]

According to David Bainbridge, *"This uniquely lengthy post-natal period of brain growth has led some scientists to claim that the human infant is really a fetus wrenched into the outside world simply so that its brain can expand, free from the restrictions of its mother's pelvis."*[100] Being born so early in the gestation period, therefore, the first skills that human babies acquire are social. Smiling, looking for mum and dad, laughing, gurgling and playing games. We can do all of these long before we can walk or run, skills that would enable us to avoid capture from hunters or be useful. Instead, we develop social skills first which helps us to bond with our parents who in turn look after us. We go on to develop social skills that allow us to bond with other people in our tribe. The tribe size was approximately 148 in Neolithic times.[101] These social skills are methods of facilitating interactions and communicating with others so that we can live successfully together. One such example is body language. Long before we developed sophisticated verbal language skills, we communicated through body language.[102] Ask someone a question, and you know what they mean if they shrug their shoulders. We know what it means when a champion raises their arms above their head in victory; there's no need for them to explain. These are remnants of our ancient ability to communicate socially with each other through visual body language and without an auditory verbal language. Most often our Intellectual Brain is unconscious of this language, but our Social Brain picks it up effortlessly and feed it back to the Intellectual Brain through feelings. Social is the new thing online, but actually, we've been social for millions of years. And over those millions of years we've developed seven DRIVERS that cause a strong reaction from the Social Brain:

- **Decision making** – people want to be able to make their own decisions.
- **Reciprocation** - we are programmed to give some-

thing back to a person that gives something to us, and we trust others to do the same

- **Interpersonal connections** - people want to be part of a group, club or tribe.
- **Victory -** people are naturally ambitious to achieve their goals to a higher level than their peers.
- **Equality** - people want equality and fairness in life.
- **Reliability -** the brain likes reliability and certainty because they are safe and uses less energy. Unreliable events are less safe and have a costly cognitive load.
- **Status** – people want to enjoy a good social or professional reputation and status. Rank compared to other people in the tribe is critical to survival.

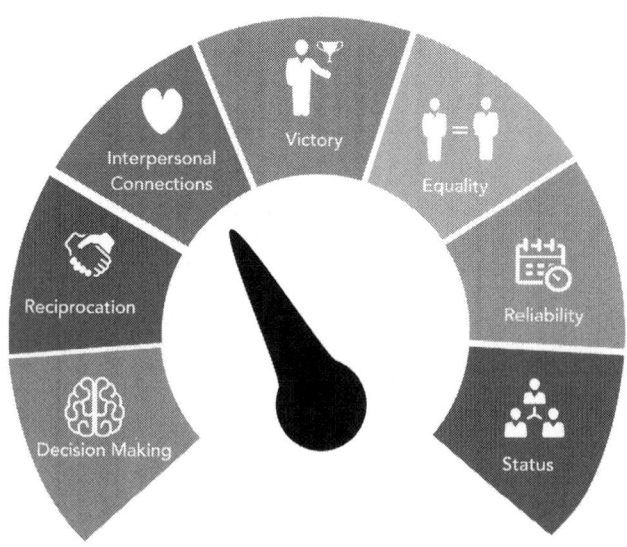

Figure 8 - Social Decision DRIVERS

Let's take a deeper dive, and find some examples:

**Decision making** – people want to be able to make their own decisions. This is so powerful that when we make decisions for other people, it can significantly increase their resistance to persuasion and cause them to do the opposite of what they actually want. Called 'reactance' people often do the opposite of what they have been asked to do, regardless if it is harmful to themselves and others.[103] **Threat example:** if we want to punish people we put them in prison where they can make fewer decisions for themselves. **Reward example:** we give teenagers increased freedom to make their own decisions as they develop maturity and responsibility.

**Reciprocation** – being from a tribe, we are programmed to give something back to a person that gives something to us. *"We are human because our ancestors learned to share their food and their skills in an honored network of obligation.*[104] *"There is an obligation to give, an obligation to receive, and an obligation to repay. Although the obligation to repay constitutes the essence of the reciprocity rule, it is the obligation to receive that makes the rule so easy to exploit."*[105] There is a lexicon of pejorative terms to describe people who do not reciprocate in society: freeloader, leech, sponge and parasite. Entitled people have a good memory for the things they've done and expect to get a return.

**Threat example:** if you lend something to a person and they do not give it back. **Reward example:** we receive a thank you card for having given a gift.

**Interpersonal connections** – people want to be part of a group, club or tribe. *"Lack of social participation and inadequate control over your life, in the sense of not being able to lead the life you want to lead, will lead to chronic stress, which in turn increases the risk of a number of diseases, heart disease among them.*[106] We saw earlier how expulsion from the tribe, in ancient times would have resulted in certain death. **Threat example:** being excluded from a peer group, being ostracized or not invited to a party. **Reward example:** being able to play for a national team, being house captain at school or fighting for your country.

**Victory** – people are naturally ambitious to achieve their personal goals to a higher level than their peers. In sales, many people describe themselves as competitive, in other words, they seek victory over another. Sport is an example of where we seek victory and most often in the absence of any financial reward. 'Keeping up with the Joneses' is an example of how victory is woven into the fabric of western society. In fact, we're so keen to be victorious over others that we prefer relative advantage over absolute advantage. In a survey of faculty, students and staff at the Harvard School of Public Health, nearly half of the respondents said they'd prefer to live in a world where the average salary was $25,000, and they earned $50,000 than one where they earned $100,000, but the average was $200,000.[107] **Threat example:** your favorite sports team loses a game. **Reward example:** being awarded the 'Top Salesperson' award.

**Equality** – people want equality and fairness in life. It is a strong driver from an early age. Children are very adept at spotting unfairness. At any age, the psychological experience of inequality can have profound effects on our body systems.[108] **Threat example:** the suffragettes fought to give women the vote due to the lack of equality. **Reward example:** somebody being treated without fear or favor.

**Reliability** – The grass is ....? Did the word 'luscious' pop into your head? The word 'juicy'? No, the words green or greener popped into your head, which is an example of your brain predicting events. The brain likes reliability because it is safe and uses less energy. Unreliable events are less safe, contain risk and have a costly cognitive load as a result. According to Andy Clark, *"To deal rapidly and fluently with an uncertain and noisy world, brains like ours have become masters of prediction."*[109] Uncertainty is an unstructured and unpredictable form of change that is outside of our control. We already know that the brain does not like change, so this extreme form of change can easily cause stress. The need for certainty increases when people feel threatened or under pressure which can drive adverse behaviors in high pressure selling environments.[110] **Threat example:** standing on the train platform and the train is late, you have no idea when it will come. If you knew the train was going to be ten minutes late, that would be OK; but you don't know. The uncertainty makes you feel frustrated. **Reward example:** knowing that you are in a job with long term security.

**Status** – Nobel Laureate economist, John Harsanyi, said that *"Apart from economic payoffs, social status seems to be the most important incentive and motivating force of social behavior."*[111] People want to enjoy a good social or professional reputation and status. Your rank compared to others in the tribe is critical to survival. It doesn't matter if you're rich or poor, we all strive to achieve status, although that may manifest in different forms. According to Marmot, good health follows a social gradient, and he calls this the 'status syndrome' where people with better status have better health.[112] In Chapter One we saw that salespeople have a very strong sense of status and that helps them to cope with rejection. **Threat example:** failing to be promoted at work. **Reward example:** a person that wins an award and is celebrated in the news.

From these, we have created the DRIVERS analysis tool for Social Brain filtering. When communicating with or challenging an individual or a team, the tool can be used to assess the potential threats or rewards concerned. Quite often we look at a situation at work or even at home and can't see the logic in it. When there's no logic to someone's motives or behaviors, that is a signal that you should look at the situation through the social DRIVERS lens. In that way you can decode the situation and hopefully resolve it. We can also use the Social

DRIVERS lens to decode many of the customs that we have in our cultures. **Liberté égalité fraternité** was the motto of the French revolution meaning freedom, equality, and brotherhood. Translated into modern-day Drivers: 'Decision making, equality and interpersonal connections.' The revolutionaries' version does sound much more compelling! It's fascinating that the rallying cry of the revolution speaks directly to the more powerful Social Brain rather than the Intellectual Brain. The revolution would not have been so successful had they cried, *"More money, more food and longer holidays!"* When Dr. Edward Miller said that 90% of people do not change their lifestyle in the face of a life-threatening illness, we know that to 'change and live' is the logical choice made by the Intellectual Brain. But the Social Brain can systematically undermine logical and beneficial choices made by the Intellectual Brain. We know that the Social Brain can process 11,534,336 bytes of data per second whereas the Intellectual Brain can process only around 50 bytes of data per second. So in a straight intellectual arm wrestle, the Social Brain will win almost every time because it is considerably stronger than the Intellectual Brain.

Can the DRIVERS help to explain the paradox that, faced with the choice of 'change or die,' 90% of individuals don't change and die younger than they should? Let's look at the 'change or die' situation through the lens of the Social Drivers:

    a. Decision making. **Threat**: the ability to decide to exercise or not, or to eat different foods has been removed.

    b. Reciprocation. **Reward**: the Doctors have helped the patient, and it will feel beneficial to reciprocate by doing as they ask. **Threat**: old friends who want to continue the lifestyle may have to be rejected which breaks the reciprocation rule.

   c. Interpersonal Connection. **Threat**: the patient may have to separate and break connections from people who engage in the old behaviors

   d. Victory. **Threat**: victories for the Social Brain are short term, so the victory of living long-term is irrelevant. The Social Brain experiences and sees poor lifestyle choices such as alcohol, cigarettes, and fatty foods as victories.

   e. Equality. **Threat**: this is unfair because other people don't have to live in such a restricted way. Loss aversion. predicts that the brain will prefer to see equality as a loss rather than a gain, where the person could think, "I'm better off than those poor people in the earthquake…" Most people see equality in terms of loss.

   f. Reliability. **Threat**: the old lifestyle has been done away with, and it is uncertain how the patient will cope with the changes. The patient is out of their routines and habits.

   g. Status. **Threat:** not being able to live in the chosen way, and make decisions in the way they want to, could make the patient feel that their status has been reduced.

Looking through the DRIVERS lens can seem illogical, and frustrating to the Intellectual Brain. But that is the conflict that rages in us all. Perhaps the worst part of this is that the DRIVERS work below the level of consciousness because they are communicated by feelings. Your 'Gut Feel.' Some people are better at recognizing and managing these feelings than others. The 10% of coronary-artery bypass patients who managed to change their lifestyles can recognize these feelings, and so deal with them more effectively. Daniel Goleman calls this dark art 'emotional intelligence' (EQ). He describes EQ as, *"The capacity for recognizing our own feelings and those of others, for motivating ourselves, and for managing emotions well in ourselves and in our relationships*[113]." A more contemporary term is 'Mindfulness,' and a first step in being able to recognize our feelings is to understand how the Social Brain works. The Social DRIVERS are the keys to decoding the behaviors that result from Social Brain thinking.

The ability of 10% of a sales population to change is a pattern that I have seen play out time, after time, after time. 90% of the people in a sales training sessions agree that updating sales skills is beneficial. 90% of the people agree that the new skills will achieve new and better results. 90% of salespeople, however, go back to their old ways in months. The reason for this is that, logically, updating sales skills is a very good idea. Everyone earns more money, has the feeling of greater success and beating the competition. Happy days. But this is the logical, Intellectual Brain making the decision, or more accurately making an intention. The Social Brain has a very different short-term agenda and has not bought into the long-term change process. The Social Brain makes most of the routine decisions for us on a day-to-day basis. Prioritizing efficiency over change, it has the motive and the power to override and undermine the Intellectual Brains' strategy of changing. The Social Brain's choices unconsciously sabotage the sales process by nudging into existing lower energy consuming behaviors. Many sales enablement programs miss this critical piece because of an over-reliance on training. This is how the 'Social Brain' can see sales the training:

- **Decision making – Threat:** it's not my decision to spend valuable selling time in the classroom. It's not my decision to change the way I operate.
- **Reciprocation – Threat:** I work my backside off, and in return, you're taking away valuable selling time from me!
- **Interpersonal connections – Reward:** I get to see my colleagues and share war stories. **Threat:** I'm away

from customers and my family

- **Victory – Threat:** I need to be on the phone to win deals, so I can get my bonuses and get into the sales 100 club. I need to look as if I know what I'm doing and with the introduction of new methods I may look inept.
- **Equality – Threat:** I don't need training, it's the other people that need it, so this is unfair on me. (Superiority Illusion)
- **Reliability – Threat:** I'm happy doing what I'm doing and certain that what I'm doing works best because I've been doing it for years. We have no proof the new system works. Customers are telling me that they do not value the differentiation, surely it would be better to spend this budget making the products and services better?
- **Status – Threat:** who are they to say that I've not been doing my job properly and needed training? I'm concerned I'll be made to look inept by trying new techniques in front of my colleagues. I'm one of the best salespeople on the team, it's not me that needs the training, it should be for the others.

Let's challenge the view described above of the 'Social Brain': *"You were only giving a negative perspective, and not all salespeople think so negatively."* That is correct, but this is the world according to the 'Social Brain' which is focused on short term social issues and is pulled more easily towards negative threats than positive rewards. Switch off the 'Social Brain' and look at it logically through the 'Intellectual Brain' and investing in sales training makes complete logical sense.

With this negative view of training, we can start to see why training is good for knowledge transfer and building understanding, but not good for behavioral change. In order to change, people need learning support when it comes to applying what they have learned, they need support solving problems and support when the environment changes. Those are the critical points when the sales person is often unsupported, and the Social Brain nudges them into doing what they've always done, and most likely that is lower energy consuming behaviors. It feels easier, which means it feels more right. This is then rationalized and backed up by the Intellectual Brain. This explains why over 70% of sales transformation programs fail.[114] According to Jane Hills, *"Leaders tell us time and again that people revert back to their old ways of working or even fail from the outset to make the shift to the new role and work methods. Incentives and threats just drive resistance underground."* [115] Hills is right about reverting back to existing behaviors which is easier and takes less energy. But in sales it's not just about sales transformation, it's about being able to adhere to the existing sales process where Social Brain driven low energy behaviors cut corners and lose deals as a result. For both of these reasons we need support inside the workflow to counter the Social Brain nudges, on a regular and consistent basis.

Sales transformation programs are not typically structured to nudge the Intellectual brain behaviors, for example pulling the sales team out of the field every 6 months for training is clearly no match for the ever nudging Social Brain. They are also not structured for getting the buy-in from the Social Brain; they are organized around getting the buy-in from the logical Intellectual Brain. Every sales transformation program that has ever happened and every sales training book ever written is clear that we need to show 'what's in it for me?' (WIIFM). I'm not saying that's not right; I'm saying that's only part of the equation because that is speaking to the 'Intellectual Brain,' but the Social Brain couldn't care less. For example, *"The company is investing $2000 in each salesperson which will result in a 10% uplift in sales which will put $10,000 extra in your pocket if you adopt the new methods."* This is logical, and shows what's in it for me. It's, therefore, tough for us to understand why the emotional brain does not buy into this especially if the sales populations say that they're on board. But their Social Brain is undermining this logic, and there is a conflict in the mind of the salesperson that the Social Brain will win over time because it is significantly more powerful. So when we're planning a sales performance intervention and we want to clarify the, 'What's in it for me?' The big question is, 'Who is me?'. The social me or the intellectual me? Hills summarizes this missing piece: *"Unfortunately traditional change management approaches are not compatible with this new understanding of the brain's functioning. Bonuses and incentives or threats of job loss will not overcome the biological reaction to change."*

We're not saying that current transformation and enablement practices are completely wrong; we're showing that logic is only part of the process of audience buy-in and a much smaller part than we may currently think. We can easily make the positive arguments that appeal to the 'Intellectual Brain,' and that's one reason we see buy-in across large parts of the sales population before the engagement. Before the sales performance intervention starts, before change happens, the Social Brain has nothing to worry about. But once the sales performance intervention starts, and we actually ask for a behavior to change, the Social Brain jumps into action by attacking the logic and undermining it at the subconscious level. It's similar to other situations that involve the Social Brain like receiving feedback. When I ask salespeople if they like feedback I typically get the answer *"Yes,"* (Intellectual Brain) followed quickly by, *"But as long as It's constructive"* (Social Brain). Let's decode that "But." The response to feedback is often negative because the Social Brain does not want any DRIVERS threats and also doesn't want to change, which is the implication of feedback. The Intellectual Brain tells the Social Brain that feedback is good for our long-term development and long-term benefit. This is the 'Yes' that comes out. But the Social Brain will be undermining this decision because there are potential social threats to deal with. This is what we typically call 'being defensive.' That's all before the feedback is even given! Once the feedback has been provided, we are then hard-wired to see it negatively thanks to loss aversion.[116] The threats to all of the DRIVERS, in the case of feedback, are felt more strongly than any potential reward, and that is why people focus on the negative when receiving feedback. If you give ten points of feedback, nine are positive, and one is negative, we all know which one is going to take the airtime in that meeting. Does the Social Brain really think so negatively about sales enablement or sales transformation? It almost certainly doesn't know what they are. The most important things for the Social Brain are avoiding change which is expensive in energy terms, and avoiding social threats, which can be fatal. And there's a ton of both of these in any sales performance intervention. Remember the 90% of heart patients who fail to change? That makes no logical sense whatsoever, and people are dying prematurely as a result. The fact that 90% of people can't change their lifestyle to save their lives only makes sense if you look at it through the lens of the Social Brain. In the same vein, failure to buy into sales performance optimization makes no logical sense. But salespeople are not consciously aware that their 'Social Brains' are thinking negatively about the situation. They just have a 'bad feeling' about it all, which is enough to start them on a journey that can result in entrenched opposition to new concepts, changes and feedback. In other words a journey towards a fixed mind-set.

Most businesses assume that explaining to the salespeople logically about their performance gaps will convince them of the need for an intervention. Unfortunately, it's the opposite. Explaining to salespeople something that is logically contrary to their emotional beliefs creates a threat response. This, in turn, makes them increasingly entrenched through self-justification. Pushing an alternative opinion towards them has the unintended consequence of making them more opposed to change over time, not less. This is how a couple of learning interventions that adversely affect the social DRIVERS can push the sales people into a fixed mind-set. From that point on, their ability to take advantage of ongoing performance support is reduced. This is why it is so important to design learning interventions that do not only talk to the logic of the Intellectual Brain, and that can potentially cause a social brain threat response. A good place to start is by designing interventions that fit in with the BASIC learning times (Chapter 11) inside the workflow, which matches more closely how sales people want to learn and need to be supported and challenged when they learn. Another way, is to look at how the sessions are communicated. Perhaps we could attach less importance, and not more importance, when communicating that 'change' is required. If we know that the customer is changing and in turn, the sales population needs to change, stopping telling the salespeople that they need to change will avoid the threat response that kick starts the move towards a fixed mind-set. Salespeople should be good at looking for and, should be good at, finding better ways to win deals. We need to tap into the way that they do this, tap into their natural curiosity and create learning interventions around this. Sales people tell us that they like to learn from each other, they like to learn in the workplace as opposed to the class room, and we know that deals are the most important thing to them. So let's use those mechanisms to create the vehicle for implicit change. That's exactly what Deal Hacks are, a vehicle for learning from each other, learning in the workplace, and working on the deals that are important to them. For these reasons the threat responses from the Social Brain are minimized and the process of developing a fixed mind-set does not get triggered.

Now that we have a working model of the brain, we can readily identify and communicate how decisions are made, and how decision making can be influenced towards consistent fixed or growth mind-sets. This allows sales leaders and sales enablement professionals to develop better strategies to build sales teams who have growth mind-sets. This should involve ways of getting buy-in that do not cause, or at least recognize and try to minimize, Social Brain thinking and defensive reactions. Strategies should recognize that the brains of sales people are hard wired to choose a lower energy and so less effective way of selling over a more effective way, because the less effective way is easier from social and energy perspectives. This can be influenced by continuous nudging inside the workflow, but not by sporadic and abstract training events. It should also include looking for learning opportunities inside the workflow when solving problems. This will allow us to design an environment that promotes growth mind-set decision making. Indeed, the organizational culture in which the sales people operate also has a significant influence over Social Brain decision making and mind-set. Dweck demonstrated that the environment can have an impact on peoples' mind-sets. In the next part we move from the individual to the organization, looking at the organizational levers we can pull to optimize the culture of the whole sales organization. This will allow us to move as many sales people as possible into a growth mind-set, to identify and plug the capability gaps that area causing the Sales Performance Paradox.

# PART 2 SUMMARY

We can change the mind-sets of our sales teams, but to do this effectively, we need a communicable model of how the brain works. We use a simple dual model of 1) the Social Brain and the 2) the Intellectual Brain. These work very differently and are often at odds with each other.

The comparative size of the Social Brain means it's hard to make logical decisions. Logic is seen as a lower priority than energy usage. This is why people often make decisions that are counter intuitive or illogical. This tells us why people avoid change that is beneficial for them, but that requires significant energy resources.

There are a set of social drivers that drive decision making in the Social Brain. Sales performance interventions often fail because they are communicated as logical gains, but received as social threats. Over time this can cause a fixed mind-set where the ability to learn and adapt to change is unintentionally shut down. The resulting situation brings limitations to sales capability and an organization's ability to grow and adapt to market conditions.

With this knowledge we can develop better strategies to build sales teams with growth mind-sets, by **avoiding Social Brain thinking and defensive reactions**, promoting Intellectual Brain thinking and growth mind-set behaviors.

# PART THREE

# CREATE A GROWTH MIND-SET CULTURE

Sales organizations have hit a diminishing return, where many salespeople are not achieving their goals despite having more resources and support than ever before. Due to cognitive biases, many sales people and sales leaders are, however, blind to the lack of capability that is causing this failure.

One of the blind spots is the use of Social Brain thinking in the sales process that cuts corners and reduces the value created in the deal. Unidentified and unchallenged, these blind spots develop into a fixed mind-set where challenging situations are avoided and the ability to adapt to change effectively shuts down. A growth mind-set culture can be created but it first needs to be defined, as do the sales cultures we seek to avoid. Chapters seven to ten are:

7) **Sales Cultures** – What are the types of sales cultures we need to be aware of?

8) **From Fixed to Growth Mind-set Culture** – What are the things that can trip us up on the journey from fixed to growth mind-set culture?

9) **Fear and the Critic** – How to avoid the pitfall of producing a fear culture

10) **Entitlement and the Friend** – How to avoid the pitfall of producing an entitlement culture

# CHAPTER 7

# SALES CULTURES

*"Culture eats strategy for breakfast"*

**Peter Drucker**

I n the summer of 1950, Professor Nevitt Sanford was fired
from UC Berkley. A popular and kind professor, Sanford
still holds the record for the longest football run, receiving the ball from the kickoff and running all the way to the end
zone, at the University of Richmond. With a Ph.D. in psychology from Harvard, Sanford became a professor at the time
that Hitler was in power. Sanford was keen to understand the
hatred of the Nazis and use the tools of science to overcome
it. He was also a champion of making college education more
accessible to minority students.[117] Sanford was dismissed because of his refusal to sign a loyalty oath to confirm that he
was not a communist. During the McCarthy purges, he was
one of the 'Fearsome Five.' Sanford never revealed his political leanings, but refused to take the oath on principal stating
later, *"My position was that no political test should be used in deciding who would be teaching at the University"* [118]

After leaving Berkley, Sanford went to Vassar College where he met a young woman who was intending to leave the college, having only recently started. Sanford could see that she was struggling with the intense level of challenge. In fact, she was not alone. Sanford undertook a study that uncovered other young women in the same situation. He contrasted this with a number of male students he had known who'd had too little challenge and who *'find quite comfortable ruts on college campuses... They learn the ropes and soon fall into a fairly complacent pattern of life*[119]*'*. From his work at Vassar College Sanford had an insight concerning the relationship between challenge and support. He saw that too much challenge leads a person to 'retreat,' as happened to the young woman. In such circumstances people perceive a threat and pull back from the challenges, and therefore cease to develop. We've all been in a situation where it's just too challenging and we 'retreat.' Like the young woman Sanford encountered, more support is often needed to cope with new challenges. Support is the stabilizing force that helps make challenge manageable. It is the support that sustains the person while new and challenging situations are undertaken. Sanford wrote, *"If people fail to find support...there is a considerable likelihood that they will find the situation intolerable and retreat."*

Conversely, Sanford could see that too much support could lead to 'stagnation.' Something he had also seen on campus. Sanford defined stagnation as, *"The non-developmental state that results from an environment characterized by too much support."* He compared this to a parent doing everything for their children; effectively stunting the child's development by offering them limited opportunities to develop and grow. Too much support can reach the point where it is counter-productive. *"The imbalance of support leads to stagnation, a lack of development, and a missed opportunity for growth."* [120] Steve Glowinkowski relates this to the workplace, *"The key point about a climate of low challenge, is that the behavioral capabilities of the employees are never fully realized, and that part of the fundamental human condition of wanting to be part of something successful is never going to be attained."* [121]

In 1950 there were a number of people ready to send the young woman back home because they considered women too weak for the challenges of college. They had what we would call today a fixed mind-set which puts a limit on the growth of people and organizations. The key as Sanford saw it was not to reduce the challenge for the young woman but to **balance** the challenge with adequate support so that the two worked in harmony. Sanford could see that the college was not being accountable for providing the support required for the young woman to succeed and that the college needed to become more accountable. He could also see that the college was not being accountable for providing the challenge required for some of the young men to succeed and that they needed to become more accountable for this too. In other words the college needed to be better and more accountable for balancing the levels of challenge and support in their organization.

An environment, like this, lacking in support can be damaging but so too can an environment lacking in challenge. Challenging involves having high expectations of people and helps to instill accountability and responsibility.[122] When a person encounters a challenge, they are required to develop new tactics to cope and overcome the challenge. Sanford wrote that, *"The challenge pushes the person to reach beyond the status quo, and beyond their comfort zone to find a solution."*[123] According to Sanford, people develop and grow in response to being challenged. For growth to occur, there must be a challenge that upsets the existing equilibrium, the status quo, and creates a situation with which existing capability is not able to deal. From this, the person creates a brand new response that can overcome the challenge. *According to Sanford, "You should work to bring the relationship between challenge and support into a state of optimal mismatch from each person so that the ideal state of development is created."*[124] Sanford's theory predicts that there is an optimal situation where success is maximized by offering people sufficient levels of challenge that require new responses and at the same time providing sufficient support to confront those challenges.[125] In the book 'Make It Stick', the authors make this connection in relation to learning which is, *"Deeper and more durable when it's effortful. Learning that's easy is like writing in sand, here today and gone tomorrow."*[126] Dr. Carol Dweck from Stanford University has also identified the link between challenge and performance, *"The more that you challenge your mind to learn, the more your brain cells grow. Then, things that you once found very hard or even impossible seem to become easy. The result is a stronger, smarter brain."*[127] Combine Dweck's insights with Sanford and we can see that a balance of challenge and support are the environment that can nurture and promote growth mind-sets.

Sanford's insight about how people develop and grow was based on solid scientific foundations. Robert Yerkes teamed up with colleague John Dodson in 1907 to undertake an experiment to investigate the relationship between the strength of a stimulus and the rate of learning. Mice were put into a box with two doors, one white door, and one black door. The mice were required to choose the white door and given a 'disagreeable electric shock' for trying the black door. The rate of learning to access the correct door was measured. What they found in the simple experiment became a classic in the field of psychology and is known as the 'Yerkes-Dodson Law.' A small shock was not enough to help the mice to learn faster, but a medium shock did, while a larger shock was too much and they retreated. The 'Yerkes-Dodson Law, therefore predicts that performance increases with physiological or mental arousal, but only up to a point. When levels of arousal become too high, performance decreases. The process is often illustrated graphically as a bell-shaped curve which increases and then decreases with higher levels of arousal. "Anxiety improves performance until a certain optimum level of arousal has been reached. Beyond that point, performance deteriorates as higher levels of anxiety are attained."[128]

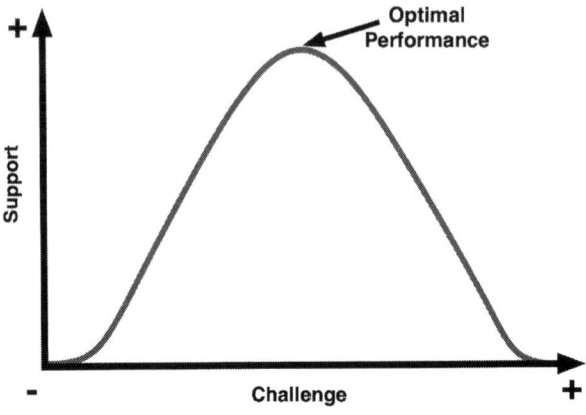

Figure 9 – Challenge Performance Bell Curve

From this, we can see that increasing challenge will improve performance, but too much challenge will decrease performance. Dr. Mihaly Csikszentmihalyi describes this optimal state, "*These periods of struggling to overcome challenges are what people find to be the most enjoyable times of their lives.*"[129]

But sometimes under higher levels of pressure, like in the college final exams, performance can reduce because of the threat response in the Social Brain. This is the drop in the bell curve. We've all been there at exam time. Too little pressure and we don't revise, so the performance is low. Increase the pressure, we revise and performance increases. If we experience too much pressure in the exam hall, we can't think straight, and performance reduces. This is also known as the Goldilocks principle. The Goldilocks principle states that something must fall within certain margins, as opposed to reaching extremes. Not too hot, not too cold, but just right. Goldilocks doesn't do extremes. So the skill we need to master is to create this balance and enable sales populations (Goldilocks) to systematically and continually grow by keeping them challenged enough to be motivated, but not so much that we create a threat response.

We've already seen how difficult walking this tight-rope can be. In Part Two, we saw how Social Brain thinking made us get a simple pricing problem wrong by changing the phrase, *"The bat costs $1.00 more than the ball"* to, *"The bat costs $1.00."* This was done to make the calculation easier to save on brain power. The pricing problem required increased challenge to wake up the Intellectual Brain and solve the problem correctly. Not enough challenge and we got the pricing problem wrong. When challenged we got it right. Too much challenge and we may have given up. Sanford's insight of creating a balance between challenge and support is a compelling one and provides a basis for us to create a growth culture in sales that is not seen as a threat by the Social Brain but allows salespeople to adapt to change and improve their skills. If we put Sanford's theory into a four-box matrix with 'Challenge' running vertically and 'Support' running horizontally, four different types of sales performance culture emerge:

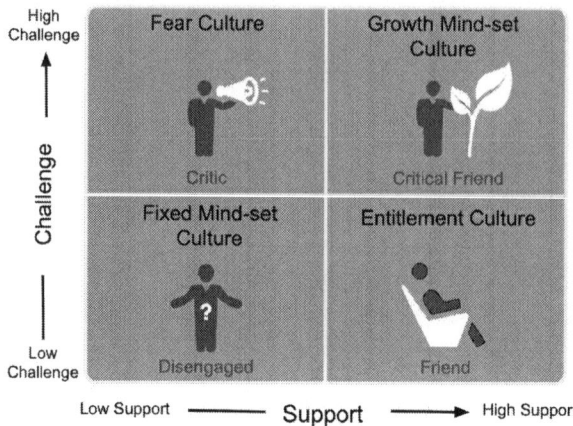

Figure 10 - Sanford Matrix

Our aim, of course, is to move the sales culture to the top right, the growth mind-set culture that will enable our organization to grow. The question you're probably wondering is how do we do that? We already know, from Dweck, that an individual can change their mind-set, and we've seen how we can enable this by helping them to manage Social Brain thinking. In the following chapters we build on this to find out how we move multiple mind-sets to create a growth mind-set sales culture. The question you may not have considered yet, that is equally important, is how do we move to a growth mind-set culture without falling into the traps of creating fear or entitlement cultures? These are cultures where the levels of challenge and support are not balanced. Too much challenge and we create a culture of fear. Too little challenge and we create a culture of entitlement.

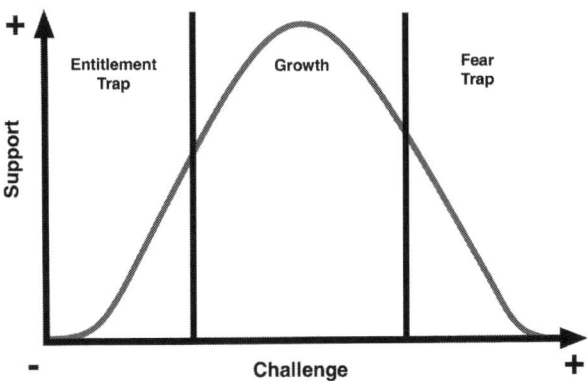

Figure 11 - Sales culture traps

As we will see in the following chapters, there are lessons we can learn on how to avoid falling into the traps of creating fear and entitlement sales cultures. We want to avoid these cultures because they produce the unintended consequence of reducing sales growth by creating fixed mind-set decision making and reducing the ability to adapt to change.

# CHAPTER 8

# FROM A FIXED TO GROWTH MIND-SET CULTURE

*"From this day forward, Flight Control will be known by two words: "Tough and Competent." Tough means we are forever accountable for what we do or what we fail to do. We will never again compromise our responsibilities. Competent means we will never take anything for granted. We will never be found short in our knowledge and in our skills."*

Eugene F. Krantz: NASA's Flight Director for the Gemini and Apollo programs.

T he CEO began his new position determined to make an immediate impact. He aimed to increase productivity in the steel company he had just joined. During an initial tour of the plant, he saw a young man leaning up against a wall in one of the offices. Wanting to demonstrate his decisive capability and to send a message to the others, he approached the young man. *"How much money do you make a week"*? He asked the young man. The young man looked surprised and responded, *"$400 a week. Why?"* The new CEO replied, *"Just wait right here!"* He went back to his office and returned a few minutes later to hand the young man $1600 in cash, Saying, *"Here's four weeks' pay, now get out and don't come back."* After the young man had walked away, the CEO asked one of the on-lookers, *"Who was that guy and what did he do around here?"* A hesitant voice responded, *"He's the pizza delivery guy."* [130]

Such an inept display of challenge is a great example of how **not** to use the challenge lever to change culture. Challenging effectively is something that needs to be planned and managed well. Similarly, we'll see shortly the difficulties and shortcomings of companies using the support lever ineffectively to drive sales culture. So the big questions we have to answer is, *how do we create a strong organizational culture where a balance of challenge and support systematically promotes growth mind-set decision making?*

According to Flamholtz and Randle, "A strong culture is one that people clearly understand and can articulate. A weak culture is one that employees have difficulty defining, understanding, or explaining. The culture may not have been defined, or it may not have been actively managed. As a result, employees are left to interpret the company's values for themselves."[131] There are three things we therefore need to define and make clear. Firstly, we need to define clearly and unambiguously what a growth sales culture is **and** what it is not. Secondly, we need to define the sales leadership styles that will deliver that growth culture **and** define the styles that will not. Thirdly, we need to define the sales behaviors of individual contributors that comprise a growth sales culture, **and** juxtapose these with those that do not. Let's start by defining a Growth Mind-set sales culture.

**Growth Mind-set Sales Culture Description:** a growth mind-set sales culture is made up of high levels of practical challenge and high levels of effective support, both combining to help individuals develop and grow. Intellectual Brain thinking is a cornerstone of the culture, and this can been seen through a readiness to adapt and change, learning, coachability, an adherence to the sales process and quantifiable value being created for customer and seller alike. This is achieved through challenging Social Brain thinking, at the same time as supporting learning and capability gaps as they arise. You know you've arrived at a growth mind-set culture when 80% of the sales population are following the defined sales process and they proactively update their sales skills and knowledge at least once a month.

**Leadership Style: The Critical Friend.** Driving the growth mind-set culture are the 'Critical Friend' leaders. Critical Friends know that their role is to challenge and support their teams. Managing challenge and support well creates a harmony where the two reinforce each other, preventing threat responses from the Social Brain and actively seeking reward responses. Critical friends know that if the level of challenge is being increased, there needs to be a corresponding and timely increase in support. Equally, if support is growing, the support is not just given, but given in return for performance improvements. In other words, support is accompanied by the challenge of ensuring the support is being utilized and maximized. Ray Dalio is the founder, chair, and co-chief investment officer of Bridgewater Associates, a global leader in institutional portfolio management and the largest hedge fund in the world. Dalio explains why he has built a culture of challenge and support in his company, *"I wanted to find the smartest people who would disagree with me to try to understand their perspective or to have them stress test my perspective. I wanted to have an idea meritocracy in which the best ideas would win out."*[132] This is exactly the reason for the Deal Hack. To 'stress test' deals using the best brains in the business, and to have the best value proposal and deal strategy that can be achieved. Critical friends achieve this as a sustainable model through critical challenge aligned with effective support. Critical friends know the sales process intimately and are the guardians of it, not allowing their own Social Brain thinking, or that of their teams, to cut corners and produce sales failures that are someone else's fault.

**Sales persona: Star.** Stars want success, so they are proactive about their development and accountable for it. Stars need to feel invested in, and so a supportive and collaborative environment is crucial. The support typically works well as, being accountable for their development, they take full advantage of what is being offered. Stars have a firm control over their Social Brain which enables them to put their ambitions to succeed before their immediate social needs. Their performance can be scrutinized and challenged without them becoming defensive and reacting adversely. Challenging feedback delivered to this person will be well received and acted upon, being used as a learning point to improve performance. Learning doesn't just come from feedback; they are obsessive about seeking opportunities to learn and improve their capability. Their interest in minimizing their Blind spots takes them outside of their immediate surroundings and enables them to build supportive networks. This type of person is coachable and will say, *"I've approached a mentor who has agreed to help with my goal of becoming the top salesperson."* Mark Roberg was the SVP of Worldwide Sales and Services at Hubspot and grew their revenue run rate from $0 to $90 million. In the book 'The Sales Acceleration Formula' Roberg says that, *"Coachability is the most significant influencer of my hiring decision. As I think back to most of the rock stars we hired, their coachability was the personality trait that really stood out in their interviews."*[133] Roberg means two things by coachability: 1) the ability to recognize capability gaps and blind spots (horizontal support axis) and 2) capacity to take on board challenging feedback and act on the feedback (vertical challenge axis). Such people are on the top right of the Sanford Matrix. Interestingly in Roberg's search for coachable salespeople, he says, "*I will say that I have probably conducted well over 1000 interviews during my six years in the head of sales at Hubspot. Across the full population of candidates I've screened, perhaps only five people absolutely crushed this.*" Finding just five out of a thousand salespeople (0.5%) that demonstrate high levels of coachability shows how rare Stars are in the sales talent pool. A Critical Friend uses interventions like Deal Hacks to improve the growth mind-set of the overall team, moving more people top right into the Star category.

The Critical Friend style of leadership gives Stars the feedback they seek to improve, but also the support they want, so they feel invested in, and the support they need to succeed. A 'Critic' leader who fails to support a Star will lose them after a time as the goodwill of Stars eventually dries up. A 'Friend' leader will not give the critical feedback Stars seeks, and Stars will leave due to a lack of challenge, as we will see shortly.

As we saw in the Chapter Two 'Blind Spot' we need to know where we're starting from, so we can build the strategies to drive to our desired destination. The opposite of the Growth Mind-set sales culture, in the Sanford Matrix, is a Fixed Mind-set sales culture where both challenge **and** support of the sales teams is low or ineffective. For a number of organizations a Fixed Mind-set Sales culture is where the journey starts from. Let's examine the Fixed Mind-set Sales culture in terms of the culture itself, the leadership style and the typical sales personas found in such a culture.

**Fixed Mind-set Culture Description:** Bottom left we find the 'Fixed Mind-set' culture, called so because it is believed that the performance of the sales people is fixed and based on their innate talent as a natural born sales person. "They have sales DNA" is the type of phrase you'll hear in this culture. In this type of culture there is a lack of challenge and a lack of support too.

**Leadership Style: Fixed Mind-set Leader:** A great example of the fixed mind-set leader is Jordan Belfort, author of 'Way of the Wolf', who describes himself in this way: "I'm one of those natural *born* salesmen who can sell ice to an Eskimo, oil to an Arab, pork to a Rabbi, or anything else you can think of...that's my gift the ability to sell anything to anyone, in massive quantities; and whether this gift comes from God or from nature, I really can't say..."[134] I know it looks like Belfort, along with his low EQ' and massive ego, has been teleported directly from the 1980s, but on amazon.com at time of writing this book is #2 in Sales Techniques, #3 in Business Negotiation Skills and #4 in Business Coaching & Mentoring Skills. This type of fixed mind-set sales leadership is amazingly popular with two types of people:

1) Business leaders who want to improve sales but have no idea about selling
2) People who want to get into sales and see it as a get rich quick scheme

Is employing sales leaders like Belfort an effective business strategy? To answer this, let's consider Belfort's online author's profile on amazon.com: *Jordan Belfort was born in Queens, New York. He hustled ices to put himself through college showing early entrepreneurial flair. His first business sent him bankrupt at 24 so he went down to Wall St with $100 in his pocket and ended up building one of the largest brokerages in America - the now infamous Stratton Oakmont. A hard partying lifestyle ended in crash and burn. Ultimately indicted by the federal government, Belfort served twenty-two months in prison, and time in rehab.*

*He's now a highly successful motivational speaker.* Clearly there's a price to pay for this type of sales leadership. The high turnover of sales staff, the orders that can't be implemented and the massive expense claims to name just a few. Belfort promises to deliver, "A system that proved to be so powerful and effective, and so easy to learn, that within days of inventing it, it brought massive wealth and success to anyone I taught it to."[135] Would anyone fall for this? To quote Charles Babbage (out of context), *"I am not able rightly to apprehend the kind of confusion of ideas......"*[136] But sadly people are still falling for this utter nonsense, and probably always will.

I asked if this was an effective business strategy as a leading question. But can we consider if this is an effective form of sales leadership? When it comes to balancing challenge and support, the fixed mind-set leadership are unlikely to invest in support as the sales people are either born to sell or they are not. When it comes to challenging their teams, they will often let the sales person get on with the job and not interfere, again because they are born to do this and so why check? I have seen this model where the sales people are left alone until the end of the quarter/half and then, like the Apprentice show in TV, either lauded for success or chastised and fired for failure. There is, as we will see, a strong correlation between the fixed mind-set leadership style and a fear culture. We explore this in detail in the next chapter.

**Sales Persona:** Fixed Mind-set sales people feel they have the innate ability to be a great sales person. If they succeed this validates their opinion. If they do not succeed they look outside for blame. Excuses include, the product is not differentiated enough, the price is too high, the competition are too cheap or the customers are just not interested. They can start out being proactive, but negativity soon sets in and explains why their tenure is so short.

Think for a moment about your own situation. What's the sales culture, the sales leadership styles and the sales personas that you encounter? There's probably a mix but an underlying dominant culture, which comes from a certain style of leadership that predominates. There will probably be a number of different sales personas, but one will predominate. Most of the sales leaders I speak to instinctively put themselves in the top right. Again the optimism bias is raising its head. I refer back to what Mark Roberge said about his experience at Hubspot, *"I will say that I have probably conducted well over 1000 interviews during my six years in the head of sales at Hubspot. Across the full population of candidates I've screened, perhaps only five people absolutely crushed this."* Roberge would put 5 out of 1000 people in the top right of the matrix. Ask those 1000 people and you'd get 1000 placements in the top right of the matrix. It's very clear that being objective about ourselves is hard, and if we're salespeople or sales leaders it's even harder.

In my experience many sales, leaders place their sales cultures in the top right. But after independently interviewing sales managers, salespeople and customers, there is evidence that they are not there. I actually see very few companies in the bottom left, because this is a staging place from where companies start from. What I typically see are companies that have a fixed mind-set culture but quickly recognize that they have sales capability gaps that can be improved. Rather than doing nothing, they start pulling on either the challenge or the support levers. This drives them either top left or bottom right.

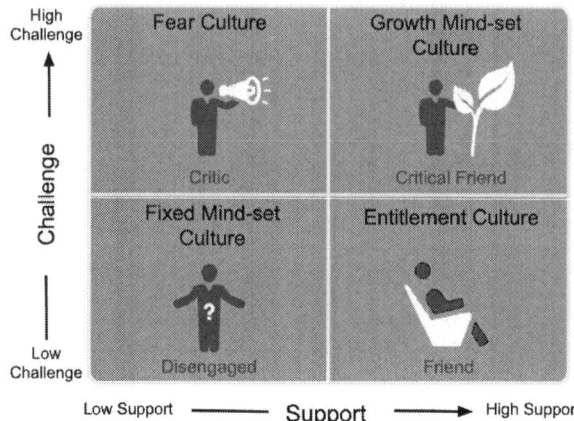

Figure 12 - Sanford Matrix

The bottom left box in the Sanford Matrix is a platform for the culture to move into 'Fear' in the top left or 'Entitled' in the bottom right. The next two chapters therefore looks at the two cultures of fear and entitlement, so that we can identify them, and build strategies to move away from them towards the top right and achieve a 'Growth Sales Culture.'

# CHAPTER 9

# FEAR AND THE CRITIC

*"The enemy is fear. We think it is hate; but, it is fear."*

**Gandhi.**

F lorida 2013: Rita Murillo dreaded the phone calls. Her regional bosses required four updates per day on progress towards aggressive sales targets. "Employees who lagged behind had to stay late and work weekends to meet goals. Anyone falling short after two months would be fired. We were constantly told we would end up working at McDonald's if we did not make the sales quotas. We had to stay for what felt like after-school detention, or report to a call session on Saturdays." Murillo said after she had resigned.[137] Wells Fargo was described by Jim Collins in 2001 as, *"A dramatic, remarkable, good-to-great corporate transformation. They had a simple formula for the transformation, Collins described this as: "Consistently increasing profit per employee. 'Run it like a business' and 'Run it like you own it became mantras; simplicity and focus made all the difference. With fanatical adherence to that simple idea, Wells Fargo made the leap from good results to superior results.*"[138] Even up to 2015 Wells Fargo CEO John Stumpf was being lauded with "CEO of the Year" award from the investment research firm Morningstar because he *"guided the bank through a difficult period in the industry and shunned activities that put profits ahead of customers."*[139]

By September 2016 Wells Fargo had been fined $100 million in penalties after employees were caught creating over 2 million unauthorized accounts for customers without their knowledge or approval. *"Spurred by sales targets and compensation incentives, employees boosted sales figures by covertly opening accounts and funding them by transferring funds from consumers' authorized accounts without their knowledge or consent, often racking up fees or other charges. According to the bank's analysis, employees opened more than two million deposit and credit card accounts that may not have been authorized by consumers,"* according to the Consumer Financial Protection Bureau.[140] Wells Fargo CFO John Shrewsberry reportedly said, *"It was really more at the lower end of the performance scale, where people apparently were making bad choices to hang on to their jobs,"* according to CNBC.[141] As a result wells Fargo *"Dismissed 5,300 employees for creating the unauthorized accounts, including some managers."* [142]

It is perhaps because of examples like this that the word 'challenge' has a bad name. That may be why companies and people shy away from having 'challenge' as a value. Examining the top 10 companies in the USA reveals that only one has 'challenge' in their values. In the UK, 'Challenge' or anything similar does not appear in the top values of FTSE 100 companies either. So there is a job to be done in selling business leaders on the need to adopt 'challenge' (or similar) as a value across organizations. This is a curious place for the corporate world to be because the political world is the opposite, and was indeed founded on the ability to challenge. Edward Samuel Corwin described the US Constitution as *"An invitation to struggle."*[143] The President, the Senate and the House of Representatives all have different mandates, functions, and levels of power. This separation of powers was designed on the basis that too much power in the hands of any one individual or institution is corruptible. *"Power tends to corrupt, and absolute power corrupts absolutely."*[144] Having three centers of power allows each institution to challenge and hold the other accountable to ensure that the people are best served when those institutions do, indeed, struggle with and challenge each other. Perhaps the corporate world has forgotten the need for effective challenge? Bardwick attributes a lack of challenge for the demise of postwar American prosperity, *"Organizations began to grant job security without regard to how well people worked and how much they contributed. They stopped evaluating employees and discharging those who were nonproductive; they failed to hold people accountable for their performance."*[145]

As always, however, there are exceptions. Hyundai is the trailblazer of corporate challenge; *"We (Hyundai) refuse to be complacent, embrace every opportunity for greater challenge, and are confident in achieving our goals with unwavering passion and ingenuity."* This demonstrates the adoption of challenge as a core value, in a way that departs completely from the likes of the Wells Fargo example. The challenge that is part of the overall culture is a mutual challenge, where it is acceptable, or even encouraged, to challenge up the corporate chain as well as down. This type of mutual challenge is intimidating to some sales leaders, and this perhaps explains the absence of challenge in the values of many companies. However, there are significant benefits to getting the levels of challenge just right, as Ray Dalio explains, *"We do it because it eliminates what I believe to be one of the greatest tragedies of mankind, and that is people arrogantly, naïvely holding opinions in their minds that are wrong, and acting on them, and not putting them out there to stress test them. And that's a tragedy. It's been the secret sauce behind our success. It's why we've made more money for our clients than any other hedge fund in existence and made money 23 out of the last 26 years."* [146]

If we'd put the Sanford Matrix in front of the Wells Fargo leadership team and asked if their culture was a balance of challenge and support, what would they have said? The optimism cognitive bias suggests that they would have told us they had a balance, and were 'top right' in the Sanford matrix. Did they have a good balance? It feels like they fell into the trap of intending to move top right into the growth mind-set box, but missed and moved top left into fear. To know for sure, we need to be really clear on what a fear culture is, who leads one and how the individual contributors behave. Here's a reminder of the Sanford Matrix:

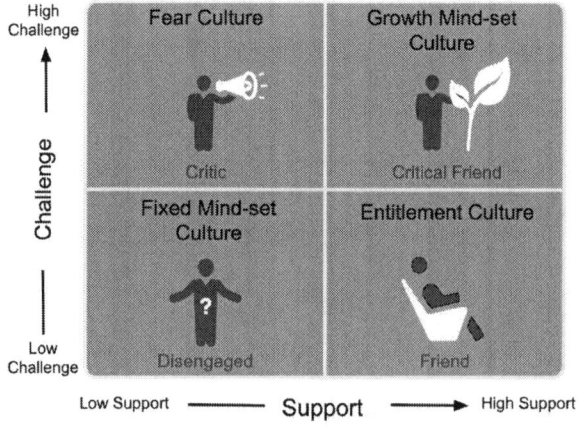

Figure 10 - Sanford Matrix

**Fear Culture Description:** a fixed mind-set culture with high levels of challenge, but low levels of support. A highly competitive, individualistic and fear-driven environment. Individual attainment is prioritized and rewarded with the concept of team being nothing more than a social concept. There is little sharing of best practice because of the high levels of internal competition. The sales strategy can be described as *"Get out there and sell!"* This culture drives threat responses in the sales population, which makes Social Brain thinking the norm inside the company and when dealing with customers. The unrelenting nature of the challenge leads to unhealthy competition where teamwork is minimal. A blame or cheating culture can exist when high standards are not met. An avoidance mentality also exists due to the negative consequences of making mistakes.

**Leadership Style: The Critic.** Critical leaders believe that salespeople thrive in a highly competitive and challenging environment. The critic can be identified by comments like, *"The sales populations need to own their targets. They are paid enough, so they should know how to sell. I'm sure she told me she could sell at the interview, so why is she not selling?"* The leadership style in this culture is a throw-back to the 1960s Douglas McGregor's Theory X, which assumes people seek to avoid work as much as possible and so need to be pushed and controlled.[147] This contradicts the latest in management thinking that, to get the most out of your team, you should actually do the opposite. There is an externalization of accountability for sales results by the leadership team, directed towards the sales team. Ironically, the more challenging the market becomes, the more critical this style of leadership becomes because they have no other direction to take. After all, the low sales figures are 'not their fault.' Unlike 'Disengaged' sales leadership, the Critic feels it is their role to intervene, and particularly to challenge. But it is not their role to support. The sales teams should be self-supporting which is a fixed mind-set trait. Critical leaders view the sales bonuses as the mechanism for motivating sales people to be self-supporting. This style of sales leadership can be seen in very traditional companies, companies who want to grow very quickly at any cost, or companies with little understanding of sales and marketing.

For example, sales targets are often set in the absence of any real market knowledge but based on what has happened previously or what is required by the business. This approach is indicative of high staff turnover, as sales people tend to retreat from this type of environment. Retreat means either lying low and disguising what they really are doing because of an absence of trust or leaving entirely if the opportunity arises. I recently encountered this leadership style when taking over from a sales regime who call themselves 'The Mafia.' They use a fear driven culture and unethical sales practices to quickly inflate sales figures in order to sell companies at a profit. They're generally not around to deal with the results of the bad deals and high staff turnover, as they have made their money and are onto the next victim. In this culture, sales gatherings are used to shame people who are underperforming. The fear of public humiliation is seen as a key motivator. Sales training sessions in a fear culture involve people being called out, and put on the spot, to make sure everyone pays attention. One such practice is called, 'Putting someone in the barrel' where the unlucky person is put on the spot to perform a task they have not prepared for. "They should know this stuff" is the justification. The reality is that people don't learn well in high pressured environments like this. Their 'Social Brains' are on fire with the status threat. If you ask them to actually recall the learnings, very little can be recalled as people are focused on saying the right thing in the moment. This is because of the 'next-in-line effect', a cognitive bias that causes people to have reduced memory for events that happen just before or after a social interaction. You've probably experienced it when being introduced to someone new and in less than a minute you can't remember their name. The effect was first documented thanks to an experiment at the University of Michigan in the early 1970s. Participants sat in a circle and took it in turns to read different words from cards aloud to the group. Afterwards, they were given a memory test in which they were asked to report as many of the words as possible. It transpires that people have a very low recall for anything that happens about 9 seconds before and after a social inter-action.[148] This loss of memory is the result of the 'next-in-line effect' and we've all experienced it. Making the 'just in line effect' last as long as possible is the reason that high pressure learning does not work. It may appear that the delegates are focused, but their 'Social Brains' are focused on protecting their status, and so the learning literally goes in one ear and out of the other, staying in place for no more than 9 seconds!

**Sales Persona: Super Chicken.** The critical and fear driven ap-proach moves down the chain, and salespeople compete with each other rather than supporting each other. Being north of the horizontal (X) axis, Super Chickens exist in a high chal-lenge environment with little support. William Muir, Profes-sor of Animal Sciences at Purdue University, coined the term 'Super Chicken' after selectively breeding super chickens to improve the productivity of egg-laying. Muir firstly selected an ordinary flock, and let it breed naturally for six gen-erations. He also created a second flock of the better egg layers, and from each subsequent generation, he selectively bred only the most productive chickens. After six gener-ations the first group, the ordinary group, was doing really well with healthy chickens laying healthy eggs. The second group of selectively bred super chickens, who were expected to have much higher egg production, were not laying more eggs. Worse, Muir found that one-third of them had pecked the other two-thirds to death, so overall egg production was actually down. He explains why, *"The reason for this perverse outcome is easy to understand, at least in retrospect. The most pro-ductive hen in each cage was the biggest competitor, who achieved her productivity by suppressing the productivity of the other hens. Antagonistic behavior is a heritable trait, and several generations were sufficient to produce a strain of psychopaths."*[149] This is an example of success at the expense of others, and this trait is strong in the top left corner of the Sanford Matrix. Most of the sales cultures that I encounter run on the 'Super Chicken' principal, which is unfortunate, but it has become so ingrained in sales, it's hard to see a way out. Margaret Heffernan, former CEO of a number of businesses questions this approach, *"For the past 50 years, we've run most organizations and some societies along the superchicken model. We've thought that success is achieved by picking the superstars, the brightest men, or occasionally women, in the room, and giving them all the resources and all the power. And the result has been just the same as in William Muir's experiment: aggression, dysfunction, and waste. If the only way the most productive can be successful is by suppressing the productivity of the rest, then we badly need to find a better way to work and a richer way to live."[150]*

Being frequently challenged means that Super Chickens are good at controlling the emotional response of the Social Brain but only to enable them to gain an advantage. Super Chickens can be proactive and deliver great results, but this can be at the expense of other colleagues or even customers. Super Chickens are common in sales cultures that allow people to behave in an adversarial way, at the expense of others. This can have a significant unintended outcome. Think for a moment of examples where a project at work has worked well and has led to sustainable success; it would almost certainly have involved a balance of long and short-term priorities. It would also have been the case that there was a collective effort capitalizing on the strengths of a team. Fear based cultures lead to short-term priorities taking precedence over long-term strategies. They also do not lend themselves to building collective intelligence and successful team selling efforts. Trying to scale the 'Super Chicken' model is particularly hard because effective scaling of expertise requires the sharing of best practice, coaching and mentoring, all of which are absent here. The antagonizing behaviors manifest in a number of ways, and one of the most important is the lack of accountability concerning values. Values often go unchallenged in sales organizations where the short-term need for sales figures override the longer term need for team selling. There is a hidden cost to working at the expense of others. Sales organizations that allow this type of behavior to persist are the ones represented in Chapter one, where only 59% of their salespeople are hitting target. Such companies will never break this ceiling because the success of some is at the expense of others. Performance is often unsustainable with high stress and potential burnout.

There is a real challenge of getting the levels of challenge right. A bit like Goldilocks, too much is bad, but too little is bad too. How do we get it to be like baby bear's porridge, just right? If you were a consultant working with Wells Fargo to improve their sales performance in early 2016 or before, how would you define their sales culture? Where would you have put them on the Sanford matrix? If you had met the leaders, it is likely that they would have steered you towards the top right 'Growth' box, and described their leadership style as 'critical friend'. But with the benefit of hindsight, and a wider view of the organization, industry, and market, it would be more realistic to put them into the top left. Especially when we heard the CFO blaming the *"Lower end of the performance scale people."* The management culture is clearly that of 'critic'. The CFOs toxic excuses suggest the leadership would not hesitate to criticize and blame their sales people suggesting a 'low trust' environment. We can see this because the management team were calling four times a day for sales reports and the employees described it as highly stressful. So stressful in fact, that Social Brain thinking would continuously dominate. Some employees, like the children in Dweck's classroom test, were cheating because of the fixed mind-set that had taken hold. Some may have been cheating out of fear because of the threats to the Social Brain. There are many ways that cheating can happen in a sales environment, in addition to falsifying orders, as happened at Wells Fargo. For example, making customers promises that can't be kept to win deals, bloating the pipeline with deals that won't be closed, working on deals that are not in their segment or territory, and claiming more meetings than have been held. According to the Sociologist Donald Cressey, there are three factors that need to be present for someone to commit a deception like this: pressure, opportunity and justification.[151] In the high pressured culture of fear, when oversight is lacking and people feel justified, this is exactly the right environment for deception and even fraud to flourish. Do you see any of these signs in your sales organization? According to Cialdini, the problem is widespread; *"Despite understanding the risks, close to half of high-ranking executives report they would act unethically to get or retain business."* [152] When individual contributors see their leaders making unethical choices, those individual contributors too are more likely to cheat. Employees with unethical leaders and unethical behaviors also show significantly less motivation.[153] Shrewsberry, the CFO at Wells Fargo, was very clear where the fault lay. It was not with him and the other leaders, but with the individual contributors that cheated. This is classic 'Critic' behavior, externalizing blame to the sales population for things that go wrong. He was completely blind to the fact that the culture he helped to shape was causing the problem. Many leaders in the top left of the Sanford model see themselves in the top right. When challenged about this, there is often the response that the sales people are 'Self-supporting' because they are paid bonuses. This is a clear abdication of responsibility that betrays a manifest lack of understanding of sales leadership.

There is a real challenge of getting the levels of challenge right in a sales organization, and the case of Wells Fargo is a good example of how easy it is to let challenge rise too high, to toxic levels. Wells Fargo continually ratcheted up the levels of challenge for their sales people, without corresponding levels of support, leading to unethical selling practices that nearly sank the whole organization. Challenging is an essential part of sales performance but the challenging itself needs to be challenged, in order to prevent it becoming too strong, too weak or detached completely from support. All of these are sub-optimal for any sales organization.

Deal Hacks increase the challenge on the sales teams in an objective, measured and controlled way. Salespeople learn to challenge themselves and each other, which is both more palatable for them and more scalable for the organization. The cross-functional team element to Deal Hacks brings greater oversight on sales activity to prevent 'cargo cult' selling practices that appear at first glance to be effective, but when examined closely are ineffective, and often counter-productive. The example of 'Wells Fargo' demonstrates a desire to increase challenge, and landing in the top left 'Fear' box by not understanding, or perhaps not caring, how challenge actually works. The increased levels of challenge in the sales organization at Wells Fargo were intended to increase performance and increase control, but due to the unethical behaviors that resulted, neither were actually achieved. The way the leaders were challenging their teams was counterproductive because of the negative effects on the 'Social Brains' of the employees. When proposing that effective challenge comes about when there is a balance of challenge and support, Sanford recognized that different types of challenges have different effects. Some challenges can be constructive, leading to growth and development. Some challenges can be counterproductive and result in a retreat like at Wells Fargo. If you want to know which challenges are counterproductive, you need to look no further than your company values, this is your moral compass at work. Corporate culture is a combination of the values, attitudes, and behaviors that manifest with shareholders, employees, customers, suppliers, the community and environment affected by a company's conduct. A healthy corporate culture is a valuable asset, a source of competitive advantage and vital to the creation and protection of long-term value.[154] Sales culture is a subset of the company culture, and the two need to be aligned if they are going to be successful. The tail cannot wag the dog, as we saw with Wells Fargo, and the sales culture is not the dog. Companies often wait for a crisis before they focus on company culture because this is when the culture is more visible. Indeed, it's sometimes more efficient to describe what a sales challenge culture is not to get the point across. Sir Roger Carr, Chairman of BAE Systems, describes this phenomenon, *"It is easier to see signs of departure from the desired culture (e.g., instances of antagonizing) than positive evidence of its existence".*[155] In addition to the methods of cheating listed above, here are some other examples of departures:

1) When a sales person cannot answer definitively about their accounts' strategic goals and is happy to provide educated guesses as facts.
2) When a salesperson blames price, or customer politics for losing a deal.
3) When a Sales Manager points the finger at operations for the loss of a sale, or at marketing for generating weak leads.
4) When a Human Resource Director facilitates and does not challenge the churn of salespeople.
5) When a Sales Leader is satisfied by his sales managers' explanations that they don't have time to coach.
6) When a board member is satisfied with the Sales Leader's explanation that an account was lost on price.
7) When there is no systematic and company-wide learning process to learn from lost deals.

We know instinctively when there is a poor sales culture,

and the above non-exhaustive list are signs of this, to which I'm sure we could all add more examples. A growth mindset culture is what Wells Fargo was trying to achieve, but they did not achieve it. As Sanford points out to us, growth can be achieved by balancing Challenge and Support. The leaderships team either did not know about the relationship between the two, or their Social Brain thinking was making decisions with systematic errors that went unchallenged, as we saw with the CFOs remarks blaming his colleagues. How ironic that a lack of challenge at the very top of the organization could have resulted in too much challenge further down the chain.

Too much challenge and unhealthy challenge like we saw at Wells Fargo, or challenge without support can lead to increased stress. In the macho world of sales, stress is often seen as an essential part of the role. But there are warning signs out there about too much stress in the working environment. A report by the Institute of Business Ethics (IBE) identified three main drivers of poor behavior at work, *"Corporate stress which led people to take shortcuts, excessive focus on short term financial targets which might of itself become a source of stress, and a ready tolerance of small breaches of the rules which allowed misdemeanor to become incremental. Corporate stress was seen as the core issue. Participants felt that any company under stress could cut corners and make mistakes."*[156] It's easy to argue that all three of these are present in many sales forces, and this goes some way to explain why 'Super Chicken' behaviors start to proliferate under the critic style of leadership. As a result, stress increases, as does Social Brain thinking and the effectiveness of the sales population reduces, which is the opposite of what is intended. We saw earlier how Sanford and the Yerkes-Dodson Law both predict that performance increases with the amount of challenge, but only up to a point. When the level of challenge becomes too high, performance decreases. So how can we get the balance right?

In Deal Hacks we significantly increase the levels of challenge that most salespeople are accustomed to, but provide support to counterbalance the challenge. Deal Coaches are trained to create an environment where people feel comfortable challenging, and being challenged, but an environment that does not resemble the type of fear culture we saw at Wells Fargo. Managing levels of challenge and recognizing the signs of threat response is key to a successful Deal Hack because in Wells Fargo they were either being missed or ignored. Perhaps if the Sanford Matrix had been used at Wells Fargo, it would have highlighted the shortcomings of their 'fear' sales culture. Using the Sanford Matrix overtly with sales leaders helps to build an understanding of the concept of challenge and support, and the types of culture that are desired. The Sanford Matrix gives a vocabulary to communicate the different types of sales culture more effectively. If we can all have an honest and open conversation about the levels of challenge and support, we can manage the situation more effectively. Left unmanaged, levels of challenge can spiral out of control as happened at Wells Fargo. In the next chapter, we look at the opposite case, where challenge levels cause problems by being too low, and the sales population live an entitled existence in their comfort of their comfort zones.

# CHAPTER 10

# ENTITLEMENT AND THE FRIEND

*"The worst thing you can do for those you love is the things they could do for themselves."*

**Abraham Lincoln**

A king in an ancient kingdom was concerned that the people of his kingdom had become lazy, too comfortable and entitled. Devising a way to change this, he placed a large boulder in the middle of a road. He sat in a discreet place away from the bolder from where he could see the situation unfold. A number of people approached the boulder, but failing to see an easy way to move the boulder or to go around it, they turned back. A merchant travelling to the city blamed the King for not managing the roads, and returned home discontented, not completing his business in the city. A priest travelling to the city to meditate at the city temple decided that to meditate there was not necessary as he could do so anywhere. Eventually a farmer came along on the way to market and tried to move the boulder. Unable to, the farmer thought about the problem for a moment and had an insight. The farmer remembered the quotation from Archimedes, "Give me the place to stand, and I shall move the earth." Grabbing a fallen branch from nearby, the farmer proceeded to lever the boulder out of the road, making the road accessible once more. Having overcome the challenge, the farmer was setting off but saw a bag lying where the boulder had been. The farmer looked around, picked up the bag and found inside a large amount of gold and a note from the King, which read, *"This gold is for you. The obstacle that was a barrier in the path of the lazy, became a path to opportunity for the strong"* The king, delighted with the actions of the farmer, left his hiding place and went back to his castle with renewed hope for his people.[157]

The story of the king and the farmer is an old Zen story showing the King's desire to create a culture by rewarding the types of behaviors that he thought would make his population thrive and removing the behaviors that would make them decline. The behavior he's looking to remove is entitlement, and he does this by rewarding the farmer for rising to the challenge and owning the problem, what we might call today a growth mind-set.

**Entitlement Culture**[158] **Description:** a fixed mind-set culture with an abundance of training and coaching, but low levels of challenge and follow up to make sure these are being used effectively. This causes the accountability for development to shift from the individual towards the company. Social Brain thinking goes unchecked and is allowed to dominate the sales process with minimal effort across stakeholder relationship management, customer knowledge, and value creation. In this culture, average or poor performers have long tenure. This culture can often be found in market leaders in a mature market, or where the company is in a naturally rising market, and poor sales performance skills are not visible. Until that is, the competition heats up, and things in the market get harder. Until that point, the sales results have been successful, and there has been no requirement to challenge sales performance above an elementary reporting level. Companies in this position either hit adverse market conditions, which reveals the poor sales performance, or they are taken over by an external third party who identifies the opportunity cost of the poor performance and can capitalize on it. Intel was an example of a company who found themselves here after many years of success. They identified it and dealt with it, moving back up into the Growth Mind-set Culture box.

**Leadership Style: Friend.** Bottom right we find the 'Friend' style of leadership, where there is a general failure to challenge the sales population. Poor performance is tolerated and often goes unchallenged. In these companies, entitlement is allowed to flourish by leaders that are reluctant to challenge the status quo and cause bad feelings. I was recently in a sales training session where a sales manager and a trainer in the client financial services company 'high fived' each other in mutual congratulation when they tried to de-rail an exercise by doing it so badly. In other sessions, other managers attempted to de-rail the training by disagreeing with the concepts being trained, and even bullying members of their team into not participating. The people were highlighted to the leadership team, but no action was taken to challenge them. This is an example of an entitled organization where entitled behavior becomes toxic because it is tolerated and allowed to flourish. Perhaps they don't know how to recognize and manage entitled people. Perhaps they have had long relationships with these people and feel sorry for them. Perhaps they are politically weaker than the people concerned. Perhaps they are entitled too. Whatever the reason, it's practically impossible to grow sales in an entitled company in a truly competitive market, and there needs to be a strong leadership team with a strong mandate to turn it around.

**Sales persona: Entitled.** Entitled people feel that they deserve good things, without actually earning them in the first place. Being right of the vertical (Y) axis, entitled salespeople are in a very supportive environment, but in a low challenge environment, they avoid taking advantage of that support. Because they are not accustomed to being challenged, their 'Social Brains' are allowed to control their response to feedback on their performance. Feedback is often taken defensively and not acted upon. Mark Manson has observed that entitled people, *"become so fixated on feeling good about themselves that they manage to delude themselves into believing that they are accomplishing great things even when they're not."* We saw this in Part One with the optimism bias inflating the results of self-assessments. Manson continues, *"But the problem with entitlement is that it makes people need to feel good about themselves all the time, even at the expense of those around them. And because entitled people always need to feel good about themselves, they end up spending most of their time thinking about themselves."*[159]

The lack of challenge creates a lack of proactivity as their sales figures plateau in their comfort zones. They depend on the status quo for the mental well-being of their Social Brain and so seek to defend the status quo above everything else. The desire to avoid being challenged means that when they are challenged, they react defensively, negatively and often aggressively so. This is the language you'll hear:

- I have given years of good service, and in return, I expect job security.
- I will always have a job even if I don't hit my targets.
- This company owes me a raise.
- I'm being headhunted by our competitors.
- I deserve that promotion because of my five years

service.
. You're not from this industry so how would you know?
. I expect my annual bonus at the end of the year.
. This company is just like one big family.

A famous study on sales performance by Neil Rackham at the Xerox Corporation revealed the ease with which salespeople plateau. In the Study, Rackham found that after 18 months, the results of new sales recruits plateaued and then started to drop. Mike Bosworth who worked for Xerox at the time recalls, "*These new batches of young kids would get better and better and better and better, but at 18 months, by batch, you could set your watch by it, they would peak, and their performance would start to go downhill quite rapidly, shortly followed by their moral.*"[160] Why? Rackham concluded that it was because they became complacent and stopped asking questions of the customer. The failing salespeople knew what the customer needed from experience and this lead to what Chip and Dan Heath refer to as, "The Curse of Knowledge."[161] As we all now know, asking the customer questions is the path to better sales, whereas telling a customer what they need is pushy, and does not work because it invokes the threat response. Rackham's observation is, as always, on point and the reason for the sales failure was indeed the change from pulling the customer with questions to pushing products. But the underlying cause of the plateauing is the lack of challenge; they became bored.

Judy Bardwick describes entitlement as, "*The result of too much generosity. We give people what they expect and we don't hold them accountable for meeting a criteria of excellence. People feel entitled when they have so much security that they don't have to earn their rewards.*"[162] Entitled people are the exact opposite of what we're looking for in a sales role. Ironically, we all know the entitled salespeople at work, and this is evidence that they can survive and even thrive in corporate environments.

This is because entitled salespeople focus on appearances and what looks good, rather than doing the right thing. Form is superior to substance, and this is accompanied by an air of superiority. But don't think that these people are just sitting around, they are super busy, busy doing what they want to do, rather than what they should do having lost sight of what's important and required for their role, their team and the organization. We typically know who they are, but they don't because their entitlement hides camouflaged safely in their own unchallenged blind spot.

*"At extreme levels, entitlement is a toxic narcissistic trait, repeatedly exposing people to the risk of feeling frustrated, unhappy and disappointed with life. Often, life, health, aging and the social world don't treat us as well as we'd like. Confronting these limitations is especially threatening to an entitled person because it violates their worldview of self-superiority."*[163] It may be counterintuitive that entitled people can be found in sales organizations given that the profession of selling is supposed to be the most performance-driven profession of all. But we often hire people who have a strong self-concept, who are ambitious and who want money and material wealth, and who are already entitled. It's easy to see that the traits of this type of person, if not managed, could quickly get out of control. Unchallenged, a spiral is created. Firstly, the entitlement creates a feeling of continuous vulnerability to unmet expectations. These unmet expectations then lead to a sense of dissatisfaction and other negative and defensive emotions. This dissonance demands a remedy, which leads to the reinforcement of superiority and the blaming of colleagues and the company.[164]

The dissatisfaction can also create something called 'presenteeism.' Presenteeism occurs when an employee wishes to leave the organization but hasn't done so yet. *"Although remaining on the job, the employee is less committed to the organization, its customers, and its other employees. Rates for presentee-*

*ism are estimated to be approximately three times higher than for absenteeism, especially in a sluggish economy when employees feel unable to find work elsewhere."* [165] The spiral of entitlement and presenteeism is common in companies that put up with mediocre sales performance and can afford to carry non-performing salespeople. This may be companies that have had a first mover advantage in a market, or who have a well-established brand. Whatever the reason, the entitlement is doing nobody any favors. The long-term personal consequences associated with entitled behavior include poor relationships, interpersonal conflicts, and depression. Of course, the business consequences are none too pretty. Entitled people blame those around them and especially the company for not giving to them what they believe they are entitled.

When it comes to having entitled salespeople in a 'Deal Hack,' the challenge could be just what some need to re-energize them and allow them to find their performing feet again. For those who are entrenched, they will struggle with the levels of challenge, particularly from cross-functional colleagues outside of sales. They will also struggle to take on board ideas, suggestions, knowledge and feedback from the 'Hack Team' because it could threaten their self-image.

Once people have become entitled, according to Manson is it hard to break them out of the entitled mind-set, *"Any attempt to reason with them is seen as simply another "threat" to their superiority by another person who "can't handle" how smart/talented/good-looking/successful they are".*[166] The overwhelming urge is to tell entitled people to 'get over' themselves, but remember these issues will not be played out in a constructive way. The danger is that the process will be undermined less overtly, for example, ideas from others on the team either not being followed up or failing because they were carried out in a way that guaranteed failure. Effective follow up on actions is essential with this population. Entitled people should only be introduced into Deal Hacks once the majority have adopted the program and Deal Hacks are an established success. Like any change initiative they will kill the program dead to make themselves look and feel good, given the opportunity.

The sales leaders I meet tend to place themselves above the horizontal line in the Sanford Model, meaning that they see themselves as 'High Challenge' and their teams as being adequately challenged and systematically held to account. But after spending time with their sales people, it becomes apparent that the leaders are over optimistic about the levels of effective challenge in their sales organization. There are often clear examples of organizational challenge but upon examination the inconsistency means thay are actually bouncing between Critic and Friend.

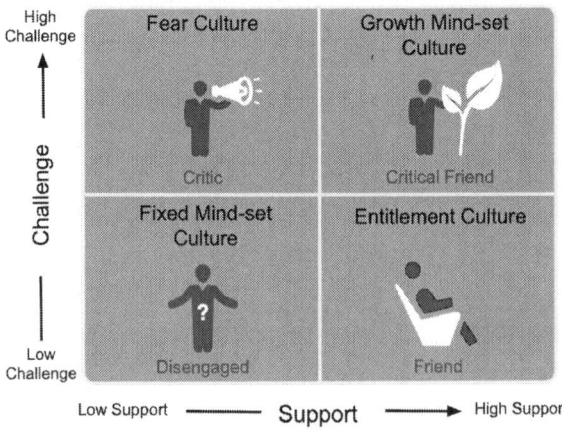

Figure 13 - Sanford Matrix

The result is the sales population lying low for protection, or as they describe it, *"Hiding from management to get some real work done."* Intense support, followed by intense challenge followed by absence. It sounds like this: *"The sales results are behind forecast. We need to give the sales team a wake-up call. I want everyone to call in daily with their activity levels and report their results into their line manager."* This is the sort of thing I hear frequently. It doesn't sound unreasonable because it is so commonplace in sales. If we look at the quality of challenge, however, can we do any better? I think we can improve this example on many fronts. Firstly, we need to be clear on why this change is required. Secondly, this challenge is being imposed on the sales teams from above, so the minute the pressure is off, the normal behavior will return. It is unlikely to be sustainable. Thirdly, we shouldn't be waiting for things to go wrong before we increase the levels of challenge. The ongoing challenge should be expected, that means planned and measured as part of the strategic sales plan, rather than ad hoc spikes in challenge that invoke a threat response and fail to get buy-in. Ken Blanchard famously satirized this as the 'Seagull Manager' in 'The One Minute Manager'. Here's an example:

The Chief Sales Officer sees that the sales figures are running under target for the third month running. Her reaction is to get the sales managers out supervising their teams more closely, and to increase the volume of reporting so that deals can be monitored more closely to prevent losses (Challenge +). After three months the trend continues, so they ask for a Training Needs Analysis and a training program is sourced and delivered (Support +). After six months the training has not worked with all salespeople so the sales managers are sent on a coaching course to improve their coaching, to help the training stick, and they increase the volume of coaching (Challenge +). Sales are still tracking under but there is a new product release, and everyone is recalled for product training (Support +).

This is not an unusual example. Sales leaders are conscious that they must challenge and support their sales populations but are unconscious about the relationship between the two. The result is that sales populations are bouncing between 'Critic' and 'Friend' and laying low when they can, waiting for the latest initiative to blow over and the next to start. The impact of this approach is that the harmony between challenge and support, where challenge and support are most effective, is not achieved. Salespeople feel threatened, and performance does not improve. We intuitively know that challenging and being challenged is an acquired taste for most people because challenging creates a threat response in the Social Brain across a number of DRIVERS:

- **Decision making** – Threat: a decision that has been made is being challenged
- **Interpersonal connections** – Threat: I feel threatened
- **Status** – Threat: if I'm challenged and proven to be wrong, my status will suffer

We want challenge because we know it's right for us, and we don't want challenge because of the potential social threats. How good are you personally at challenging other people? Are you good at holding others to account? Rate your capability from one to ten. One being, 'Really Bad, I always avoid challenging other people,' five being the average and ten being, 'Nothing gets past me, I'm world class.' What is your score? Do you have the number?

In the book Crucial Accountability, the authors describe experiments where they observe the behaviors of people in situations where accountability should be challenged. For example, someone barges in front of a queue of people, or someone makes distracting noises in a library. They found that when people were asked if they would hold others accountable for unacceptable behaviors like this, all participants unanimously responded that they would. What they found, through observational experiments, was that people almost always failed to do so. At best people would give a look, or criticize the perpetrator to another person, but they almost always failed to hold the person to account.[167] This gap between intention and execution is our old friend the optimism bias, helping us to be overly optimistic about our capabilities once again. The same pattern can be seen in workshops when I ask sales managers about their ability to hold their sales teams to account. Again, I've never had any manager score themselves less than a five, but as we all know, it is statistically impossible for all managers to be better than all other managers. When I analyze the deals that sales teams are working on, I almost always find significant gaps that should have been picked up by sales managers or sales leaders with the most rudimentary of challenges. If sales managers and sales leaders were good at holding their teams to account, I would not see these systematic gaps, and arguably I'd not be writing this book. So why are people so poor at challenging one another? People naturally avoid challenging other people because challenging someone rarely passes the value equation. The value equation predicts that if we value something enough we'll do it, and by value, we mean that the reward is greater than the pain. The pain of challenging someone could be a ruined interpersonal relationship. It could make future events uncertain. It could be that you're made to look inept. It could be the spark of a conflict and the challenger might not come off best. Challenging someone is high stakes and high risk, so there needs to be a significantly higher reward for doing so, and that is why people generally avoid challenging others. In the moment, when the decision to challenge is made, it feels like it's just not worth the hassle, especially when there's a cubic mile of spreadsheets, pie charts, and reports to hide behind.

If we look at the cultural example set by Hyundai, we should be able to challenge up and down the corporate ladder. On a scale of one to ten, one being, 'Really Bad,' five being the average and ten being, 'Nobody and nothing scares me; I'm a world class challenger.' How good are you at challenging up the corporate ladder? Do you have the number? When it comes to challenging upwards, the situation gets worse. For a Growth Mind-set sales culture to take root, there needs to be the ability to challenge up and down the management chain. This is especially the case in sales where the salesperson is the customer's representative in the selling organization. In sales training sessions, the delegates often raise the need to challenge their colleagues and managers to get the best deal for the customer. If they feel that they cannot challenge upwards within their organization, the voice of the customer may be heard less, which is harmful to any organization. So, how do the sales people in your organization fare at challenging upwards? How are you at challenging upwards? A famous experiment carried out by Stanley Milgram in 1963 sheds light on our ability to challenge authority. In the experiments, a participant was paired with another person who they thought was another participant, but was, in fact, a member of Milgram's team. Lots were drawn to determine who would be the 'learner' and who would be the 'teacher.' The learner had to learn a list of word pairs and the teacher had to test them on the pairs. The draw was fixed so that the real participant was always the teacher, and the learner was always a member of Milgram's. The learner (the colleague) was taken into a separate room, strapped to a chair and had electrodes attached to their arms. The teacher and researcher went into the room next door where there was an electric shock generator. Unknown to the participant, the researcher was, in fact, an actor. The teacher could not see the learner but was asked to test the learner on the word pairs over an intercom. If the learner got an answer wrong, the teacher was asked to give them an electric shock, increasing the level of shock each time. The generator had a row of 30 switches marked from 15 volts (Slight Shock) to 375 volts (Danger: Severe Shock) to 450 volts (XXX). The learner gave mainly wrong answers (on purpose), and for each of these, the teacher gave them an electric shock. The rooms were located such that the participant could hear the screams and pleading of the learner to stop. When the teacher refused to administer a shock upon receipt of an incorrect answer, the experimenter gave a series of challenges to ensure they continued. If they did not comply, the researcher read out the next challenge, and so on:

- **Prod 1**: Please continue.
- **Prod 2**: The experiment requires you to continue.
- **Prod 3**: It is absolutely essential that you continue.
- **Prod 4**: You have no other choice but to continue.

The results of the experiment were extraordinary. 65% (two-thirds) of participants (i.e., teachers) continued to the highest level of 450 volts (XXX). All the participants continued to 300 volts. When participants could instruct an assistant to press the switches for them, 92.5% shocked to the maximum 450 volts (XXX).

Milgram summarized the experiment: *"I set up a simple experiment at Yale University to test how much pain an ordinary citizen would inflict on another person simply because he was ordered to by an experimental scientist. Stark authority was pitted against the subjects' [participants'] strongest moral imperatives against hurting others, and, with the subjects' [participants'] ears ringing with the screams of the victims, authority won more often than not. The extreme willingness of adults to go to almost any lengths on the command of an authority constitutes the chief finding of the study and the fact most urgently demanding explanation."*[168]

In the Milgram experiment, all of the participants challenged the researcher, but two-thirds allowed nothing to change as a result of their challenges. In other words, the challenges were futile. One-third of the participants challenged the researchers to the point where something changed. What sort of sales population do you work with? Do they challenge and nothing changes? Or do they challenge until they get the required changes? From the Milgram experiment, we can see that two-thirds of people are inclined to stick with the status quo rather than challenge effectively, even when it means they are killing another person. It may seem so, but selling is not life and death, and salespeople have a lot to lose from challenging upwards. Salary, bonus, relationships, and reputation are all on the line when we challenge upwards. There is potentially a lot to lose. The participants in the Milgram experiment did not have anything to lose; they were only told to torture a stranger by an authority figure in a white coat. People in 'Deal Hacks' need to be able to challenge each other, because that is what creates a better deal. People in the Deal Hack need to be able to challenge each other productively and sustainably, and that includes upwards and across different functions. They are required to do this but bear in mind that at least two-thirds will struggle with this. Fortunately, help is at hand. There is evidence that showing someone how to challenge helps to re-balance the value equation by increasing the reward and reducing the pain.[169] It enables the person to reduce the risk of harming a relationship, increases certainty and improves the chances of a successful outcome. For these reasons Deal Coaches create an environment where challenge is objective and measured, balanced with support, and so produces the desired outcomes. Coaching is the present day performance intervention that is designed to be a balance of challenge and support. Standing alone in this capacity is why it appears like the silver bullet to improve sales performance. When sales leaders position their sales organizations above the horizontal line of the Sanford Matrix, putting themselves in the 'High Challenge' part of the matrix, coaching is frequently given as an example to substantiate this position. This is understandable because coaching is intended to be a way of holding the sales population to account. But according to John Blakey and Ian Day in their book Challenging Coaching *"Much coach training is biased toward supporting others rather than challenging them. We noticed that this bias was also reflected in the many coaching books that exist and in the accrediting stand-*

*ards used by the different professional coaching bodies: an empathetic emphasis on listening and asking questions in a nondirective style, as opposed to a provocative emphasis on providing feedback and holding to account in an honest, direct style."*[170] Blakey and Day are referring to traditional coaching in companies, which is based on time-honored models like GROW. They offer a welcomed and updated model of coaching that focuses more on challenge and is a credible alternative model for coaching in a sales environment. Their astute observation is all the more pertinent when it comes to the sales environment where traditional coaching models like GROW have become the de facto standard. Coaches need to be more adept at challenging the strong self-image of sales people, and scrutinizing at the deal level. To be effective in the sales arena, traditional coaches must build their skills in challenging more robustly **and** in more effectively scrutinizing deals. When we recruit sales coaches are they trained in value identification, value creation, value quantification and value communication? Do coaches have the capability to, in the words of really Ray Dalio, stress test a deal? [171] Do they have the mandate and the specific knowledge required to challenge at the deal level and demonstrably increase the chances of a better deal outcome? There needs to be a clear distinction between a traditional personal development coach, and a Deal Coach who has the mandate and the capability to challenge live deals. Traditional coaching holds the coachee as the focus, a Deal Coach holds the deal as the focus and that is an important and philosophical shift from present-day practice that many coaches will struggle with.

When we ask sales managers and sales leaders why they are not holding their sales teams to account, their answers invariably come back to time and opportunity. A coaching session is an ideal opportunity to hold people to account, but according to the Sales Management Association too little time is spent coaching. *"Salespeople don't get enough coaching, in management's opinion. A mere 15% of respondents believe their firms provide the right amount of sales coaching. An overwhelming majority (77%), think the sales force is offered too little coaching. On average, managers spend 36 minutes per week in one-on-one coaching interactions with each direct report salesperson, and just under four hours per week across the sales team managed."*[172] If we're going to challenge sales populations effectively on deals, we can either free up our sales managers to be able to have the capacity to do this, or we can implement a process like the Deal Hack so that salespeople and colleagues can start holding each other to account, and fill the accountability gap. To summarize the picture for conventional approaches to sales coaching, given the low volume of coaching and the lack of challenge in traditional coaching, together this creates a supportive environment that lacks challenge, which is according to Sanford, an ineffective environment for performance improvement. Training is probably the biggest tool in the sales enablement toolkit and, like coaching, can be considered a balance of challenge and support. To understand the level of challenge in training, we need to be clear on how to build 'Challenge' into training in the first place. The absence of any recognized model or way of doing this is perhaps indicative of the fact that training designers are not consciously designing with 'challenge' in mind. To make up for this, I've developed and use the TEST model to analyze learning interventions and test the levels of challenge they contain:

**Test:** to define areas of weakness
**Express:** the learning in the context of their own environment
**Solve:** a problem before being taught the solution
**Try:** the skill in the workflow

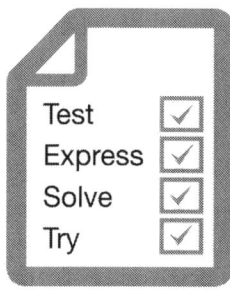

Figure 10 - TEST Challenge Model

How can we TEST the level of challenge in sales training?

**Test:** using a tool to identify and highlight areas of weakness is one of the best ways to improve overall performance. This takes many forms in classroom training from conventional recall testing to testing the application of skills in, for example, role-plays. The reason for the testing and the intended use of the results needs to be 100% transparent. There is a justified concern from delegates that the results will be used as performance management information. If this is the case, then this needs to be clear and the session treated as an assessment center rather than training. In some countries, like Germany, the testing needs to be approved by the unions or worker's council in advance.[173] If the testing is designed to improve learning, then it's a good idea to refer to it as informal testing, for example, a quiz.

The ability to incorporate informal testing is a real barometer of the culture. Some salespeople delight in informal testing, and the tests can be a fun way to engage and reward with prizes. However, plateauing and entitled salespeople are keen to test other people, but avoid being tested themselves because it challenges their self-image by potentially exposing them.

**Express:** this is the process of giving new concepts meaning by expressing it in the context of your own environment, for example, using your own words and connecting it with what you already know and do.[174] Training designers and trainers are well aware of this and look for opportunities for delegates to do this. The one that's often missing in sales, which can bring about the desired change, is the use of live deals. Training designers replicate live deals in the form of role-plays and simulations. But these are abstract and provide many opportunities for cynical delegates to play the card, *"That doesn't happen in the real world."* Learning is more successful when the abstract is made concrete, personal and meaningful. That is, best done in real deals. Why do we shy away from real deals in sales training? The answer is uncertainty. A live deal that is selected for use in the moment during a training session could, by chance, illustrate the required concepts, or the deal might prove to be irrelevant and not support the learning points at all. Inside the training room the trainers are working to the clock, and going off script is a big risk for them. It's far easier and less risky to write and scale an abstract role play. I've seen sales training companies use role plays that are not even from the same industry, and this is done to cut down on development costs. The client is told that the role plays stretch their people, and coming out of their normal environment provides a leveling effect for the sales team where experience can give an advantage for some over others. The aim is to demonstrate the skills not to demonstrate how to actually sell it. It is clear that people believe this because I've witnessed it many times in my career. Personally, I don't buy it, and I know that training companies do this because it is more scalable and more profitable, not because it is in the interest of the learners. In my experience, the learning needs to be more like the learner's environment and not less. Making it less so is easier for the training team to scale but it invokes the threat response in some delegates because of the lack of relevance.

**Solve:** Solving a problem before being taught the solution is one of the best-known ways to learn through challenge. Trainers often use a Socratic model of conversation with the group, proposing problems as a way to manage the flow of learning. However, during classroom sessions, the temptation is to explain the concepts and tools before the delegates trial them. This is primarily because it is more time efficient, but also it leads to better feedback scores as the learning is less challenging. Solving a problem before being taught can also be done through pre-work, where tools and concepts can be tried before the session. However, in my experience of sales training, other than in Asia where compliance levels are high, it is unlikely that more than 30% of delegates will do pre-work.

**Try:** we all know that if we don't use a skill, we lose the skill, so repeated practice is essential. Attempting a complex skill in an abstract form and then not having the immediate opportunity to try it in the workplace with accurate feedback, is one of the most significant reasons that new behaviors fail to take root. Working on live deals inside the workflow is how to circumvent this because it allows for immediate and ongoing practice. Because the mechanism for follow up of live deals are already in place, sales management coaching, it provides an immediate jump on point for coaches to reinforce.

Sales training programs use, to a lesser or greater degree, all of the STEP components: Solve, Test, Environment, and Practice. But it's certainly worth challenging the design and delivery team to ensure that these opportunities to challenge the delegates are being activated. Reducing the duration of the program is the most assured way to sacrifice the effectiveness of the STEP components. With the delegates, sales managers and sales leaders all wanting to get out of the classroom and back into the workflow, this unrelenting pressure brings with it a stark opportunity cost of reducing the effectiveness of the intervention through the subsequent removal of challenge activities that cost 'time.' This is a good example of short-term economic interests overriding long-term interests leading to unintended consequences. According to two cognitive scientists Henry Roediger and Mark McDaniel who dedicated their careers to the study of learning and memory, *"When they (learners) hear a lecture or read a text that is a paragon of clarity, the ease with which they follow the argument gives them the feeling that they already know it and don't need to study it. In other words, they tend not to know what they don't know; when put to the test, the find they cannot recall the critical ideas or apply them in a new context".[175]* If we reduce the time available in a training session and extract the STEP activities that challenge the delegates, we're left with a more 'lecturing' approach, to get the information across as quickly as possible. 'Fire Hosing' as we affectionately call it in the trade. This, in turn, feeds the 'Illusion of Superiority' we saw earlier. If you've ever wondered why some people leave sales training saying, *"That was a waste of my time, I knew all that,"* It could be an indicator that they didn't actually know it, they don't know it in sufficient depth and they almost certainly won't apply it in the workplace. Relying on such feedback happy sheets to measure the effectiveness of a training program can be extremely misleading for this reason.

Sales performance interventions are typically undertaken outside of the workflow. This increases the time pressure on the design, which reduces the already reduced opportunities in large-scale social environments to challenge an audience. Without the requisite amount of challenge in the interventions, the interventions cease to be effective. Judy Bardwick explains why, *"Too little challenge is destructive. It deprives people of the experiences that create confidence. They never learn how to push past risk to success. They never have the opportunity to develop the skills of coping, of somehow managing to pull it off even when being unsure."* [176] It's really up to the sales leaders to specify the level of challenge that a training program contains, but a weakness I frequently see is that sales leaders are not consciously aware of the relationship between challenge and support. This means they sometimes inadvertently scupper the opportunities for challenge in training by actively seeking to reduce the challenge component in sales training programs. If sales leaders were more aware of the relationship between challenge and support, I'm sure they would be asking for the challenging volume to be turned up and not down.

Entitlement in the sales profession is something that is more frequently recognized by those outside of the sales profession than by those inside the profession. This is because entitlement sits so perfectly in a person's or organizations' blinds spot. Until entitlement is recognized, it will remain untouched, reducing the effectiveness of any sales organization where it finds itself. Entitlement comes from a lack of effective challenge, and we've seen some good ways to increase challenge in sales forces. But we'll now see how entitlement can be exacerbated by the very learning interventions aimed to tackle it. In this next part of the book, we look at how Deal Hacks help to build a solution to this by keeping learning in the workflow, where sales people learn best, and Social Brain reactions are managed more effectively.

# PART 3 SUMMARY

We want sales people with growth mind-sets, which collect-ively we call a growth mind-set sales culture. We achieve a growth mind-set culture when we manage social brain think-ing in the workflow through a balance of challenge and sup-port. When levels of challenge and support are ineffective or imbalanced we get Social Brain thinking that creates non-growth sales cultures.

In the journey from fixed mind-set to growth mind-set cul-tures we need to be conscious of how we balance challenge and support. The unintended consequences of many trans-formation initiatives is that we can drive people into fear or entitlement cultures, both of which will limit sales growth.

An entitled culture has an abundance of training and coach-ing, but low levels of challenge and follow up to make sure these are being used effectively. This causes the accountabil-ity for development to shift from the individual towards the company. Social Brain thinking goes unchecked and is al-lowed to dominate the sales process.

A fear culture is a highly competitive, individualistic and fear-driven environment. Individual attainment is prioritized and rewarded with the concept of team being nothing more than a social concept. Social Brain thinking, again, goes unchecked and is allowed to dominate the sales process reducing sales effectiveness.

Deal Hacks help to drive a balance of challenge and sup-port. They reduce entitlement by increasing challenge. They reduce fear by adopting a healthier approach to challenge.

Deal Hacks reduce Social Brain thinking in the sales process through effective feedback and form the backbone of a growth sales culture.

# PART FOUR

# KEEP THE LEARNING
# IN THE WORKFLOW

Sales organizations have hit a diminishing return, where
many salespeople are not achieving their goals despite
having more resources and support than ever before.
Due to cognitive biases, many sales people and sales leaders
are, however, blind to the lack of capability that is causing
this failure.

One of the blind spots is the use of Social Brain thinking in
the sales process that cuts corners and reduces sales effectiveness. Unidentified and unchallenged, these blind spots develop into a fixed mind-set where challenging situations are
avoided and the ability to adapt to change effectively shuts
down.

A fixed mind-set is often exacerbated by the very learning
interventions designed to drive performance improvements
because they can create social brain reactions. Further attempts to improve sales performance can result in fear or en-

titlement when challenge and support are not balanced.

In this next part of the book, we look at how Deal Hacks help to build a solution to this by keeping learning in the workflow, where sales people want to learn, they learn best, and where the impact is direct, immediate and measurable. Part four is divided into:

**Chapter 11 – Learning Inside the Workflow**. How do Deal Hacks compare to traditional learning and development interventions?

**Chapter 12 – Deal Hack Structure and Process.** What's the Deal Hack process?

**Chapter 13 – Why Anything?** Why should prospects buy anything?

**Chapter 14 – Why Us?** How can we get prospects to choose us?

**Chapter 15 – Why Now?** How can we get prospects to buy now?

# CHAPTER 11

# LEARNING INSIDE THE WORKFLOW

"Falling over is definitely the best way to learn."

Richard Browning, founder of Gravity Industries Ltd.

T he islanders lit the fires on the makeshift runway. The glow from the fires could be seen in the darkness, miles away from Vanuatu, a Pacific island in the South Pacific Ocean. Alongside the runway was a wooden shack with what appeared to be a bamboo antenna constructed on top of it. In the hut sat one of the islanders with a headset made from coconut shells, and spectacles made from bamboo. At the end of the runway was what appeared to be an airplane, but on closer inspection, was a mock-up of an airplane made of bamboo and dried brown leaves. The islanders waited patiently for the airplanes with the cargo to arrive. Seventy years after the last cargo planes had left, the islanders would be in for a very long wait.

The John Frum cult on the Pacific island of Vanuatu undertook such rituals in an attempt to entice back the cargo planes that landed on their island during World War II. During the Second World War, the US military constructed temporary runways across many of the Pacific Islands to transport cargo to the front lines. The islanders had not previously been exposed to such technology, and were suddenly enveloped in a swarm of airplanes transporting supplies for the war effort. Some of the supplies were shared with the islanders, including food, like tins of corned beef, clothes, and personal items. In 1945 the airplanes left as quickly as they had arrived just a few years earlier, leaving the islanders nostalgic for the days when supplies would seemingly arrive as gifts from the sky. To this day, the John Frum cult worship 'John From America' an American GI from the war, in the hopes that they can entice the cargo planes back with their gifts from the sky.

I'm sometimes reminded of the John Frum cargo cult when I'm invited to look at how companies are attempting to improve their sales results. The essential components of sales performance improvement are seemingly in place, but like the cargo planes, over time the results do not come. Many of the essential building blocks of their sales enablement engine are like the bamboo airplane at the end of the makeshift runway. They look real from a distance but, upon closer inspection, they lack what is actually required to produce the desired results. To understand why this is the case, we need take a look at the operational infrastructure that supports sales performance in sales organizations, the sales enablement function. Are they doing a good job of supporting sales performance and maximizing sales effectiveness?

In larger companies, the sales organization traditionally received performance support from learning and development professionals in the human resources (HR) department to help improve sales capability, and responsibility for improving mind-set would have fallen here. This may still be the case, but over the last 15 years in most companies, sales perform-ance support has morphed into a specific sales enablement function charged with performance optimization within sales populations exclusively. The sales enablement function typically sits outside of the learning and development func-tion and inside the sales organization. While the salespeople have their heads down selling, the mandate falls to the sales enablement function to have their heads up looking for change, systems and innovation to drive across the sales population, to increase sales effectiveness and productivity. This separation has happened because the sales enablement function can more exactly support the needs of sales than traditional learning and development departments based in HR. Sales enablement functions, for example, often comprise people from the sales function itself, whereas you'd rarely hear of salespeople in the learning and development function. So there has been a move by organizations from traditional learning and development towards sales enablement because sales enablement teams are nearer to sales and they under-stand sales more intimately. Sales enablement should, there-fore, be in a place to drive growth mind-sets and performance improvements within sales populations. Problem solved? There has indeed been a move away from learning and devel-opment into sales enablement, but training and coaching re-main the primary tools of choice for both functions, unques-tioningly so. Sales enablement functions use the tools handed down to them by their learning and development cousins, but these tools were designed for general learning and develop-ment across whole organizations, not learning in a commer-cial sales environment. For example, when designing learning interventions, I sometimes hear learning and development people asking *how* the audience learn? What's their learning style? They ask this to make the learning more adapted to the styles of the audience. There's a ton of reference material on this from Honey and Mumford's four learning styles, through Walter Burke Barbe's VAK model to Neil Flemming's VARK model (Visual, auditory, reading and kinaesthetic) if you'd like to learn more. Whilst this is interesting stuff, I've always struggled to see the direct connection between this and sales enablement. The people I meet in sales are a mixture of all of the learning styles. I, therefore, find it almost impossible to effectively diagnose and apply learning styles when I'm designing sales enablement interventions in any meaningful way. I'm sure it's applicable to traditional organization wide learning and development, but for sales enablement, I think a far more interesting and impactful question is not *how* do people learn, but *when* do they need to learn? If we ask *when* salespeople need to learn, we can start to really impact on performance. If we was *when* salespeople need to learn, we find there are five BASIC learning times that sales people need to learn to remain effective at selling:[177]

- **Brand new learning:** when you need a brand new skill for something you've not done before
- **Additional learning:** when you need to build on an existing skill, to go to a deeper level
- **Solving Problems:** when you meet a problem in applying the learning, and it does not work out as planned
- **Implementing learning:** when you act on what you've learned, which includes adapting to your unique situation
- **Changing behavior:** when you need to change what you're doing and adopt a new method of working

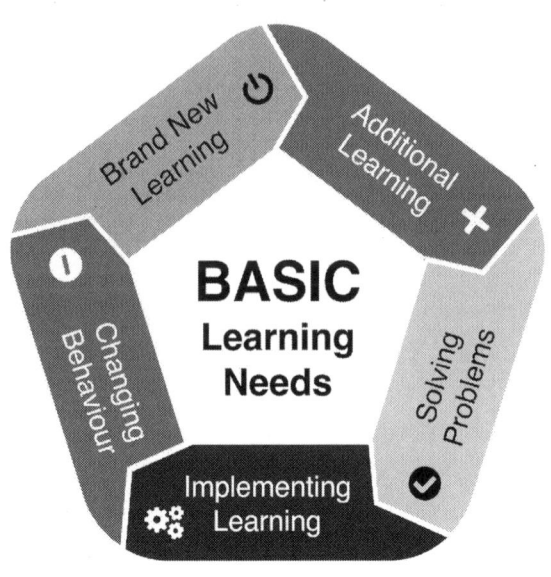

Figure 14 - BASIC learning times

Different learning times require different types of learning interventions. We intuitively know that training and coaching are good for Brand New Learning and Additional Learning. But what about the other three? Firstly, what about when a person is implementing learning in the workplace after attending a training course? This is a big issue because, even if the implementation of the learning is the next day, we know from Ebbinghaus,[178] approximately 60% of what has been learned will have already been forgotten. But how many people can implement the learning from a training session the next day anyway? Sometimes it's weeks and even months later that they find the opportunity to apply the skills they learned. When the delegates have delays in implementing learning, do you send them on another training course? A bite-sized e-learning training course? Coaching would perhaps provide better support for the learner in that case, but with minimal coaching actually available, the result is that new behaviors learned in training are all too easily forgotten, and legacy behaviors come back to fill the void. We know this because we see it happening around us all the time.

Secondly, what about when the sales people need to solve real world problems that are time critical in the workflow? They typically ask a colleague or they look for the answer in a sales enablement system like Seismic. *"When employees are stuck, they need the answer quickly. It doesn't help them to sign up for a class that will happen three weeks from now and sit through a four-hour session to get the answer they need this minute,"* says Consultant Britt Andreatta, Ph.D. [179] Coaching could help here, but training is not responsive enough to this learning need and that is why we see more and more sales enablement systems like Seismic emerging. Thirdly, how effective are training and coaching when Changing Behavior? People 'do' what they believe to be right and their beliefs are based on their experiences built up over a significant amount of time. We'll see later, in detail, that training people to change their behaviors is like cold calling a prospect, telling them to buy your product and expecting them to compliantly buy it from you. If the prospect was already looking for your product then that may just about work, and you've found the needle in the haystack. But we know that to get buy-in from prospects we need to use the sales process to drive the buying process. Using training for behavioral change shows sales people what they need to do if they did change, but the process of building new beliefs should precede the training. Building new beliefs is more that just telling them how they'll benefit. Again, think of how badly that approach works with prospects in the sales process. Building new beliefs for behavioral change involves deconstructing the legacy beliefs by creating new experiences, before, during and after the training. Training is a part of the process but used alone it is unlikely to be able to drive any sort of meaningful change. Once again, coaching could help here. Coaching does always seems to be the catch-all response to the limitations of training programs translating into workplace behaviors. The get out of jail card, if you like. But, as we saw earlier, too little time is spent coaching in sales environments which means that in reality it is not a viable option to plug the gaps when sales people need to implement learning, solve problems or change behaviors.

If we're clear on *when* people need to learn, in order to be effective, we can then design performance interventions that have greater individual and business impact. Asking *when*, also helps us to understand why there are problems with the current approach to sales enablement in many sales organizations. Common problems like the lack of adoption, and lack of application of the learning in the workflow come from **not** asking this question. Interestingly, when I put the BASIC learning times model in front of a sales audience and ask them what they want, guess where they point to? They point to 'solving problems'. They want performance support inside the workflow when they hit a problem. They don't want to be taken out of the field every six or twelve months to go on an intensive course. Even if it is designed around their learning style. When I put the BASIC learning times model in front of sales leaders and ask what they want, guess where they point to? They point to 'behavioral change'. They want their sales people to be able to adapt to changes in the market, and embrace the latest methods of selling. But, training alone is good for neither of these. The over reliance on training, coupled with the lack of coaching, is a significant reason why so many sales people and sales leaders become disengaged from sales enablement interventions. When I put the BASIC learning times model in front of sales enablement leaders and ask what they want, where do you think they point? Typically, they point to 'Implementing Learning', which is level three on Donald Kirkpatrick's industry standard scale used for measuring learning success[180]. Achieving this for any learning intervention is a sign of success. Implementing new behaviors in the workflow is the bit that all learning and development, and sales enablement departments talk about but it's the bit they really struggle with. The controversy has been around since the 1980's when learning and development departments were the new kids on the block. The reason for the controversy can be explained with these types statistics:

1. Formal training is the source of only 10 – 20% of what we learn at work, although it accounts for about 80% of spending in business education.
2. Only 20% to 30% of what is being learned in formal training is actually transferred to the workplace in a way that enhances performance.
3. 80-90% of what employees know of their job, they know from informal learning.[181]

These statistics, and many more like them, shine a light on the problem of over reliance on training for performance improvement. The genus of the over reliance on training is the unquestioning adoption of legacy learning and development techniques that are inadequate for the corporate world and are particularly inadequate for sales. The proof is all around us. Getting salespeople to actually *do* in the field what they have learned in the training sessions is extremely hard, and gets harder over time due to Social Brain thinking short-cutting the sales process. The diagnosis of the learning and development community is that we're failing to 'transfer' the learning from the classroom to the workplace. That's why the concept of Deal Hacks is so annoyingly good and irritatingly obvious. There's no need for the transfer of learning, because there's no transfer to be made. Deal Hacks, work on live deals inside the workflow. The traditional transfer problem gets dispatched with surprising ease, because the traditional methods of scaling learning and development are not being (mis)used.

Another topic that rages in the world of Learning and Development is demonstrating the results of the learning interventions, Level Four on the Kirkpatrick scale. I've always found this to be relatively straight forward when designing interventions in sales because there are so many KPIs to attach to. For example, the number of leads generated, the number of phone calls converted into meetings and the number of sales made, etc. Unlike many other functions, in sales we're in the fortunate position of being continuously measured and have a number of metrics to attach learning to. Having these KPIs clearly in mind during the learning design process, along with researching and testing the customer buying process and sales workflow, means it's not hard to make sure you achieve them. But because learning and development has traditionally been designed around the entire organization, and not the sales organization specifically where metrics are more common and better tracked, the opportunity to use the metrics and clear KPIs in the sales environment is often being missed. A good example of this is achieving a return on investment (ROI) through training, known as 'Level Five' on the Kirkpatrick scale. Having originally only developed four levels, this is very much the 'stretch goal' for the learning and development community. But here's where the John Frum cult analogy comes in. The right pieces seem to be in place, but in reality nobody can actually point to any credible evidence of how organizational learning can support anything remotely like a credible ROI. James Kirkpatrick, son of Donald Kirkpatrick who developed the measurement scale used by most companies today, has admitted defeat and coined an alternative to ROI, the Return on Expectation or ROE. Here's what he has to say, *"ROE lies in contrast to ROI, which attempts to isolate the value of the training program alone and is done after the fact. ROI is a defensive and reactive tactic that calls for little or no collaboration between training and the business."* I'll give Kirkpatrick Jnr. the benefit of the doubt that this is the case in traditional learning and development organizations. But it's not the case in any sales enablement function I've set up. When using Deal Hacks we're not just *collaborating* effectively with the business, we *are* an integral part of the business. We can track ROI because we're improving deals, killing bad deals that waste time, increasing margin and driving the KPIs that bring in revenue. If sales enablement functions followed Donald Kirpatrick's advice we'd not get the funding we need to run Deal Hacks because we'd be asking for the budget using ROE when everyone else in business uses ROI. This gives another example of why sales enablement departments have moved away from learning and development, and Deal Hacks are an example of moving further away. Personally, I'm happy to take the good parts of traditional learning and development with me, but equally happy to leave behind the elements that are holding sales organizations back, like ROE. The real art, of course, is knowing which is which. So let's look a little deeper into what works for sales enablement and what doesn't.

In the BASIC learning model, we can clearly see that training is good for brand new learning, like onboarding new sales people. Training is also good for 'Additional Learning' provided there are no existing experiences that need to be treated as behavioral change. But, and it is a big but, training alone is not good for solving problems in the workflow, not good for implementing learning and not good for behavioral change. Three of the five learning times in the sales organization are missing if you're only delivering training, and we've already seen that training accounts for about 80% of spending in business education. Sales organizations need to understand that there are five BASIC learning times and use those to guide the design of sales enablement interventions. Sales enablement functions that use training for all of the five BASIC learning times are wasting valuable time and resource. But what if there's more to it than just throwing money down the drain? What if this is actually harmful and not benign? What if this

177

over reliance on training is causing a corresponding increase in fixed mind-sets, and that is why we are experiencing the diminishing return of the Sales Performance Paradox?

It transpires that using training in this indiscriminate way can be harmful to sales effectiveness because it unintentionally develops and reinforces fixed mind-set behaviors. Unproductive training interventions can push people towards a fixed mind-set because they reduce the value sales people see in learning interventions overall. Many sales people say they see sales training as a necessary evil, time away from selling that they can ill afford. Sales enablement functions see this response as a fixed mind-set where the person does not want to learn. What the sales person means is that they want learning support inside the workflow when they hit real life problems but they don't have the vocabulary to articulate this. Understandably they do not want to be taken away from selling to solve abstract, make believe problems in the classroom. This is not a bad thing, it's a good thing! It may not be that they have a fixed mind-set after all, but ironically by the time they walk out of another unproductive sales training session, that's exactly what they'll have.

One of the biggest complaints from salespeople is that they are being taken out of the workflow for sales training. And when shown the BASIC learning model, they identify that they want timely learning support inside the workflow to help them solve problems. Why aren't we listening to this? Why are we misdiagnosing this as a fixed-mind-set? Maybe we have the fixed mind-set in sales enablement? Let me explain. The training and coaching mechanisms handed down from our learning and development cousins are the predominant tools in the enablement toolkit. If you were designing learning and development interventions from an organizational perspective using these tools makes total sense. But, if you design learning and development interventions from a sales perspective, the world begins to look very different. From a sales perspective we **can** design interventions around the deals we're driving, and that is the Deal Hack. This may not be appropriate for non-sales audiences, and so this is where sales enablement takes another evolutionary step away from their learning and development cousins. This is an opportunity for a step change in sales enablement. A change in which we need to bring our learning and development, and sales enablement colleagues with us. It's not just the sales people that need to change, for a change. It's therefore time to reflect the mind-set mirror back onto our learning and development, and sales enablement colleagues to see how they will cope with this evolutionary change.

We know from the 90% of heart bypass patients that Social Brain thinking nudges them towards taking the easy path, which fails. So we need to make sure that Intellectual Brain thinking is being supported in the workflow. Such support would provide the nudges in the opposite direction, away from Social Brain thinking which can harm decision making in the sales process through short-cuts. The question to challenge ourselves with is, *"How do we move sales performance optimization into the sales workflow where it is wanted, needed, and can nudge salespeople to use Intellectual Brain thinking to add value for customers in the sales process?"* The need for this to happen is one reason why there is a macro trend for learning to move from being a formal process outside of the workflow to an informal process inside the workflow. But for informal learning to be effective, salespeople need to be effective at learning in the first place, and as we saw in Chapter One, the sales profession is particularly weak at learning. But it's not just salespeople struggling in this space, Learning and Development professionals are struggling too because of the historical approaches to designing and scaling performance interventions that are too cumbersome, too slow and do not align with the audience's needs. Coaching is currently the most effective way to provide learning support to a sales population dynamically inside the workflow, but as we have seen and experienced, sales managers, for a myriad of reasons, are not spending enough time coaching their teams. The system is broken, like many educational systems that are not coping with the transfer to a knowledge economy. Ken Robinson asserts that *"Human resources are like natural resources; they're often buried deep. You have to go looking for them, they're not just lying around on the surface. You have to create the circumstances where they show themselves. And you might imagine education would be the way that happens, but too often, it's not. Every education system in the world is being reformed at the moment and it's not enough. Reform is no use anymore because that's simply improving a broken model. What we need is not evolution, but a revolution in education. This has to be transformed into something else. One of the real challenges is to innovate fundamentally in education. Innovation is hard, because it means doing something that people don't find very easy, for the most part. It means challenging what we take for granted, things that we think are obvious. The great problem for reform or transformation is the tyranny of common sense. Things that people think, "It can't be done differently, that's how it's done."*[182]

Robinson was speaking about education in general, but his words encapsulate perfectly the niche situation concerning sales enablement today. The unintended consequence of the present status quo is that the window of opportunity for learning inside the workflow, when it is needed most, when it is being asked for by salespeople and sales leaders, and ironically when learning is most effective, is being completely missed and squandered. That is why the Deal Hack is such a refreshing and needed change because it creates opportunities for learning support inside the workflow when it is needed most, when it is being asked for by salespeople and sales leaders, and when learning is most effective. The biggest impediment to this change is *"The tyranny of common sense. Things that people think, "It can't be done differently, that's how it's done".* Can you lead the revolution by pulling sales learning back into the workflow by working on live deals instead of abstract training? The Deal Hack is a great place to start, so let's do just that.

Here's a recent conversation with a sales trainer who was observing a Deal Hack. *"I've no idea what that was, but I can't do it,"* he said as we were walking out of a Deal Hack. *"That was a Deal Hack. It improves decision making in the deal process through objective, cross-functional teamwork,"* was what I thought to myself. *"It's been a long day, let's find a bar,"* was what I actually said. I was hopeful that he would become a 'Deal Coach' for me because he was a first class sales trainer. At the time I was surprised by his bewildered response, but it helped me to realize just how different the Deal Hack concept is, compared to the training and coaching that traditionally support sales performance. *"I've no idea what that was",* told me that even a seasoned sales trainer of many years had no frame of reference for what the Deal Hack was. When describing the concept of the Deal Hack, I find it helpful to anchor into familiar concepts like training and coaching, so people can understand what I mean. Equally, however, it is necessary to differentiate from these existing concepts too, and therein lies the challenge. To do this, let's see an example of how different interventions map to the needs of a typical sales enablement project in the corporate B2B environment. The intervention map shows that overall no one type of intervention type matches all the criteria required for a successful sales program, and that is why a mix of interventions is usually used. You can see that operationally e-learning is an attractive choice. If a message needs to get out to an audience quickly across a large geography, it's operationally the best option. But if the message is complex and needs to be tailored to the individual, you'd likely have a live webinar, with questions and answers, delivered to segmented audiences, or move across into face to face training or coaching. I'm sure the table will create significant debate as it is subjective.

| | | E-learning | Classroom | Coaching | Deal Hack |
|---|---|---|---|---|---|
| **Operational** | Speed to deployment | 🙂 | ☹️ | 🙂 | 🙂 |
| | Scalability and language | 🙂 | ☹️ | ☹️ | ☹️ |
| | Cost per learner | 🙂 | ☹️ | ☹️ | ☹️ |
| | Can be matched directly to business results, immediately | ☹️ | ☹️ | ☹️ | 🙂 |
| | Provides oversight in the workflow to show that the skills are being applies | ☹️ | ☹️ | 🙂 | 🙂 |
| | Provides insight on sales performance in live situations | ☹️ | ☹️ | 🙂 | 🙂 |
| | Provides insight into sales results forecasting | ☹️ | ☹️ | ☹️ | 🙂 |
| **Learning and behavioral** | Team-based and social | 🙂 | 🙂 | 🙂 | 🙂 |
| | In the workflow of the learner | 🙂 | ☹️ | 🙂 | 🙂 |
| | Based on needs of the individual | 🙂 | 🙂 | 🙂 | 🙂 |
| | Self-paced with learner time flexibility | 🙂 | ☹️ | 🙂 | 🙂 |
| | Allows for expert input and experience sharing | 🙂 | 🙂 | 🙂 | 🙂 |
| **BASIC Learning Need** | Brand New Learning | 🙂 | 🙂 | ☹️ | ☹️ |
| | Additional Learning | 🙂 | 🙂 | ☹️ | ☹️ |
| | Solving Problems | ☹️ | ☹️ | 🙂 | 🙂 |
| | Implementing Learning | ☹️ | ☹️ | 🙂 | 🙂 |
| | Behavioral Change | ☹️ | ☹️ | 🙂 | 🙂 |

Figure 15 - Intervention Map

I notice that when I show the table to e-learning developers they put smiley faces down the whole e-learning column, as coaches do in their column, as trainers do in theirs! However, it is hoped that debate helps to form a view of how the different interventions can combine together to satisfy the changing needs of sales performance improvement.

If you ignore the Deal Hack column for a moment, you can see that the combination of e-learning, classroom and coaching cover nearly all criteria. On paper the current system works well, we can impart knowledge and then get it applied into the workflow through coaching. Most performance optimization is built this way, but that ignores three significant issues with the traditional approach:

1) As we saw earlier, classroom and e-learning can cause a threat response in the Social Brain when used across all five BASIC learning times. With a threat response from the 'Social Brain,' the learning does not get transferred to the workplace and applied. In some cases a fixed mind-set is built, and reinforced.

2) Coaching doesn't happen enough, so the critical support in the workflow does not happen at the times when we need it most: to solve, implement or change.

3) Training and coaching connect indirectly to business results. What do sales leaders want above all? An immediate and direct impact on business results.

From the table, we can see that the Deal Hack is more similar to coaching than to the other interventions. So a pertinent challenge is, why don't we just increase the volume of coaching in the present system? The first reason concerns the team-based nature of the Deal Hacks, where wider expertise is pooled for better decision making and deal outcomes. This allows sellers to start matching the buyer investment which we know from Neil Rackham is critical to sales success. [183] It also creates the forum for team-selling, bringing in the sales support functions behind the sales organization. The second reason is that, being more deal focused, Deal Hacks are much easier to match directly to business results. Existing coaching is 'coachee' focused and indirectly focused on deals.[184] The third reason is that the Deal Hack can also be used as a vehicle for imparting knowledge. Deal coaches can be trained in new tools, insights, and techniques and these can be applied directly into the workflow and impact deals immediately. Again, traditional coaching aims to find the answer from the coachee and is not used in this way. Lastly, we know that sales people are over optimistic about their performance and their deals. Having the mandate to challenge sales forecasts and deals, is something that traditional coaching does not normally have.

Some learning and development professionals almost certainly have an attachment to specific methods of enablement. I can still recall very clearly such an instance when I first set up a sales enablement function. *"I don't believe in e-learning,"* said one of my colleagues bluntly to me and the team. We were trying to introduce e-learning to align with the strategic objective from the CEO of accelerating innovation from engineering to the customer in a global software organization. This colleague had no intention of implementing the new learning technology and the conversation turned rapidly into a pantomime argument of *"My method of training is better than yours."* This fixed mind-set response spawned one of my first blog articles proposing that enablement departments could benefit from borrowing the concept of 'enablement mix' from our marketing cousins who use the 'marketing mix.' The marketing mix is a foundation of marketing and can be described as a set of marketing tools that a company uses to pursue its marketing objectives in the target market.[185] Any tool in the marketing mix is not better than another, and you'd never hear a marketer say, *"I don't believe in advertising."* What they would say is, *"Advertising is not appropriate for this audience, we need to use a combination of mailshots and cold calling to raise awareness and drive the required actions."* This is the level of conversation we should be aiming for in enablement functions, but we often fall into the fixed mind-set *"My way is better than yours"*, argument. If you find yourself here, stuck with someone saying that they prefer training, or coaching to 'Deal Hacks.' It's a bit like a mechanic saying they prefer using wrenches to screwdrivers. It doesn't make any intellectual sense because all of these are different tools for different jobs. We need to get to the place where we recognize the differences between the various types of performance interventions and how we can create synergies by using them together as a complementary 'mix'. We need to elevate the debate significantly to diagnose what types of interventions fit best into each sales enablement situation. Sales enablement need to challenge themselves on mind-set as much as the sales audiences they look after. The Deal Hack alone is not a silver bullet to transform sales forces, but it plugs significant gaps that exist between the current interventions. The best way to undertake a sales enablement program is to create a blend of these interventions based on the operational needs and goals of the organization, the learning requirements of the sales population, and the resources available. Deal Hacks can spearhead a sales transformation or sales enablement program because they can be deployed immediately, no learning needs analysis required. The learning and messages get straight into the deals without delay. Notice that I didn't say that they get into the population straight away. That's because in Deal Hacks we're focused on the deal and not the person. We do this because if you get the deals right, the people will follow the success naturally. Sales leaders will be able to see an immediate and measurable impact, and credible stories can be created of how the desired changes to sales practices are helping to win more/better deals. This is important because it helps create buy-in for any training and coaching to come. Adding Deal Hacks into the mix enables companies to improve the responsiveness of the sales population to change, matches the buyer investment to create more value for customers, and supports learners when they need to solve, implement or change inside the workflow.

Deal Hacks can be readily embraced by some trainers and coaches as an opportunity for them and the organization, but sometimes they are not. As we saw earlier, it can be difficult for some trainers and coaches to get their heads around the concept because it is such a significant departure from current thinking and practice. This is because there are a number of potential Social Brain threats for them:

1) **Reliability** – working with live deals is uncertain. The Deal Coach needs to make the diagnosis live in the session and work with ambiguity. There is no script as you find in training. For coaches, they'll need to change to focusing on deals and not people, and for some that it might be hard to change how they work.

2) **Victory** – If the deals do not close, the Deal Hack could be perceived as a failure. Currently sales trainers and coaches are connected indirectly to deal wins and losses. This makes it hard to link them to success, but a benefit to them is that it is also hard to link them to losses. Removing this protective shield will be too much for some.

3) **Status** – Failure to close a deal could adversely affect their status. Not knowing how to implement Deal Hacks could also negatively impact their status.

From these possible threats to coaches and trainers, the Social Brain could take over and Deal Hacks could be seen as a threat. So to reduce the risk of a threat response, it is worth taking time to make it clear that Deal Hacks are not a replacement for training and coaching, they sit along-side and will help with these. Deal Hacks can inform the diagnostics that will be used to create the training and coaching interventions that follow.

They are the 'Third leg of the stool' as my friend and CSO Chris Doggett likes to say. For those who would like the challenge of becoming involved in live deals, this is an exciting opportunity for personal development and to make a name for themselves. In other words, there are possible victory and status rewards for the 'Social Brains' for the right people. Which begs the question who are the right people? When looking for a Deal Coach, these are the competencies I look for:

1) **Facilitation:** the ability to facilitate a room of senior level people who may push against or fight the process
2) **Sales Process:** the ability to apply a sales process to a sales opportunity and identify where there are gaps
3) **Commercial Acumen:** the commercial ability to diagnose what is in the commercial best interests of customers and the vendor
4) **Challenge:** the ability to challenge senior level people to get to the 'reality' of the situation
5) **Objectivity:** someone remote from the sales opportunity who can remain emotionally detached.

I've eluded to the goals of the Deal Hacks already, but it's worth being really clear that they are two-fold:

1. To improve the deal by identifying gaps and risks, then putting a close plan in place to fill the gaps, mitigate the risks. The result should be an increased chance of closing, sooner at an increased margin.
2. To identify and fill the skills gaps of the sales people in the Deal Hack.

Number two is a secondary goal and it is only achieved if the first goal is executed effectively. The roles of those involved in the Deal Hack are:

1. **Deal Owner** – this is typically the salesperson who owns the deal. They are the main source of information in the Deal Hack and they will:
   a. Give an overview of the deal
   b. Grade the deal
   c. Act as the primary source of information and interaction
   d. Decide what actions to commit to
   e. Agree and own the actions
2. **Deal Coach** – is a person trained to facilitate the room, optimize challenge with support, and select the most appropriate analytical tools to find the insights that will improve deal outcomes. The Deal Coach is responsible for delivering the 'Close Plan' which is agreed with the Deal Owner. In addition, they will:
   a. Set the agenda and timings
   b. Contract with all stakeholders at the event
   c. Organize the roles and resources
   d. Collect the information for the tools
   e. Write up a report on the deals and the capabilities of the delegates

**3) Subject Matter Expert** (SME) – a person invited to attend the Deal Hack to contribute an area of expertise.

**4) Hacker Tracker** – a person trained to capture the outputs of the sessions, in particular, the outputs from the analytical tools and actions. This person has been trained in the use of the tools and will have a technology platform for sharing the outputs like trello.com.

In his address to Caltech in 1974, Richard Feynman used the Cargo Cult analogy to address what he considered to be the missing components in newly developing areas of pseudo-science. *"Now it behooves me, of course, to tell you what they're missing. But it would be just about as difficult to explain to the South Sea Islanders how they have to arrange things so that they get some wealth in their system. It is not something simple like telling them how to improve the shapes of the earphones. But there is one feature I notice that is generally missing in Pseudoscience... It's a kind of scientific integrity, a principle of scientific thought that corresponds to a kind of utter honesty—a kind of leaning over backwards. For example, if you're doing an experiment, you should report everything that you think might make it invalid—not only what you think is right about it."*[186] Here, Feynman helps us to understand another root cause of poor sales performance, and that is a lack of objectivity and oversight. Deal Hacks help us to report what makes a sale invalid, not only what we think makes it likely to succeed. Deal Hacks force us to be more honest with ourselves, to challenge ourselves, to improve the deal. In traditional deal reviews with a sales manager, the sales people put forward what they think to be right about their deal, that's just human nature. The sales manager is the objective back stop, who challenges the deal. But they too are paid on the deal, so how objective can they actually be? We know from earlier that Sales Leaders are over optimistic, and financial incentives are only likely to increase that natural cognitive bias. We need something more objective in the system. From a more objective standpoint, the Deal Hack team firstly look for what makes the approach invalid, not just what makes it valid as those with a vested interest are programmed to do, thanks to the optimism bias we saw in Chapter Two, 'Blind Spot'. From this more objective view-point, with a clear understanding of what is wrong, two things can happen:

1. A plan can be made to improve the health of the deal, to make it healthier and more likely to close as forecasted.
2. Learning gaps can be identified and filled

Some sales leaders react negatively to having someone from outside inspecting their deals. I think this is understandable because it sets off a number of social drivers, in particular the status driver. I've heard things like, "Thanks for the Deal Hacks, we know how to run them now, so we'll take it from here." We need to recognize that it's nearly impossible for sales people and sales managers to be objective about their deals, thanks to cognitive biases. If they could inspect their own deals, we'd not need the Deal Hacks in the first place. Again the problem is not teaching them how to do this stuff, they already know how to do it. The problem we're overcoming is that due to cognitive biases they are not doing what they should be doing, and it takes an objective eye to see this and an objective process to check there is the optimal close plan for the deal. And as we've just seen, that objective eye needs to be in the field alongside the sales people, not remote in a classroom. In the next chapter we look at how the Deal Hacks are structured to achieve this.

# CHAPTER 12

# DEAL HACK STRUCTURE AND PROCESS

**"Everybody has a plan until they get punched in the face."**

**Mike Tyson**

I n 1980 Fuji Xerox won the legendary Deming Prize for Total Quality Management. Some-time later at a seminar, a process expert from Fuji Xerox was explaining why process orientation is the key to building competitive success. Someone in the audience asked him rhetorically, "But Michelangelo followed no process?" Unflustered, the expert replied, "First, be Michelangelo. Everybody else, he said, must follow the process."[187]

Deal Hacks are far less structured than training because all deals are different and they are all at different stages. However there is an underlying process to keep the Deal Hack on track. I use a simple four-stage process that you can remember with the acronym GOAL:

1) **Grade:** the deal owner grades the deal in relation to four key indicators: decision makers, decision criteria, deal value and decision process. The deal is then forecast in terms of value and closure date.

2) **Overview:** an overview of the deal by the deal owner answering the question, why would the prospect buy this? (known as the why anything question).

3) **Analysis:** review the health of the deal using analytical tools answering two questions:
   i. Why should the buy from us?
   ii. Why should they buy now?

4) **List of Actions:** prioritize and allocate actions in the form of a 'close plan'

The process is the same for all Deal Hacks but the duration of each Deal Hack depends on the size and complexity of the deals involved. I've worked on deals worth over $100m and we've had a cross-functional team working on the deal for two days. I've got regional teams of sales people together for Deal Hacks where we cover up to four deals in a day, each deal worth around $100k to $5 million. For this reason, it's imperative that you run a number of pilot Deal Hacks to get a sense of how big the events are for your deals, because the first question you'll be asked is, *"How long will this take?"* And you need to have a good answer! The only way to answer that is to hold pilot Deal Hacks. Another frequently asked question is, which deals should we bring into the Deal Hacks? Unfortunately, the answer to this takes some thought and planning on your part. It can be the sales manager and the sales team who decide which deals are most important to them. Or it can be the sales leadership who decide that Deal Hacks should be run at a specific time in the year, or when certain deals of a certain size reach a particular position in the pipeline. For example, all deals forecast to close in the quarter could be put through a Deal Hack at the start of the quarter to make sure they close as forecasted. I've worked with companies where all deals over a certain revenue size are put through deal hacks. I've worked with companies where all deals at a certain level in the pipeline are put through deal hacks. I'd suggest putting a team together to look at the volume of deals and the Deal Hack resources available to find the optimal mix for you. Chapter 16 'Crossing the Chasm' will help you to plan this. Let's look at each stage of the Deal Hack process in more detail.

**Deal Hack Step 1: Grade**

The very first stage is to determine the comfort level of the sales person on the four key indicators:

1) Decision Makers
2) Decision Criteria
3) Deal Value
4) Decision Process

The deal is then forecasted and the results stored in the deal tracker using Red, Amber and Green (RAG) like this:

| | Why Us? | | Why Now? | | |
| --- | --- | --- | --- | --- | --- |
| | Decision Makers | Decision Criteria | Value | Decision Process | Forecast |
| Deal Name | GREEN | AMBER | RED | AMBER | GREEN Q3 |

When grading the four key indicators, red means that the situation is not understood and so we are not in control of that element of the deal. Amber means that the situation is somewhat understood and so we are partially in control. Green means that the situation is completely understood and we are in complete control. When grading the forecast, Green means that there is a high likelihood of the deal closing, because we are in control of the key elements of the deal. Amber means that there are gaps and so there's a chance that the deal will close, as we are not in complete control. Red means that it is unlikely that the deal will close because we are not yet in control of the deal. One reason that we do this is because the aim of the Deal Hack is to get all of the boxes to turn green. The RAG color system allows the sales leaders, at a glance, to see the areas they need to focus on to improve sales results. Another reason is that the Deal Coach also makes an identical assessment of the deal after the Hack is complete, based on what they actually found. This allows us to see how good the sales people are at gauging their own performance, which is an indicator of their mind-set. Needless to say the sales person's view is typically far more optimistic than the Deal Coaches view.

**Deal Hack Step 2: Overview of The Deal**

The Deal Owner provides the context of the deal to the room. The Deal Owner will want to tell the story of the deal, and this should be allowed to come out naturally. It is inevitable, however, that they will need help to communicate the full picture, and so here's a checklist of information that the Deal Coach can use to make sure the overview is as comprehensive as possible, without taking too long:

1) Why should the customer buy anything? What is the problem to be solved or opportunities to be realized?
2) When did the deal start? If the deal has been around forever it tells us a lot about the health of the deal.
3) Who kick started the process, the customer or the sales person? This tells us if the customer is actively buying and has a project to buy, or if we are attempting to move them away from the status quo and we're selling to them and we need to get them into the buying process, a much tougher sale.
4) Where is the deal in the sales process and the customer

in the buying process?

The Deal Hack starts with the overview from the Deal Owner and the information will be coming thick and fast. The Deal Coach needs to know how to document the information and start to build the visual and collaborative tools. The initial tools being used will be:

1) **Facts and Risks** – this acts as a holding place for all information initially before the other analytical tools are used.
2) **Goal and Timeline** – this tool will be built continually through the session.
3) **Sales Process/Buying Process** – not recognizing where the deal is in the sales/buying process, or trying to deviate from the agreed sales process is a surprisingly common issue. Continuous checks to agree process alignment by the 'Deal Coach' is essential.
4) **Stakeholder map** – names come out quickly at first. I find it helpful to give the deal owner a pad of post-it notes along with a pen so they can write the names and titles of stakeholders. This reduces the, *"How are we spelling the name..."*
5) **Opportunity chain** – is a list of the departments in the prospect company, along with their goals, initiatives and challenges. Any company relevant information will go here.

These tools can be found in the toolkit at the end of the book.

### Deal Hack Step 3: Analyzing the Deal – Why Anything, Why Us and Why Now?

Deal Analysis is the largest part of the Deal Hack. In the analysis we have three basic challenge questions that anchor the session:

1) Why do they need to order anything? (Why Anything?)
2) Why will the choose us? (Why Us?)
3) Why will they choose us now? (Why Now?)

Known as the three whys, if we can answer these three questions in detail and with certainty, against the challenge questions of the Deal Coach, we are in a really good position to close the deal.

## Why Anything?
1) **Challenges** – why should the customer buy anything at all? What are the challenges and opportunities that can be satisfied by our solution? This is covered in the introduction by the deal owner. If there is no 'Why Anything' then there's no deal to hack. Typically, there is and we focus on the next two questions. If you're digging around and can't find a reason the prospect should do business with you at all, cut the Deal Hack short and move on to a better deal.

## Why Us?
2) **Decision Makers** - Who are the decision makers? Build a clear picture of all the people who have an influence over the customer buying process and develop an aligned coalition in both the buying and selling organizations.
3) **Decision Criteria** - Why should the stakeholders choose us? What is their decision criteria? What are the alternatives? What is the clear and visible differentiation of the value we are creating against the other propositions being considered? How is this being measured? What do we score against the competing alternatives?

## Why Now?
4) **Decision Process** – what is the buying process and

how does that align with the sales process? What are the decision gates the customer must go through? What process steps do we need to undertake to complete the sales process?

5) **Deal Value** - what value is being created? Build a visually clear and communicable picture of where the proposal adds value to the decision makers, and the buying organization as a whole. What is the 'Investment' and what is the 'Return' for the customer and is that compelling compared to the alternative options?

Because of their importance to the success of the Deal Hack, we cover the three whys? in detail in the following chapters. If you have your own sales methodology, it is in the analysis part of the Deal Hack that you would put the methodology and tools.

**Deal Hack Step 4: List of Actions**

The outcome of the Deal Hack is a list of actions that form a plan to ensure the deal closes as forecasted by the 'Deal Owner.' The aim is to get all of the boxes to green. The actions are collected throughout the Deal Hack and agreed with the 'Deal Owner' as they are collected. At the end of the Deal Hack the 'Deal Coach' ensures that the actions are prioritized and SMART - specific, measurable, achievable, reviewed, time-based. When there's a significant number of actions, it is essential that the 'Deal Coach' prioritize them with the 'Deal Owner'. The 'Deal Coach' should ask, *"What do you anticipate could get in your way?"* This will pre-empt any problems and offer an opportunity for the wider team to contribute. *"What will you commit to? Will you have time for all of the actions you've listed? Which are the top three that cannot be sacrificed?"* These basic coaching questions allow the actions to be prioritized which increases the likelihood that the right actions will be completed.

The final part of the session is to ascertain when the follow up should be, what format it will take and who will be there. Over time the Social Brain thinking will take over and encourage shortcuts to be taken. The follow up makes sure the Intellectual Brain thinking continues and the actions are completed as agreed. Recently we agreed in a Deal Hack that we would not give pricing to a customer who was using us as a pricing exercise. It was not worth the time and effort to create the pricing and proposal. This was agreed in the room. One week later pricing was sent out which was against what we had agreed. The sales person never heard from the customer again, which was no surprise to those in the Deal Hack. The Social Brain thinking of the sales person kicked in with the approach of, "*What do I have to lose?*" In that case it was control of the deal, reputational damage and loss of time and resource. So the actions agreed in the Deal Hacks need to be stuck to, and therefore following up on the actions by authority figures is essential.

We use a specific toolkit to manage information flow, creativity and decision making in the Deal Hack. The toolkit makes the sales opportunity visual and allows a group of people to physically interact with the data. Author Alan Briskin proposes that our ability to cooperate and see the opportunities of working together is undermined by the complexity and the daunting nature of what confronts us. "*When faced with too much information, people often default to the simplest explanation*"[188]. We know from Part One that this is the Intellectual Brain being overridden by the energy saving Social Brain. When the Intellectual Brain switches off, there is a reduced ability to intellectually understand the full facts, resulting in emotional and narrow-minded positions. The toolkit helps to prevent this. Deal Hacks generate a lot of information. Information about the prospect company, the people, and the competition. One of the challenges for the Deal Coach is to collect and organize that information so that the room can work collectively and interact with it. For this we have the 'Deal Hack Toolkit' consisting of:

1. Deal Progress Tracker
2. Facts and Challenges
3. Goal and Timeline
4. Stakeholder Map
5. Opportunity Chain
6. Competition and Decision Criteria
7. Value Frame
8. Action planner

Please see the end of this book for copies of these tools. The Deal Hack toolkit is designed to maximize individual working memory, maximize collective creativity, to create an environment where cross-functional teams can succeed in a complex task and create artifacts that can be used to re-create the deal hack event in the future. The Deal Hack does this by using the Toolkit to get around the Social Brains' dislike for complexity and it's structural inability to hold comfortably more than four chunks of data in working memory at any one time.[189] We learned in Part Two that the brain is built with energy conservation in mind. One of the best mechanisms for saving energy in the brain is the use of visuals when communicating. For this reason, the Social Brain loves visuals like the Deal Hack toolkit. The majority of information we consume comes through the visuals senses. Approximately 50% of our brain is dedicated directly or indirectly to visual functions, and around two-thirds of the electrical activity of the brain is devoted to vision when the eyes are open. Vision is responsible for the bulk of the arousal effects in the brain and reducing the response to this stimulation is one reason why we close our eyes when we want to sleep, because it disconnects us from the outside world[190]. Vision is the dominant sense: it provides the brain with over 80% of what it knows.[191] The primate brain has around fifty times as many cortical neurons devoted to processing visual as to auditory information.[192] We all know that it is the dominant sense, just stick a blindfold on and try to find the bathroom and use it. John Medina goes further by describing vision as an antagonist. This is because it tries to persuade our brain that what it is sensing through vision is the only reality, whether the perception is accurate or not. In his book Brain Rules, Medina says that *"About 60 percent of our smell-related genes have been permanently damaged in this neural arbitrage, and they are marching toward obsolescence at a rate fourfold faster than any other species sampled. In the crowded, zero-sum world of the subscalp, something has to give."*[193] It appears that we're not only intensely social creatures, but we're intensely visual too. In 1856 the Nurse and campaigner Florence Nightingale graphically showed how deaths from preventable diseases far outstripped deaths from wounds in the Crimean War, using visual charts.

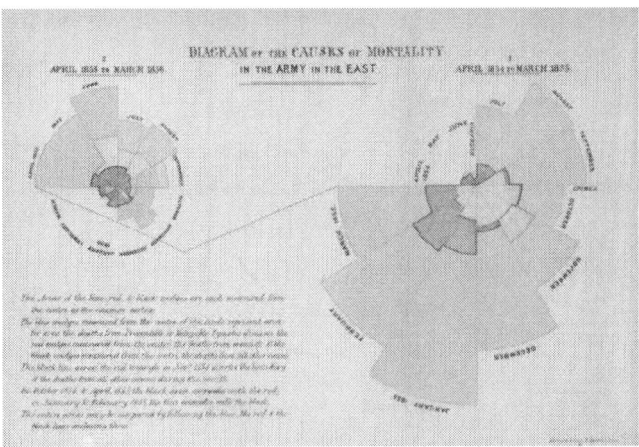

Figure 16 - Diagrams by Florence Nightingale[194]

Nightingale was lobbying members of Parliament and civil servants who would have been unlikely to read or understand the underpinning statistical reporting. The Charts illustrate the large number of deaths that occurred in the Crimea from preventable diseases (in blue), compared with those deaths which were a result of wounds or other causes (shown in red and black). These visuals saved countless lives and prevented immeasurable suffering. Bringing us up to date, Hubspot tells us that visual content is 40 times more likely to get shared on social media than other types of content.[195] It appears that we have a preference for visual information over text information because it is easier to consume and easier to see correlations and insights. It's also easier for images to be recalled, in other words, images are stickier. We can recall images far easier than text data, something called the 'Picture Superiority Effect.'[196] If the information is presented orally, people remember about 10 percent, tested 72 hours after exposure. That figure goes up to 65 percent if you add a picture.[197] If you can convert language into an image, you're making life easier for the people whom you're communicating with. People are more likely to take notice of your communications, more likely to understand them and they are more likely to be able to recall them. Images convey more meaning, more easily and more quickly, as well as being recalled more easily. In such an information rich environment, it would be easy to base the work in Deal Hacks around text alone, such as spreadsheets and reports, but the Social Brain would check out pretty quickly. For this reason, Deal Hacks use a visually engaging toolkit. Using the 'Deal Hack Toolkit' increases engagement and interaction from the group by engaging the Social Brain. It is a powerful way to resolve misunderstandings that can arise, which could waste time and lead to failure. It is also a powerful way to generate new insights from the collective group that can improve group decision making. Years of running Deal Hacks show that people enjoy interacting physically with information, and this drives engagement and success. Often this can be information that would otherwise be sat in a CRM or, worse, sat in a person's head. Once in a visual format, this information often generates insights that are pivotal in making the team gel, and helping them to win the deal. When seen end to end, the Toolkit helps the group to see the bigger picture. Almost every sales leader I've ever met has asked me to improve the strategic thinking of their sales populations, and there is no better way to achieve this than through being able to actually see and interact physically with customer information and to see the value that is being created across the whole customer organization. This creates a central theme for the 'Deal Hack Team' to work around, but it also creates a visual output of the value being created for the customer to see in the customer pitch. The Deal may have to be re-Hacked, and the Tool Kit can be captured as artefacts to improve group memory and accountability over time. This is key to making sure the actions are followed up which is a challenge for all programs in all organizations.

Hopefully this chapter gives you a feel for what the Deal Hack is. It is, of course, a little tough to communicate this without the reader having experienced it. The best thing you can do is to make contact with a company that run Deal Hacks and see one in action for yourself. What you'll see is a cross-functional team working collaboratively and positively to make sure the deal comes in as planned. In the next three chapters we cover how the Deal Hacks are delivered using the three why's framework:

1) Why should they buy anything?
2) Why should they buy from us?
3) Why should they buy now?

# CHAPTER 13

# WHY SHOULD CUSTOMERS BUY ANYTHING?

*"Look wide, and even when you think you are looking wide, look wider still."*

Lord Robert Baden-Powell

*"T*he problem was that everything was sticking to everything!"* Harry Coover reminisced about his botched experiments in 1942 to cast new precision plastic gun sights for the military war effort. Coover was experimenting with cyanoacrylate, an acrylic resin he had developed, but the experiments were a disaster because the acrylic stuck to absolutely everything it touched. The project was abandoned when the government cancelled the contract, so the acrylic was shelved and forgotten about. Six years later, when working on casting materials for jet airplane canopies, Coover shared his cyanoacrylate work to his development team. Warning them that the substance could break

the lab equipment because it was so sticky, the team started experimenting by gluing objects together. It was only then that Coover realized the potential of the acrylic and one of the most successful commercial products of all time was born, Superglue.[198]

There's three crucial things that make superglue a commercial success:
    1) It solves problems
    2) It solves problems better than alternative options
    3) It solves problems quickly and easily when you need it to

If we reverse engineer these three factors we get a commercial test that can be used to measure the likely success of any commercial sale, namely the three Whys?

    1) Why should the customer buy anything?
    2) Why should the customer buy from us?
    3) Why should the customer buy now?

Superglue passed the three whys for a significant market segment and went on to become an astonishing commercial success. In Deal Hacks we're dealing with a lot of information about the deal and we find the three why's to be a very simple yet powerful way to organize the session and keep everyone on track. Let's start by looking at how we use the 'Why Anything?' question in a Deal Hack.

The Deal Owner will most likely give a good account of why the customer needs to buy something, after all, if there's no challenge or opportunity for the solution to attach to, then there's no deal to hack. We often find in the 'Deal Overview' the customer needs articulated by the 'Deal Owner' can be narrowly focused, often focusing on one or two people in just one department. However, when we ask the 'Deal Owner' how many departments are affected by the solution, there are a number of departments affected, and sometimes the whole company. If more of the company is affected by the solution, then it makes sense to understand how those other departments are affected. Similarly, if we can attach the solution to the strategic goals of the business, then it's going to be easier for us to get buy-in across the senior stakeholders and budget holders. Peter Cheverton describes how people in companies today work in a chain, and what happens in one department most often has a knock-on effect on other departments. Cheverton describes how to identify these chains: *"We have to analyze their dynamics to see where the true opportunities lie, for our proposition, for our value and for our reward."* To make a complete analysis of how a solution affects a whole company Cheverton developed a concept called the 'Opportunity Chain'. From this we've developed an analytical tool for sales people to quickly understand the opportunity (why anything?) across a whole business, and for that reason we use the 'Opportunity Chain' in the Deal Hacks. It's the tool that helps us to answer comprehensively the question, *"Why should they buy anything at all?"* and is often the tool we start with first.

The first step in creating the 'Opportunity Chain' is to list the departments or functions in the company that will be impacted by the solution. Then attach the people from the 'Buyer Team' onto their relevant departments. For each department we need to ask three questions"

1) What are your objectives or goals?
2) What initiatives do you have to achieve them?
3) What challenges are you experiencing in these initiatives?

If we put the answers to these questions into a grid, we build a visual representation of the customer organization, what they are actively working on and what is critically important to them. From this 'landscape analysis' we begin to see far more reasons for the customer to buy something, more reasons than we started with at the beginning of the Deal Hack. As the picture builds we can see in greater detail how our solution affects the objectives and goals, the initiatives and challenges of departments across the whole business. In the first few deal hacks, we build the opportunity chain in the session, but once the 'Deal Owners' see how useful the opportunity chains are, they come to future sessions with them already filled in. When this happens, the Deal Hacks move from being about finding information to building strategies to win the sale, which is a far more productive use of time. I've trained people to use opportunity chains in the sales process and they rarely get used after the training. But after one Deal Hack, and after seeing how the opportunity chain positively impacts their deals, the delegates start using them on other deals. This means that the other deals become more strategic, better run and are more likely to close too. Use of the tools increases if the Deal Hack toolkit is left on the walls of the sales office, for deal reviews and conversations. Another positive impact of using the opportunity chain, is that deals can be lost because another similar program is happening somewhere else in the business that we didn't know about. Using the opportunity chain, and having a more complete understanding of the customer's business, will help to reduce the risk of this type of deal loss. The opportunity chain builds the stakeholder mapping exercise we undertake in the next chapter, and it also builds the platform for the value analysis we do later. The opportunity chain is the backbone of the Deal Hacks and worth spending the time getting right.

In Deal Hacks I often see deals that have a 'Why anything?' and the sales person sees the deal as being in a position to close, and scores themselves 100%:

| | Why Us? | | Why Now? | | |
|---|---|---|---|---|---|
| | Decision Makers | Decision Criteria | Value | Decision Process | Forecast |
| Deal Name | GREEN | GREEN | GREEN | GREEN | $500k Q3 |

What happens next is that we drill down into the four key indicators and we get a big fail:

| | Why Us? | | Why Now? | | |
|---|---|---|---|---|---|
| | Decision Makers | Decision Criteria | Value | Decision Process | Forecast |
| Deal Name | RED | RED | RED | RED | $500k Q3 |

Understanding that the customer has pain, or a problem you can solve is the starting point, and not the end. In the next two chapters we answer the next two questions, why they should buy from us, and why they should buy now? Doing so is how we convert this red table into a green table and increase our chances of winning the deal. Let's start by answering the next question, if they buy something, why should they buy it from us?

# CHAPTER 14

# WHY SHOULD CUSTOMERS CHOOSE US?

*"Madness is the exception in individuals, but the rule in groups."*

Friedrich Nietzsche

*"I* have nothing left to fight with,*"* the Commander shouted. *"Am taking to the woods. I can't wait for you"*. Then the radio went dead. The Bay of Pigs invasion met its ignominious end in the afternoon of 19th of April 1961. Three days after the invasion force of 1,400 Cuban emigres landed at the Bay of Pigs, the C I A officers who planned the assault gathered around a radio in their Washington war room while the Cuban Brigade's Commander transmitted his last signal. He had been pleading all day for supplies and air cover for his outnumbered and outgunned troops, but the promised support had been cancelled by President John F. Kennedy him-

self. [199] 1,200 of the invasion force surrendered, and many were later executed. In the following days JFK described the 'Bay of Pigs' invasion as a, "Colossal mistake," that left him feeling depressed, guilty, bitter, and in tears. *"How could we have been so stupid?"* he asked his group of advisers. One historian later called the Bay of Pigs fiasco, *"One of those rare events in history, a perfect failure."* [200]

In the years following the 'Bay of Pigs' failure, a faculty member of Yale University was analysing the events, and in particular the decision making that lead to the 'perfect failure'. Irving Janis wanted to answer the question, *"How could bright, shrewd men like John F. Kennedy and his advisors be taken in by the CIA's stupid, patchwork plan?"[201]* Janis later wrote in 1971, *"Stupidity certainly is not the explanation. The men who participated in making the Bay of Pigs decision, for instance, comprised one of the greatest arrays of intellectual talent in history of American government.... My conclusion, after pouring over hundreds of relevant documents, is that the groups that committed the fiascos were victims of what I call 'groupthink' "[202]* 'Group Think' is the classic theory of psychology that describes the tendency of groups to try to minimize conflict and reach consensus without sufficiently analyzing, challenging and evaluating their ideas. Janis himself described it as, *"A deterioration of mental efficiency, reality testing and moral judgement that results in group pressures."* [203]

In complex business to business deals there are a lot of decisions to make and, like the Bay of Pigs, many of them are collective decisions. We've already seen that creating value for the selling and buying organizations requires effective decision making. We know that effective decision making can be eroded by the short cuts favoured by Social Brain thinking in individuals. Here we move from individual decision making to group decision making.

It will comes as no surprise that the individuals in collective decisions are prone to exactly the same cognitive biases as we saw before in the individual. If we look at the decision making in the Bay of Pigs examples through the social DRIVERS lens we can clearly see both **status** and **interpersonal connection** biases playing a role in reducing the effectiveness of the decision making. So all that we learned in Chapter Five about why decisions are hard, is relevant here. But as Janis pointed out, there is the additional dynamic of the group at play here too, but in selling there are two principal groups. We want to see effective decision making by the teams on the buying side, **and** on the selling side, and so in this chapter we look at how to manage that group decision making dynamic.

When it comes to buying decisions, a critical question is, "Is it a group buying decision at all?" Sales people have been trained for years to look for 'The' decision maker, or 'The' economic buyer. For this reason, the initial 'Deal Overview' by the 'Deal Owner' often reveals a single point of contact on the seller side, with little or no signs of collective decision making. What we often see, initially, is that the majority of communication in the sale or negotiation is exclusively through the salesperson and a single buyer, which looks graphically like this:

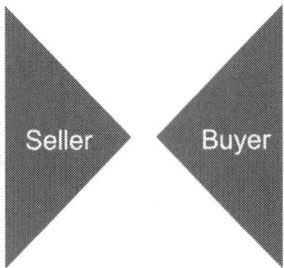

All communication goes through two solo contacts. Let's call this 'Solo' selling. This is classic Social Brain selling because it is the easiest way to conduct business. There is no bigger shortcut than this. But it's not the best way to generate a successful sale because there are more people on both sides, we just don't know who they are yet. In Business to Business sales, there's always two groups of people in the sales/buying process, the Selling Team and the Buying Team. The buying team need to be aligned with each other, so they can come to a consensus over the purchase decision criteria. At the start of the Deal Hack we may not know who is on each team, and so we start to dig:

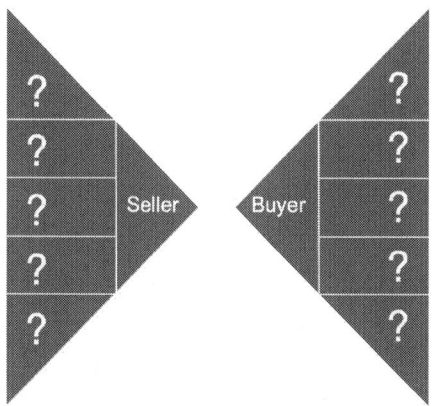

**The Selling Team**
By putting the Deal Hack together, we want to promote objective Intellectual Brain thinking and do this by pulling a selling team behind the seller like this:

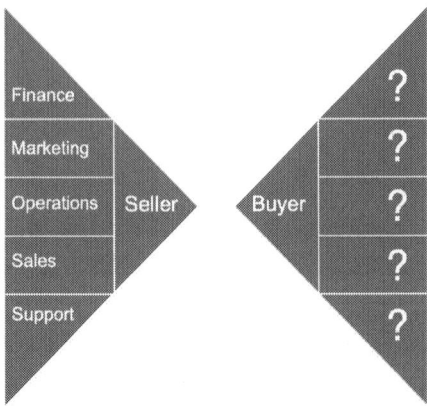

This helps us to match the customer investment, and also allows us to start working on how to complement their buying team. Very few sales people take the time to gather a support team behind them, as this takes time, but it is best practice as Ray Dalio, the American billionaire investor explains, *"We work in teams because it elevates ourselves above our own opinions so that we start to see things through everybody's eyes, and we see things collectively. It's been the secret sauce behind our success."*[204] The Social Brain of the salesperson may see potential status threats in this approach because they are now more visible to the business and open to challenge, so there may well be push back from those in a fixed mind-set. Ray Dalio explains how being part of a team helps to avoid a fixed mind-set, *"There's a part of our brain that would like to know our mistakes and like to look at our weaknesses so we could do better. I'm told that that's the prefrontal cortex. And then there's a part of our brain which views all of this as attacks. I'm told that that's the amygdala. In other words, there are two you's inside you: there's an emotional (social) you and there's an intellectual you, and often they're at odds, and often they work against you. It's been our experience that we can win this battle. We win it as a group."* [205] The Deal Hack makes sure that the sales person is not alone, and creates the 'Selling Team' behind the seller.

**The Buying Team**

All salespeople know if you're going to make a sale, you need to be talking to the decision-maker. While this is obviously true, the simplified manner in which the 'decision maker' is applied results in 'Solo' selling which greatly reduces the likelihood of closing a complex business-to-business deal. There is often an assumption that there is 'a' decision-maker or 'an' economic-buyer, when there is more likely to be a group of people who have an influence over the decision, and who act as a formal or informal buying team. How many people are in the buying team? The CEB put their collective necks on the line and said that there is a group size of 6.8 buyers in each business to business deal.[206] This aligns with my experience that there are between six and ten people on the buyer side in deals between $100k and $1 million. As you'd expect, when the value of the deals increase, so does the number of people with influence over the deal to mitigate the increasing risks. However, all deals are different, and it's up to the 'Deal Coach' to challenge the room to make sure that all of the people who can influence the purchase are accounted for. This process can be accelerated by having access to an organizational chart for the customer's business, but it is surprising how often this basic information is missing when asked for. As a result, in some organizations it has become mandatory to bring 'org charts' to Deal Hacks. The Deal Coach will challenge the sales team to think wider across the customer using the opportunity chain tool. For each department they will ask who the relevant people are in those departments. This will increase the number of people about whom we need to know. The job of the salesperson is to build a coalition of buyers from across the business behind the solution. In the book '*Leading Change*', John Kotter suggests that there needs to be a, "*Guiding coalition*" to drive any organizational change. Kotter says that one person alone can't generate enough momentum to overcome the status quo singlehandedly. Instead, he says, *"Putting together the right coalition of people to lead a change initiative is critical to its success. That coalition must have the right composition, a significant level of trust, and a shared objective"*[207]. Kotter was referring to organizational change, but when a business buys a new service or system, this is itself organizational change. Finding the buying team is a journey, and we often see a pattern in Deal Hacks relating to how relationships develop between buyer and seller teams. During the first Deal Hack we work to understand the buying team better. In these early stages, we're often moving from Solo selling, and so we're trying to find out basic information on the people impacted by the purchase, or who influence the purchase. It's normally the case that the sales person knows a quarter of the people they really need to know, often less. As time progresses in the Deal Hack, we're working towards the 'Bow Tie' model of communication:[208]

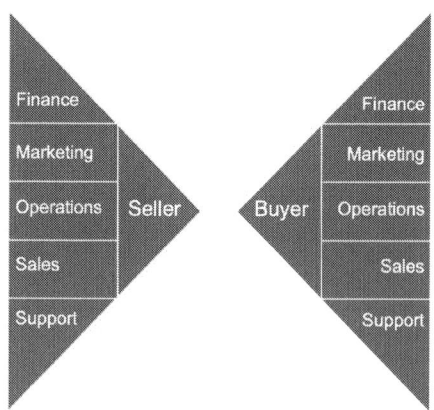

The Social Brain may resist this type of work with phrases like, *"I don't have time to do all that extra work"* or, *"They're just not interested, this is a waste of time."* However, with a room of experienced 'Intellectual Brains' this fixed mind-set can be challenged effectively to produce a better outcome. Once we have enough basic information for the 'Bow Tie,' we can progress to building strategies to align the buying team behind our solution. What often emerges as a strategy is the diamond model of contact where a number of the buying team and the selling team are in contact with each other, building relationships and working together, coordinated by seller and buyer. Here we start to build relationships at multiple points of both companies, what we call 'Relationship' selling:

In the 'Relationship' selling phase, the salesperson uses influencing skills to build a coalition in the buying organization, alongside and often driven by a coalition in the selling organization. There's a number of fairly obvious benefits to this model. The salesperson saves time because the selling team can take on some of the spadework. If the salesperson leaves, the other relationships remain intact lowering the risk to the company because the customer is more 'sticky.' There is a better flow of communication and improved relationships which will add value to the sale, and that value is easier to see and measure. Conversations are less price based, and there is a longer-term focus. What's not to love? The move from 'Bow Tie' to 'Diamond' looks attractive and it's incredibly easy on paper. However, in real life, it is a cultural change that is surprisingly difficult to achieve. If it was easy, our 'Social Brains' would ensure that we'd all be doing it already. It's perhaps an excellent example of the Intellectual Brain seeing a future opportunity, with the Social Brain seeing immediate threats. Decision-making, reliability, victory, and status can all be threatened by the move to a model where there is less control and more initial work to do. This is why training people to operate like this does not work. Intellectually it makes perfect sense, but outside of the classroom and with limited support in the workflow, it does not happen. It get's put into the 'too hard to do' pile by the Social Brain because it takes a considerable amount time and effort compared to the alternative of not doing so. The analysis of the buying team is a reliable indicator, or barometer, of how much focus and effort a salesperson is really putting into the sale. If they arrive with a Bow Tie or a Diamond to the Deal Hack you know that the Deal Hack will move quickly and be able to create insights and strategies quickly. However, if they arrive with a Solo selling model, there's a lot of spade work to be done just figuring out who's who, before the strategizing, insight building and value creation can really start.

The benefits of diamonds are evident for both sides of the transaction, but sometimes the buyer may feel that they do not want the selling team to contact their colleagues in this way. Especially if they are a trained purchaser and want to tightly control the purchasing process tightly. They may resist the move to 'Diamond' but will probably welcome a move to 'Bow Tie.' In which case work over time to build relationships across multiple points of contact. A tool that helps to make sure the coalition fits the 'Diamond' model is the 'Buyer-Seller' matrix that has the buying team along one side and the selling team along the other:

| | Jeremy - Sales | Jane - CFO | John - Ops | Jenny - Service |
|---|---|---|---|---|
| James (CFO) | Good relationship | Have not met | Good relationship | Acquaintances |
| Ian | Good relationship | Have not met | Acquaintances | Acquaintances |
| Robert (CFO) | Good relationship | Have not met | Have not met | Have not met |
| Linda | Acquaintances | Have not met | Have not met | Have not met |
| Margaret | Good relationship | Have not met | Acquaintances | Acquaintances |

| | |
|---|---|
| 🙂 | Good relationship |
| 😐 | Acquaintances |
| ☹️ | Have not met |

From this matrix, we can see that Jeremy, the salesperson, is managing a 'Bow Tie' relationship. If Jeremy leaves, the account could be at risk. The operational team has limited contact, which could easily be enhanced. Jane the CFO should reach out to make contact with her peer in the buying company as a first step. There's work to be done regarding adding more value in the sales process and reducing the risk of losing this customer or account.

Buyer Roles

Within all of the stakeholders that we identify in a Deal Hack, there are three 'buyer roles' that we concentrate on to maximize our chances of success in the deal. The three buyer roles we identify are:

1) **Coach** - a coach is a person who is outside of the buying process, but has an interest in helping us in the deal. Coaches can be outside or inside of the organization you're selling to. Their role is to help us with information that can inform our discovery. For example, you may speak to someone who used to work at the prospect company, or who knows someone who does, or the coach

may be a supplier. Equally, it could be a first or second level LinkedIn contact who works at the organization but works outside of the area you're hoping to sell to. Coaches have information and can help you, but they have no influence over the sale. Deal Coaches will challenge the Deal Owners to come up with more coaches than they typically want to. The collective team can often contribute coaches from their network which can help build knowledge and influence in the deal.

2) **Champion** - is the person who has access to the Economic Buyer, along with the power, influence and credibility to sell on our behalf inside the customer organization. Without someone selling on our behalf inside of the organization, it's unlikely that the deal will close in our favor. There are often two types of champion, a deal champion **and** a technical champion if there is a strong technical component to the deal. There are four stages to champion building, ABCD:

    a. **Ascertain** – who is the person in the customer organization who has access to the economic buyer, and has the power, influence and credibility to sell on our behalf?

    b. **Build** – how can we build our relationship with the Champion so they will knock down doors and run through walls on our behalf?

    c. **Challenge** – look for opportunities in the buying process to check that they will fight for us. Will they go to the economic buyer with our value proposal? Will they give us the information we need to craft our offer for key stakeholders?

    d. **Do** - use the champion to do things on our behalf, for example sell and negotiate, particularly behind closed doors when we are not there.

3) **Economic Buyer** - this is the person or people who can

sign off the contract and has the ability to say 'no' or veto the deal.

The Deal Coach will ask questions to determine who fits into these roles, and then challenge the allocation of roles. There are usually gaps to be found around the strength of the champion, *"Will they really put their neck on the line for us when the decision is to be made?"* This is usually because they have not been **Ascertained** correctly, not been **Built** sufficiently, they have not been **Challenged**, or that they have not been asked to **Do** what we need them to do. The Deal Coach will ask questions in all of these areas to determine the gap. There's also typically ambiguity around who the Economic Buyer is because of the lack of questioning and lack of challenging the customer. One area the Deal Coach will challenge is the assumption that a particular title in a company makes that person a Buyer Role, for example the CFO is the economic buyer. We tend to find a lot of assumptions here, and this is a big issue because misidentification of the Champion and Economic Buyer can be fatal to a deal. So the Deal Coach will diligently and deliberately drill into these roles, test them with challenging questions and build a list of actions to gain clarity and control over the buyer roles in the deal.

In Part One we covered the difficulty of making individual decisions because we often become conflicted between Social Brain and Intellectual Brain thinking. Take a moment to think about how difficult it is to make the right individual buying choices when it's an important choice to make. For example, which college to attend, which house to buy, what to have for lunch.... Now add another seven people into the mix. The CEB estimate that 6.8 buyers are involved in the decision making for each deal, and experience tells us that it is probably more.[209] All of these people with a voice, all with different opinions, different needs and their own political agendas. Making a collective buying decision is hard because the group has to align around a single choice, and opinions as to which option to choose will almost certainly differ. As we saw from the 'Bay of Pigs' example, even the most intelligent people can become highly dysfunctional and ineffective when making challenging decisions. The difficulty in making a collective decision is one reason why so many deals lose, not to a competitor as we might expect, but to the status quo. Anyone who has been involved in a complex buying process will agree how difficult it can be to manage the collective decision making process within a buying team. Sales people have the unenviable task of managing this process from outside of the buying company, where the remoteness makes influencing the collective decision making group much harder to exercise. It is surprising how many sales people have not been involved in complex buying initiatives within their own companies. It would be surely to everyone's benefit to let them see, first-hand, how buying works locally before we ask them to undertake influencing it remotely.

Because of the complexities and difficulties of managing a complex buying group, the Social Brain will be looking for shortcuts. One shortcut it invariably finds is, as we've seen, to deal with a single point of contact and Solo sell. Another shortcut is to let the customer decide on their own decision making criteria and for the customer to prioritize this themselves. We've seen already that prioritization is an Intellectual Brain activity that is avoided by the Social Brain because of the high levels of energy required to complete it. This is a potential area for the sales person to add value. When we know who's in the buying group, we start by asking them how they will make their decision. *"What is important to you in this project? What is the most important? Is this more or less important than that?"* Often the buyers are not sure about this, and so they can be helped with insights like, *"Our customers usually consider installation and security as their most important criteria, are these important to you?"* You'll end up with a number of decision criteria that are prioritized by each person like this:

| Criteria | Jeremy | John | Jane | Jenny | James | Justine | Jade | SCORE |
|---|---|---|---|---|---|---|---|---|
| Installation | 4 | 3 | 4 | 3 | 4 | 3 | 3 | 24 |
| Currency | 3 | 2 | 1 | 4 | 3 | 1 | 4 | 18 |
| Security | 2 | 0 | 3 | 0 | 1 | 4 | 2 | 12 |
| Time | 1 | 4 | 0 | 2 | 0 | 2 | 0 | 9 |
| Color | 0 | 0 | 0 | 0 | 2 | 0 | 0 | 2 |
| Finish | 0 | 1 | 0 | 0 | 0 | 0 | 1 | 2 |
| Size | 0 | 0 | 2 | 0 | 0 | 0 | 0 | 2 |
| Duration | 0 | 0 | 0 | 2 | 0 | 0 | 0 | 2 |

Here we can see that installation is the most important criteria, followed by currency, security and then time. You can probably already see that playing this back to the buying group delivers insights that can help them reach a better buying decision. But this is just one decision they need to make. They will also need to decide which vendor should be chosen to supply these criteria.

To help the customer with this, list the top criteria and then give each a weighting to differentiate the most important criteria. Then award scores for each of the alternative options for each alternative option. In a Deal Hack, the scoring can be done from the collective experience of the team in the room, but can also be gleaned from the customer. Under competition law, the customer is not allowed to give you bid information on competitors. However, they can help you to understand the competitive landscape without revealing who the competitors are. You should end up with a table like this:

| Decision Criteria | Weight | Option A | Option B | Option C | You 'Y' |
|---|---|---|---|---|---|
| Installation | 4 | 6 | 4 | 4 | 7 |
| Currency | 3 | 5 | 7 | 5 | 7 |
| Security | 2 | 7 | 8 | 6 | 8 |

| Time | 1 | 4 | 4 | 7 | 7 |
|---|---|---|---|---|---|
| Weighted average performance | n/a | 14.25 | 14.25 | 12.5 | 18 |
| Price performance | | 6 | 7 | 5 | 6 |

All value decisions are influenced by price, so comparing the performance of your solution with price performance will allow you to create an overall performance measure for each of the different options to help the prospect make a robust decision.

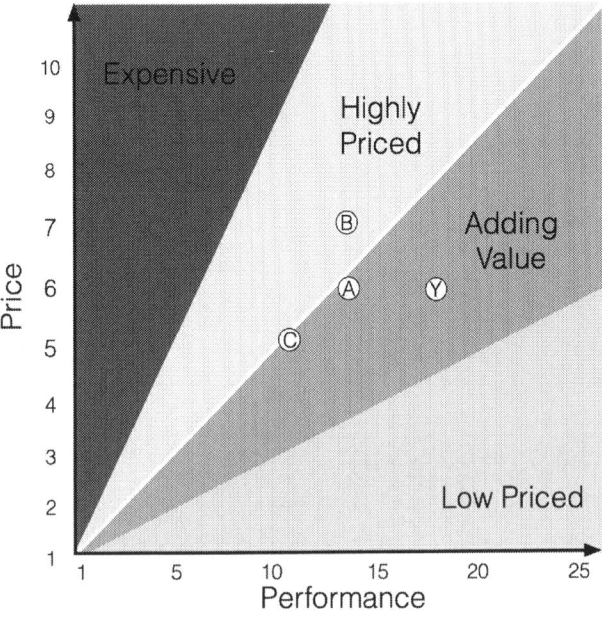

Here on the map taken from the grid, you can see the relationship between price and performance. The diagonal white line is the line of fair value where price and performance are equally balanced. Moving left of the line will be more expensive and moving right of the line will bring greater value for the price being charged. Company B are unlikely to be chosen as they have the same performance as A but are more expensive. In this example, option 'Y" is the furthest right of the line which means Y are creating the most value and are equivalent in price to A. So a choice between A and Y should deliver Y as the chosen solution, because it performs better against the customer's criteria at a similar price. C has a lower price but does not perform as well as Y, so will only be chosen if the additional benefits that Y deliver are not worth the increase in price. To defend the higher price position, option Y need to be clear on the differential value, they are creating against C. To reduce the price of Y, a purchaser could approach Y with the quote from C, telling them that the business prefers C (e.g. the FD has an existing relationship from a previous company and they still play golf together) and ask them to match the price of C to win the contract. The easy thing to do here is lower the price to equal C and win on performance. The best salespeople know this is happening and hold their price by defending the differential value that they have created in the sale. But to do this they would need to know who has an influence over the decision, what their buying criteria are, how they are measuring success and how the competition rank against these criteria. This takes a lot of time and Intellectual Brain work and it's easy to see why the Social Brain shortcuts are so attractive here. The Social Brain can save considerable energy and time by simply going back into their own business and asking for a discount to match C. Professional purchasers make a ton of money for their own organizations this way. Without the groundwork of knowing the wider stakeholders, knowing how value is created for them, and how the competition rank, the sales people are unaware of the reality of what is going on and so are powerless to compete against this tactic. Perhaps the bigger problem is when the sales leadership are also unaware that their sales people are falling for this simple purchasing tactic. This can be seen when the sales leadership are not challenging the performance of their sales people correctly, and a tell tale sign of this is not only low margins, but sales leaders who see Deal Hacks as an inconvenience rather than a help.

Conducting this type of price performance exercise is clearly Intellectual Brain thinking, and that is why it rarely happens to this level of clarity in sales. It's far easier to let the customer figure out their priorities and how these compare, and that is why this exercise is the staple of professional purchasers. Once we know who's in the decision making group, and we know how they feel about our performance, we can build strategies to align them behind our solution and increase our chances of winning the deal. The stakeholder map[210] is ideal for this and is one of the first tools we use in the Deal Hack. When the 'Deal Owner' is giving their overview, it is inevitable that names will be given, and these should be captured on post-it notes in anticipation of placing them on the stakeholder map when the overview is complete.

To build the stakeholder map, the first question we need to ask is do they have influence over the purchasing decision? Do they have power in this decision or not? What Buyer role do they have? Move the post-it along the horizontal axis, back and forth until the 'Deal Owner' is happy with the position. Then you need to understand if they are aligned with our solution, or are they against it?

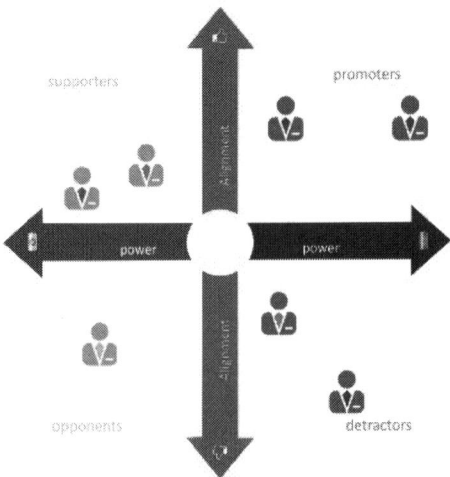

Move the same post-it up and down to gauge the agreed level of alignment. Be careful not to change this second question into do they like us or not? This is because they may like us, but might not be aligned with our solution. This is about alignment with the proposed solution. In other words, does our solution fit their buying criteria? So when working out alignment, detail the buying criteria for each person and score them like we did above. This will mean a meeting or at least picking up the phone to them, to understand their decision criteria and what they *really* think of your solution.

Asking these two questions allows you to distribute your decision making group onto the stakeholder map. I usually write a big 'C' on the person who is allocated the role of Champion. Then a big 'E' for the person who becomes the economic buyer. Once on the map you can then create strategies to move them top right, and to align them. Remember the aim is to secure a coalition of people powerful enough to secure adoption of your solution, lead by the Champion and sponsored by the Economic Buyer.

Khrushchev, the President of the USSR, saw President Kennedy's poor decision making as an opportunity to put atomic weapons into Cuba, America's back yard, after the 'Bay of Pigs' failure. Fortunately, President Kennedy had the self-awareness not to blame others for the poor decisions that were made, and had contributed to the failed invasion. Instead, following the 'Bay of Pigs' failure, he set up a system of 'Independent Challenge', to challenge thinking when making important decisions in his administration. When it came to deciding what to do in the Cuban Missile Crisis that followed, often considered the closest the World has ever come to full-scale nuclear war,[211] thankfully Kennedy made much better decisions. But the story allowed us to see that group decision making is hard, even with the best brains available. When it comes to selling, influencing decision making in the buying organization is one of the hardest things we do, and it is therefore not surprising that it succumbs to Social Brain thinking. For this reason, we find that it is one of two of the most beneficial areas to focus on in Deal Hacks. It allows us to answer with confidence the *'Why Us?'* question. "Why will they buy from us and not from someone else?" To answer this question, we need two things:

1) **Decision Makers:** a coalition of customer stakeholders aligned behind our solution, lead by the Champion and who can influence the Economic Buyer

2) **Decision Criteria:** an intimate understanding of the decision criteria of each of the stakeholders, that align with our solution.

Once we know why the customer will 'Buy Anything', and we know why the customer will 'Buy from Us', the final piece of the jigsaw is to know if the customer needs to 'Buy Now' or not, and we cover this final piece in the next chapter.

# CHAPTER 15
# WHY SHOULD CUSTOMERS BUY NOW?

**"The trouble is, you think you have time."**

Jack Kornfield

T he woman was in a trance-like state, rocking back and forth on the Serpentine Column, which was a bronze tripod and cauldron, positioned high over a large crack in the floor. Surrounded by priests in the dark underground chamber, Pythia was engulfed by clouds of sweet-smelling ethylene smoke wafting up from the cracked floor in the magical ritual. Over time, her face became pale, and her voice dried up, becoming deeper and hoarse as she uttered her prediction to the priests who then interpreted it for King Croesus of Lydia. The richest King of his time, Croesus is credited with issuing the first true gold coins. The name of Croesus remains, to this day, a synonym for a wealthy man in

Greek and Persian cultures.

In the ancient world, the Delphic Oracle was the highest religious authority. Found on the slopes of Mount Parnassus in central Greece, the Oracle was open for consultations one day each month, except during winter. Predicting the future on behalf of the God Apollo, the priestess Pythia was consulted by those with a burning need to know the future, and those who also had the ability to pay. From Alexander the Great to Nero the Roman Emperor, her predictions changed the course of history. On this particular day, King Croesus wanted to know if it would be advantageous to wage war against the traditional enemy the Persians, or whether he should alternatively seek an alliance and peace. Pythia told him that if he did wage war, *"He would destroy a great empire."* Taking this as a sign of victory, Croesus launched a military offensive, attacking Persia. Pythia was right in her prediction, Croesus did indeed end up destroying a great empire, but sadly for him, it was his own.

The writer Isaac Asimov once said, *"If I were asked to guess what people are generally most insecure about, it is the content of the future. We worry about it constantly."*[212] Indeed, we know from the human DRIVERS that the human brain craves reliability and certainty and this is absolutely the case in business where making the right moves translates directly into competitive advantage and business success. In the case of King Croesus, he sought reliability and certainty from the Oracle at Delphi. The irony is that Pythia was reliably right, if ambiguous in her prediction. The problem lay with King Croesus himself, failing to heed the aphorism 'Know Thyself,' inscribed on the forecourt of the temple as he entered. We learned in Part Two that the human brain craves reliability because reliable events allow the brain to use less energy. The human brain is designed to save energy, and to do this the brain prioritizes running on autopilot through familiar and likely scenarios.

Moving outside of likely scenarios feels bad because of the costly cognitive load. The Social Brain will, therefore, seek reliability at every opportunity, only deviating from reliability into risk when there is a substantial 'pay off.' The ancients increased the reliability (mitigated the risk) of uncertain, high stakes events through the likes of the Oracle at Delphi, or other diviners who provided insights into the future. Today people still use astrologers in much the same way, but the modern world of business has moved from individual esoteric fortune tellers to an industrial and scientific approach to prediction. The Global Prediction industry is a multibillion-dollar industry, covering financial services, business planning, economics, technology, weather, and populations. Describing it as the 'Second oldest profession' going back some 5000 years, the author William Sherden provides some examples, *"According to the Employee Benefit Research and Investment Company Institutes, tens of thousands of money managers provide investment predicting advice in managing $7.5 trillion in pension, endowment, and mutual funds. Weather forecasting is approximately a $5 billion business employing 6,000 schooled meteorologists and a large number of forecasters. There are 172,000 loan officers predicting whether you will default on your business loan, mortgage, or credit card, and 15,000 actuaries busily crunch statistics about when you are likely to die, be disabled, wreck your car, or suffer damage from a hurricane or an earthquake."[213]*

Being able to predict events with accuracy in business is extremely valuable. There are two fundamental areas that successful businesses can predict better than unsuccessful ones:

1) **Revenues:** how much revenue will come in and from where?
2) **Expenditure:** how much do we need to invest and where to achieve revenue targets?

The ability to predict successful investments that can drive revenue growth, is key to a successful commercial organization. Not unsurprisingly, therefore, a fundamental tenet of business is that in order to make money you have to know how to spend money. Both of these business practices, making and spending money, involve predicting the future and both can be helped by sales people. Enlightened sales people help the customer through the buying process when they spend money, but the best sales people link this to revenue and growth, showing the buyer how they can make more money. To do this the sales people need to be able to demonstrate how an investment can help the company to achieve their strategic and tactical objectives. For this to happen a sales person needs to have an intimate knowledge of the company, and we've already seen tools like the opportunity chain and the stakeholder map that can help achieve this. The tools we've already seen can help to answer the 'Why buy anything?' and 'Why choose us?' questions. But they can't answer the final question, namely, 'Why will the customer buy now?' that we shorten to 'Why Now?' There are two major components to the 'Why Now?' question, two of the four Ds:

1) **Deal Value:** Is the quantifiable value to the business sufficient for them to invest?
2) **Decision Process:** Is there an identifiable and timely buying decision process that can be driven by the sales process?

If we can answer both of these questions positively, we have a strong 'Why Now?' and we're more likely to close the deal. Let's look at Deal Value first, which I find to be the area with the biggest gaps in Deal Hacks. Part of the reason for this is the word 'value' itself, which means different things to different people. In Deal Hacks were interested in quantified financial value because this helps us to communicate the impact of our solution more effectively. The international language of business is, after all, finance. This is because different departments in any business will understand their own measures and KPIs, but they don't always understand each others'. This limitation is overcome by strategic business leaders using a common language across the whole business, and that language is finance. The language of finance is universal and applies not just within companies, but between companies, in any industry, anywhere in the world. There are a number of financial tools that can be used to articulate the value created in a sale, and to cover them all would require a whole new book. So let's cover the most basic tool for articulating value in the sales process which is the '"innovation adoption' tool.

If we simplify business finance to the simplest level, there's always two sides to consider: money coming in or being saved (revenue and savings) and money going out (expenditure). When it comes to expenditure, the money going out is almost always linked to revenue and savings, because it is expected that any expenditure will help money to come into the organization or be saved in some way. For example, increased sales, increased customer retention, increased operating efficiencies or cost savings. To make a financial decision, two questions need to be answered:

1) What are the total costs?
2) How much will this impact on revenue or savings?

Sales people will always give a price to the customer for their solution, so that it can be paid for. This answers part of question number one, by telling the buying company the required expenditure, or how much money will be leaving their organization on that solution. But, to get to the total cost they'll need to add the internal costs of change to this. Total costs are, however, only half of the information the business needs to make a financial decision. Those making the decision on expenditure will have alternative options for spending any budget, and they will most likely choose the option with the biggest impact on revenues or savings. If we're helping the customer to make a purchase decision it makes sense, therefore, that we provide 1) the financial costs, **and** 2) the financial impact on revenues and savings. Sales people all provide the direct costs in a proposal, however, rarely do they supply a CFO ready business case that includes the positive impact on revenues or savings. In line with sales methods that are over 100 years old, sales people today are often still giving the generic un-quantified 'benefits' of their solution and letting the customer figure out the financial impact on the finances of the business. In other words they let the customer figure out the value that the seller is creating for them. So the sales people answer these two questions:

1) How much will this cost?
2) What are the benefits?

But these are not the questions being asked. This is a classic Social Brain shortcut. Remember the bat and ball problem? The Social Brain substituted the relative *'More than'* statement in the problem (the bat costs $1.00 *more than* the ball) with the absolute statement (the bat costs $1.00). This made the problem easier to solve. If a ball and bat together cost $1.10 and the bat costs $1.00, then the ball does indeed cost ten cents. But that's not the question that was asked. The same type of 'switch' has been made here. The work load for the Social Brain of the sales person is reduced significantly by asking, "What are the benefits?". But the original question still needs to be answered. All that has happened is the workload has shifted over to the customer, along with any chance to influence the process. Remember, benefits are not what are required to make a financial decision. Benefits are just the starting point for calculating financial impact, not the end as they are often treated.

In recent years, this fairly obvious void has been filled by two mechanisms. Firstly, as we saw in Chapter 1, buying companies have created purchasing departments to improve purchasing decision-making. Secondly, sellers have started using business value consultants to help their sales people to quantify the potential impact on the customer's overall finances. Whilst the implementation of business value consultants on the seller side is a good move, it often comes late in the buying process and can be seen by the buyers as a way for the sellers to defend value, and so it not always accepted by buyers. I've also see sales people avoiding using the business value consultants because they see more work and perceive it to be a slower process. Classic Social Brain thinking. What's clear is that companies that are buying solutions need to know the negative and positive financial implications of the purchase to make the best decision. This means that they need to know the quantified impact on savings and revenues as well as costs. Sales people who only provide quantified costs without a quantified return are living nostalgically in a world that ended long before the close of the last century, and are missing a massive opportunity. Exactly who makes the prediction of quantified benefits and how that prediction works its way into the buying process is up for grabs. There is a significant opportunity for sales people to help customers to make better buying decisions by helping to predict the positive and negative implications for the company's finances. This is why we focus on this area in Deal Hacks and turn the Social Brain thinking into Intellectual Brain thinking.

The first step in doing so, is to look at the 'Opportunity Chain'. From the goals, initiatives and pain across the whole business, we can see where the value can be realized, what Cheverton calls 'Value Hotspots'. And if we cross reference with the stakeholder map, we can see how far the decision makers are from the areas of value, what Cheverton calls 'Decision Hotspots'.[214] From these 'Value Hotspots' we can start the process of quantifying the value. Here's an example: *"HR are having problems recruiting 20 sales people next year, what's the impact of them not being able to do this? What would be the cost of a solution that they would have to spend to solve this problem?"* Clearly here we are coming up with the figures, but the next stage will be to validate these with the customer. Lots of actions and questions come out of this exercise.

Go through the functions affected one by one, listing how they will be affected, and then answer the questions, *"What would it cost if they if they didn't have that, and had to do it the old way?"* Once you've reached exhaustion, get the hack team to chunk the benefits into a maximum of six categories. Calculate the benefits for each category. We should have now six categories with six amounts. Here's an example:

a. **Increased revenue: $700,000**
b. **Increased productivity $60,000**
c. **Increased customer retention $50,000**
d. **Reduction in risk $30,000**
e. **One stop shop $30,000**
   **Total Potential Value Year 1 = $870,000**
   **Total Potential Value Years 2 and 3 = $1,740,000**

The question from this approach is, how do we know this is true? For example, how do we know for sure that risk can be reduced to the tune of $30,000? Why not $25,000? Well, the short answer is that we don't know for sure, yet. We're on a journey to become 'more sure'. The figures above are a value hypothesis, not the final position. Often, when we start the process of calculating value, the sales team will say, *"You can't calculate the value of that benefit, it's intangible!"* For example, the benefit could be *'it makes them sleep better at night.'* Can we calculate the benefit of this? Yes, we can, but we need to be significantly clearer and less abstract. The benefit is not 'sleeping better', that's an analogy. We dig deeper by asking,

*"What's the risk you're concerned about? What does it look like when it happens? What happens if it manifests? What's the impact of that to you, and your colleagues? How can we quantify that? How much would it cost to fix? How long would you be unable to work? What's the likelihood of it happening?"* Working in this way with the customer allows us to come to a justifiable value that we can use in the 'Value Hypothesis'. What we find in the Deal Hack is that a 'Value Hypothesis' is essential to generate discussion and to provoke the generation of new and better figures in collaboration with the customer. The rigor applied in the Deal Hack allows the salesperson to bring the customer into the process of value quantification, and to jointly create an amount of value that the customer feels happy with and will stand beside. The process starts with brainstorming and best guesses but finishes with a validated, tested and robust CFO ready business case that the customer champion can confidently take to the buying group and sell on your behalf. Taking the 'Hack Team' on this journey is the hardest part of the 'Deal Hack.' The Deal Coach must be able to challenge the thinking of the Hack Team and take them outside of their comfort zones. There will be significant objections from Social Brain threat to status, reliability and victory:

a)   I don't have the time to do all that investigation
b)   It's not possible to quantify those things
c)   I'll look stupid in front of the customer

This is a clear departure point from training and coaching because the 'Deal Coach' needs to hold their ground and produce an outcome. If we can't do this bit, if we can't formulate the 'Value Hypothesis', we can't communicate value to the customer or capture value, and we will not win the sale. This is not a 'nice to have' this is essential and worth fighting every inch of ground for.

To complete the business case, we need to develop a full picture of the value being created, and quantify the **complete** costs to the customer of the solution. Not just the costs of the proposal, but the cost to the customer of implementing the solution and changing their working practices. Normally salespeople want to ignore or limit these costs, but think like the customer and address all relevant costs to build trust and credibility, like this:

    f.  Product cost: £200,000
    g.  Project team: $90,000
    h.  Customer service impact: $40,000
    i.  Training time on new systems: $30,000
    j.  Down time due to changes: $30,000
        **Total Costs Year 1 = $390,000**
        **Total Costs Years 2 and 3 = $0**

These are the costs that the 'Social Brains' of salespeople normally want to ignore but are essential for a CFO ready business case. When this complete picture is used with the customer, it can be used to tell the story of impact across the business, including costs and returns. A CFO ready business case accelerates the decision and because it shows a far deeper understanding of their business than the competition, who will probably only provide solution costs, it makes it more likely you'll win the deal too.

With a CFO ready business case in place, we still have to know the roadmap of making the decision. When it comes to decision process, unless the sales person has recently arrived from Mars, they will know that they need to know the customer's decision making process in order to close the deal. Surprisingly, however, when we put a visual representation of the decision process on the wall in Deal Hacks, there are gaps that occur time and again that can cause the deal to **miss**. These are:

    1. **Mis-aligned buyer and seller goals:** the most fre-

quent is the seller trying to shoe-horn the decision into a shorter timescale. Scope of the project is also a common mis-alignment.

2. **Missing steps from the buying and sales process:** the most common mistake when decoding the buying process is the sign off. Most corporate buying decisions are a two stage process where the project is given the go ahead as the first gate and then the selection of alternative vendors is the second gate. Many sales people misunderstand the first gate as the decision to buy from them, and it is not. It is always worth challenging the customer decision process as there are invariably missing steps. The really surprising thing is the frequency that I see missing sales steps. Lack of goal alignment will invariably manifest as shortcuts in the process. Ultimately these shortcuts reduce value or increase risk and have a detrimental effect for buyer and seller.

3. **Mis-understood roles and authority:** this is a commonly recognized and understood issue in sales. The common themes we see are unsurprisingly finding Champions who do not have the power and authority to sell on our behalf, or Economic buyers who do not have sign off authority. These come to the surface in Deal Hacks when looking at the decision process and also the stakeholder map when we look at Decision Makers. A lack of ability to challenge the buyers is the root cause of this. The sales person using their manager as a 'Higher Authority' to play the bad cop can help the sales people to have the challenging conversations with their customers that their Social Brains want to avoid.

We know from our study of the Social Brain that people crave certainty and reliability. At the start of this chapter we looked at the most successful prediction business of all time, the Oracle at Delphi, and we looked at the high level of demand today for prediction services in business. When companies are choosing what to buy, they are trying to predict the best outcome for their business and this impacts both expenditure and income. Sales people can play an active role in that process by contributing to the certainty of a robust decision. This involves helping the customer to analyze the quantified value being created across the whole of their business, and the complete costs of the project, so that the best decision can be made. Creating a complete picture of quantified value like this and managing multiple stakeholders are the two most significant gaps we see in Deal Hacks and the reason that Deal Hacks are so successful in improving closure rates.

# PART 4 SUMMARY

Deal hacks create targeted learning opportunities inside the workflow that satisfy a number of the BASIC learning times that sales people have. This makes them a great compliment to existing forms of training and coaching. Deals Hacks do this at the same time as directly impacting on deals and causing less Social Brain reactions, avoiding the development of fixed mind-sets.

Deal Hacks have a structured process called GOAL. 1) **Grade:** the deal owner grades the deal in relation to the four key indicators: decision makers, decision criteria, deal value and decision process. 2) **Overview:** an overview of the deal by the deal owner answering the why anything question. 3) **Analysis:** review the health of the deal using analytical tools answering the three whys? 4) **List of Actions:** prioritize and allocate actions in the form of a 'close plan.'

Deal Hacks focus on answering three fundamental questions about any deal. 1) Why Anything? Why should prospects buy anything? 2) Why Us? How can we get prospects to choose us? 3) Why Now? How can we get prospects to buy now?

# PART FIVE

# SET-UP A DEAL HACK PROGRAM

Sales organizations have hit a diminishing return, where many salespeople are not achieving their goals despite having more resources and support than ever before. Due to cognitive biases, many sales people and sales leaders are, however, blind to the lack of capability that is causing this failure.

One of the blind spots is the use of Social Brain thinking in the sales process that cuts corners and reduces the value created in the deal. Unidentified and unchallenged, these blind spots develop into a fixed mind-set where challenging situations are avoided and the ability to adapt to change effectively shuts down.

A fixed mind-set is often exacerbated by the very learning interventions designed to drive performance improvements because they can create social brain reactions. Attempts to fix the problem can result in cultures of fear or entitlement when challenge and support are not balanced.

We can create a growth mind-set culture, firstly by highlighting the blind spots to reveal the real reasons that sales results are not being achieved. We then set up a Deal Hack program that avoids Social Brain thinking and reactions, and keeps learning in the workflow, where sales people learn best, and where the impact is direct, immediate and measurable.

In part five we now look at how to set up a Deal Hack program in a complex sales organization. Part five is divided into:

**Chapter 16 – Crossing the Chasm.** How do we roll out Deal Hacks?
**Chapter 17 – Measuring and Reporting.** How do make sure the Deal Hack program stays on track?

# CHAPTER 16

# CROSSING THE CHASM

*"There is nothing more difficult to plan, more doubtful of success, nor more dangerous to manage than the creation of a new order of things."*

Niccolò Machiavelli, The Prince (1513)

E verett M Rogers was born on March 6, 1931, into a poor farming family in Iowa during the Great Depression. Hard economic times meant a tough life. With no internal plumbing, heating, or electricity his family survived the sub-zero winters together in Iowa. Rogers recalled his early life: *"One's hands got red and chapped from wearing wet gloves or mittens while doing chores, and from milking the dairy cows."*[215]. In 1930 during the Great Depression Roger's father, Rogers Snr, had a choice to make. Should they farm the new hybrid seed corn that yielded 25 percent more crop, and was resistant to drought, or should they continue with the corn seed variety that they had traditionally used? Rogers Snr. was part of a study by two sociologists, Ryan and Gross, who were examining how independent farmers were adopting hybrid seeds, equipment, and new farming techniques.[216]

Rogers had seen that his father liked electro-mechanical farm innovations, but was highly resistant to adopting biological-chemical innovations like this. As the spring of 1936 approached, the Rogers family hoped that the drought of the last few summers was over and the heavy winter snowfalls had been a sign that rain would follow. As summer approached, the Rogers and other farmers searched the sky for signs of rain. But it didn't come. Dust from the South-West blew into Iowa creating drifts of dust two to three feet high around fences and buildings. Dust sifted into houses, under doors and through cracks in windows frames. Dust filled the air, sometimes blocking out the sun. While the hybrid seed corn survived on the neighbors' farms, the traditional crop on the Rogers' farm wilted in the dry, dusty environment. After eight years of crop failure, Rogers Sr. was finally convinced to adopt the new hybrid corn.

This experience had a deep effect on Rogers who went on to win a scholarship to study agriculture at Iowa State University. His father's reluctance to adopt biological and chemical innovations, despite him seeing the benefits on other farms, showed Rogers that adopting innovations was more than a rational economic decision. More influential seemed to be the opinions of neighboring farmers, especially those that his father respected. Adopting innovations seemed to be a social and communicative process, involving the exchange of ideas, persuasion, and personal influence. These social aspects of innovation diffusion formed the basis of Rogers' graduate work at Iowa State.[217] His doctoral dissertation dealt with the adoption of weed spray in two Iowa farm communities, similar to the study his father had been part of by Ryan and

Goss. The doctoral committee didn't think much of Roger's dissertation but was intrigued by his review of literature chapter. In this chapter, Rogers reviewed the existing studies of the diffusion of all kinds of innovations — agricultural innovations, educational innovations, medical innovations, and marketing innovations. *"I was convinced that the diffusion of innovations was a kind of universal process of social change,"* said Rogers.[218] He found several similarities in these studies, for example, innovations tend to diffuse following an S-Curve of adoption. In 1962 Rogers published these insights in his first book, *"Diffusion of Innovations"* when he was a 30-year old Assistant Professor of Rural Sociology at Ohio State University. He quickly became a global success, and his Diffusion of Innovations theory is now the second most cited study in social sciences.[219]

Rogers witnessed first-hand how hard it was for his father to change from one brand of seed to another. We saw in Part Two why individual change is hard. We saw in Part Three that organizational change is hard, because of the need to build a growth mind-set culture across leaders and individual contributors. This chapter helps identify and prepare for the predictable levels of apathy and skepticism that will come with any organizational change program. Sales performance optimization programs tend to follow a common approach where the whole population is pushed through the events as quickly as possible. The sheep dip. An unintended consequence of this is that the practices are not adopted universally, as we'll see. Here we use Roger's Diffusion of Innovation theory to overcome this and successfully launch the Deal Hack into sales organizations.

What sort of phone do you have? Bit random? The way you answer that question will determine your place on the Diffusion of Innovation graph that Rogers produced. Rogers developed five categories describing peoples' approaches to when and how they adopt an innovation:

**Innovators:** the obsession that innovators have with new ideas leads them to seek out innovation and other innovators. Communication and friendships with other innovators are common. Typically, they have sufficient resource to help absorb the possible losses from unprofitable innovation. They can understand and apply complex technical knowledge, and their status is bound up in their technical superiority. They can cope with a high degree of uncertainty. They queue up outside the Apple Store to get the latest iPhone.

**Early adopters:** seek information about new ideas. They have a high degree of exposure to information sources and their interpersonal networks reach beyond their immediate environment. They can cope with high levels of uncertainty about innovation. They are opinion leaders, and their status is bound up in respect. They are the people we check with before we adopt a new idea and are essential to achieving critical mass in a market. They have the latest iPhone.

**Early majority:** they adopt new ideas just before the average member of the system. They interact frequently with peers but rarely hold positions of opinion leadership. They hold an important position in the diffusion of innovations process, connecting the early adopters to the late majority. They have a good iPhone.

**Late majority:** they adopt new ideas just after the average member of the system. Economic necessity and peer pressure form part of their reasons for adopting. They do not adopt until most others in their system have already done so. Most of the uncertainty about a new idea must be removed before the late majority feels that it is safe to adopt. They have an old model iPhone.

**Laggards:** are the last in the social system to adopt an innovation. They possess almost no opinion leadership.

The point of reference for the laggard is the past, and decisions are made regarding what has been done previously. Similar to innovators, they tend to mix with those with similar values, but in this case traditional values. They are suspicious of innovations and change agents. They are proud to have a 'brick'.

Where would you put yourself on the diffusion of innovation curve when it comes to cell phone technology? Where would you put yourself on the diffusion of innovation curve when it comes to cars? Where would you put yourself on the curve when it comes to sales skills innovation? When we poll salespeople on this latter question, they typically put themselves in the middle of the early adopters. Being better than average, the early adopters adopt new concepts and ideas just before the average. This is perhaps once again the illusion of superiority talking. Not only is it statistically unlikely for everybody to be an early adopter, but the inability of the audiences that I encounter to talk knowledgeably about the latest concepts in sales effectiveness does not reflect this proposition at all.

When trying to drive the adoption of innovation into a market, or an audience, the diffusion of innovation theory suggests that innovators must be won over first. They will then pull the early adopters, who will then pull the early majority, who will then pull the late majority who finally pull the laggards into adopting. Geoffrey Moore came up with a remarkable insight that built on Roger's work. When studying technology companies, he found that technologies often failed to get full market adoption because they failed to bridge the gap between early adopters and the early majority. Moore famously called this the 'chasm'. The chasm has caused the death of many a technology company, and it turns out that it has also caused the death of many a sales transformation program too.

In sales organizations, we see a similar problem to that experienced by many technology companies, a lack of adoption. I hear sales leaders regularly saying. *"We have pockets of excellence, but we're not where we need to be across the board."* That's because they are in the chasm. The pockets they are referring to are the early adopters, who actively seek out best practices and use them. They are the opinion leaders, and the people others check with before they adopt a new sales concept. The early adopters pull across the early majority, an essential step towards adoption. But they are failing to do so because the whole sales organization is being treated like one homogeneous mass, instead of distinct audience segments. If we overlay the diffusion of innovation categories with our sales personas, we can see how Moore's theory of the chasm applies to sales organizations. 'Stars' are the innovators and early adopters, from whom we easily to get buy-in and adoption and on side of the chasm. On the other side of the chasm, the opportunistic, entitled and survivor categories make up the early majority, late majority and laggards respectively. The question is no longer how can we drive adoption of sales effectiveness ideas and techniques across a sales population. The question is, how do we cross the chasm to get the early and late majority on board? This might sound like the same question, but it is different. Different because the segments of the diffusion curve require different approaches. We know that we can pull the early adopters on fairly easily. If we pull them on board first, we can then pull on board the early majority, the late majority and laggards in turn. This enables us to reach critical mass, where the audience works for the change instead of against it, allowing the new techniques and ideas to diffuse more naturally across the whole sales population.

The diffusion of innovation theory has been around since at least the early 1960s, and in different guises even before that. Do we currently use it to segment audiences in sales transformation programs? The sales transformation programs that I experienced with sales training consultancies over the years were all segmented along the lines of the job role. I never saw segmentation by mind-set. Why? Because all of the stakeholders involved in sales transformation were keen to get the salespeople through the sales interventions as quickly as possible. What we call in the trade the 'sheep-dip' process. All salespeople in a similar role go through a sales training program together. They are put through regardless of their levels of knowledge, capability, accountability, and irrespective of their desire to do so. I agreed to have 12 people in a session once and walked into a room of over 50 people. This is common because the sales leaders want as many people through as quickly as possible and the training companies get paid more for more people. We force people through the process and in doing so cause a threat response in their 'Social Brains' that triggers the fixed mind-set and self-justification as we saw earlier, leading to a rejection of the intervention. How can we avoid the threat response and get buy-in from the Social Brain for the Deal Hack? To mix some metaphors, It's time to put this sacred cow through the mincer and get rid of the sheep-dip mentality. It doesn't work in any other frame of commercial reference. Can anyone point to any audience/market where the innovation diffused across the whole audience/market in one move? No innovators, no early majority, just everyone moving across to adopt the innovation in one homogeneous mass. This approach is just fantasy driven by ignorance and greed. Who wouldn't want everyone to move across to a new innovation in one go? But the science has been telling us for over fifty years that it just doesn't happen like that. Ken Blanchard is famous for saying, "*Change—even organizational change—happens one person at a time. This important fact is overlooked in most organizational change planning.*"[220] Blanchard makes an insightful and accurate point, and in the sales arena at least, this seems to be **the** most sabotaged component of any sales performance transformation program.

Everyone involved intellectually understands that change does not happen over-night and that people change at different rates. Then without waiting to draw breath, the sales transformation team process everyone through as quickly as possible, and altogether. It's a classic Intellectual Brain V Social Brain conflict. The Intellectual Brain understands the concept of changing one person at a time, and almost certainly agrees. But it's just too much like hard work for the Social Brain who's looking to cut corners and get immediate gratification. Remember what Dr. Miller said, *"If you look at people after coronary-artery bypass grafting two years later, 90% of them have not changed their lifestyle."* We intellectually know what is good for us, but most often seem to do what's easiest.

The challenge that surfaces when segmentation and prioritization is suggested is, *"Well we're holding the classes anyway, so just let them all attend."* NO! What would happen if Apple gave a segment of laggards the latest i-Phone on the day of the new product release? The reviews would be terrible, *"It doesn't do what I need it to do. I couldn't navigate my way around it. Loads of features I just don't need."* The reviews online would be shocking and other people would be warned against buying it. It would be a complete commercial disaster. So why do we do that in sales transformation? When you put entitled people into a class they are soaking up time and ruining the experience for everyone else. Entitled sales managers and leaders can kill the program dead in short order. Some do it overtly, and some covertly. There is no long-term commercial situation where this approach has proven to work. The reasons we do this are:

1) The sales population want to go through as quickly as possible because they feel they don't need the training, after all they're all above average performers and it's the others who need training.
2) Sales performance optimization teams are reacting to

what the sales leaders want instead of leading them. This is often because they are much smaller and politically weaker.

3) The sales training companies and consultants are maximizing their revenues and margins because there are more people going through in less time

There seems to be a shortage of 'Intellectual Brains' on the team with concern for the future saying, *"Hang on a minute, this short-term approach makes no **long term** commercial sense!"* If we look at the stakeholders involved in a sales optimization intervention, the majority have a short-term interest in it being over and done with as quickly as possible. Robert Merton described this type of situation as *"imperious immediacy of interest,"* and a primary cause of unintended consequences. [221] The unintended consequence that we see time and again are the creation of fixed mind-sets and the rejection of the learning we're trying to get across. The desire to get through the sales performance interventions as quickly as possible happens because the audience do not buy into them. Not buying-in is the part we need to change, and we can only do it by following Roger's Diffusion of Innovation, which breaks down how people buy-in, into three phases.

**Phase One – Cross-Functional Leaders**

Before we embark upon a sales performance intervention and execute the diffusion of innovation strategy, we need to make sure we have business leaders on board across the wider organization. We know from Peter Cheverton that value is created across the whole organization and it is that complete organizational value that we want to harness in the Deal Hack. Leaders across the different functions of the business will be supporting the Deal Hacks and so will have to buy into the concept and be clear on what is expected of them and their teams. There will be leaders who are early adopters and can be identified by them stepping forward as volunteers. These Early Adopters should be welcomed into stage one with open arms. They can be champions, promotors and evangelists for the cause, and may even become Deal Coaches.

**Phase One – Sales Managers**

Before executing the diffusion of innovation strategy with the sales population, we must segment the sales managers, the line managers of the individual sales contributors. We're looking for sales managers who challenge and support their teams well. We're not looking for leaders who have the biggest territories, we're not looking for leaders who have big deals, we're not looking for leaders we like, and we're not looking for leaders who return great results or leaders who return poor results. We're looking for leaders who have the mind-set to consistently challenge and support their teams. The importance of the attitude of the sales manager was brought home to me the last time I, very reluctantly, agreed to take part in a 'sheep dip' approach to sales optimization. It was one of those situations where I agreed to class sizes of 12, but I was over-ruled by the client and a former colleague who saw no reason why we shouldn't have 30 people in the room while I trained two other trainers at the same time. I also gained assurance that a senior person would be there to introduce me and the program and spoke to that leader in advance to make sure we were aligned. When I asked him to address the room crammed full of people to say why we were there, he said, *"I don't know why we're here. We're the best and don't need to be here."* You may think I'm taking his words out of context and perhaps he was joking, but that is not the case. The result was an unmitigated disaster, not just for that team but the whole program. Prior to the engagement and in front of senior colleagues, the sales manager had agreed to address the team, and claimed he was looking forward to the sessions we had planned. He was clear on the messaging and his role. However, when the time came he didn't actually turn up to the first morning when he was due to address his team. When he did turn up and was in front of his team, his Social Brain kicked in and the status Social Driver took over. I don't lay the fault at the feet of the sales manager for the failure of the intervention. In a rush to execute a 'sheep dip,' we did not take the time to segment the sales managers effectively. We had selected a manager based on the size of the territory, who had told us he was bought into the process, when in fact he had not. This had not been challenged or tested. To make matters worse, he had a 'Friend' style of leadership. His inability to challenge his sales team had resulted in an entitled team culture which responded negatively to the changes in working practice intended in the performance intervention. The learning for us is clear. Sales managers are pivotal in the success of Deal Hacks, think of them like the champion in a deal. They have the power in their hands to make or break it. The risk is that they can break any sales performance optimization program they choose, so we need to segment the sales managers in the program first. Build the program with the ones who can be your champions and satisfy two criteria:

1) They have proactively bought into the concept, and are not paying lip service to appease their political masters. For example, they have a personal interest bound up in the success of the project.
2) They have demonstrated the ability to challenge and support their sales teams, so they appear in the top right of the Sanford Matrix. This enables them to be able to defend the program on your behalf when you are not there to do so.

Sales managers who fall short in either category are the biggest liability to the success of any sales transformation program. If they are allowed to take part in a program early on, it is within their power to kill the program dead if they want to. This is a risk not worth taking because if they kill the program, this will have the long term consequence of increasing fixed mind-sets across the whole sales organization. The program needs to be in safe hands and should be allowed to grow to a critical mass within the organization before entitled, and critic styled sales managers are invited to participate. The risk of doing otherwise is that Geoffrey Moore's prediction will come true and you will not cross the chasm from early adopter to early majority and onwards and the program will not be a success.

**Phase One – Sales Population**

With trusted, keen and capable sales managers acting as champions, we next segment the sales population. We're going to segment the target audience based on two criteria:

1) The Sanford Matrix
2) Deal attractiveness and achievability

We're aiming to get up to 16% of the total sales population in the first wave. According to Rogers, this is the combined size of innovator and early adopter profiles.[222] We've already segmented the sales managers, so their teams are the total viable population for phase one. This population should then be segmented using the Sanford matrix, and Stars should be selected for phase one. Stars are good at being challenged and take advantage of support when given, so they are the ideal cohort to make a success out of the first wave of 'Deal Hacks.'

Once we have a clear view of the people we want to engage, we can then look at the deals that this group will use in their deal hacks. We segment the deals based on attractiveness to the seller organization and achievability to land the deal. You will need to select five criteria for each, here's an example:

| Attractiveness Criteria | Score | Achievability Criteria | Score |
|---|---|---|---|
| Size and margin | | Clear differentiators | |
| Complexity of deal | | Available sales resource | |
| Closure date* | | Internal political support | |
| Strategic fit | | Technical ability to satisfy customer needs | |
| Future revenue opportunities | | Operational capability and resources to supply | |
| **TOTAL** | | **TOTAL** | |
| **Total Deal Score** | | | |

* Prioritize deals with forecasted closure dates in the mid-near term.

By segmenting against your own criteria, you'll be able to focus on deals that are a good use of the Deal Hack resource. It will be the case that not every Deal Hack will result in a win. It's been the case that Deal Hacks have killed deals that needed to be put out of their misery because they were not good for the selling company and were wasting precious sales time and resources. The Deal Hack is not alchemy, it cannot turn terrible deals into gold. Charles Babbage, the inventor of the first computer, was once asked, *"Pray, Mr. Babbage, if you put into the machine wrong figures, will the right answers come out?"* His response was. *"I am not able rightly to apprehend the kind of confusion of ideas that could provoke such a question."*[223] The modern phrase is, *"Garbage in garbage out."* So let's feed as little garbage into the Deal Hack machine as we can, at least at the start.

We've segmented the audience and segmented the deals. The aim is to get 16% of the total sales population into phase one. There will be trade-offs, but that's what we're aiming for. We sell the (16%) targeted cohort of salespeople on the concept of Deal Hacks based on the reward of scarcity. Creating a situation of scarcity creates a reward effect with the Social Brain DRIVERS, and in particular 'status.' *"This is only open to a select number of salespeople who have been selected based on performance criteria."* Innovators and early adopters are driven by scarcity, so they will be attracted by this type of approach.[224] If you look at highly successful marketing campaigns, they tightly control the flow of a product into a market at launch. Limiting the volume of a product into a market stimulates the early adopters who compete for the product and pay a premium. Look outside an Apple store and see them queuing when they release a new iPhone. In the same way, we will tightly and deliberately control access to the 'Deal Hack.' This strategy will stimulate demand and prevent de-railing by people who are not yet ready for it. Scarcity drives demand, so be prepared for people asking to be included in the program. Put additional Stars on a waiting list, and park everyone else for now. Run Deal Hacks with this segment only. We're looking for two outcomes from the first wave of Deal Hacks:

1) **Social Proof** - Captured anecdotal feedback from the team members to build the social proof of success.

2) **Results** - Clear and measurable results that can be communicated, for example, increased closure rates, decreased time to close and increased margin. Again, to build social proof.

We need enough successful deals and experiences to build enough 'Social Proof' to pull over the early majority into adoption. While early adopters are motivated by scarcity, that is not the case for the early majority. Being more risk-averse, and more attached to the existing status quo, the early majority require social proof to pull them on board. Back to the sales manager who told his team that they did not need to attend the performance intervention. He had not bought in. He needed time for the early adopters to test the new methods, achieve success and socialize that across the organization. This would help him to see that if he doesn't adopt, he will be losing out. This is the point the Deal Hack turns from a threat to a reward in the Social Brain and opens the door to organizational adoption. Before this point, he was not ready to adopt but was being told to do so. Being told to adopt was a threat to his social DRIVERS, in particular, decision making and status. A fixed mind-set ensured that when he was due to sell his team on the benefits of the intervention, outside of the political pressure of other sales leaders, he could not do so.

**Phase Two**

You're looking for around 16% of the sales population to have had successful experiences before opening up the program to the targeted early majority which is phase two. That could be anywhere between 2 and 4 months depending on the time to close the deals concerned. You'll be there when there's enough social proof to get the early majority across. Before that outcome is achieved, phase two should not be activated.

Phase two should be launched with a communication to the remaining 84% of the sales audience, opening up the Deal Hack to them by application. The application process is key, because those who have been stimulated by the social proof of phase one will engage, and according to Roger this is about 34% of the population. I'm not saying that 34% will respond to your internal communication campaign and be hammering down your door! 16% of the sales population has been through the program. Of the remaining 84% of salespeople, 34% will be in favor of joining the program. They still need to be brought on board with an effective marketing communication program, which will be led by the social proof created in phase one. The communication program needs to be proactive by reaching out to people and to 'nudge' them on board. Sales populations are busy! Actively target people who fit the profile, and who have deals that score highly.

**Phase Three**

The program has so far been executed in a voluntary and supportive way. By the end of the first two phases, we should have had 50% of the sales population through 'Deal Hacks.' This means that 50% of the sales population are actively using Deal Hacks as part of their sales process. In phase three we throw a little more challenge into the mix, in two specific areas:

1) **Major Deals** - we go back to our deal segmentation and pull out the higher value Deals. Select the ones that can have a significant effect on the organization. These deals are then put through 'Deal Hacks.' Those salespeople who have been through the process will simply continue. Those who have not been through the process yet will be required to do so. They should be paired with members of the leadership team who have been through the process already, and have the experience to bring back into other 'Deal Hacks.' This is to counter the risk of 'Entitled' salespeople reacting adversely to the process.

2) **Postmortems** – a lost deal is the best opportunity for learning about selling in the workflow. It tends not to happen because we move on to the next deal so quickly. It is difficult for many salespeople to learn from lost deals because of the threat response of the Social Brain. The Deal Hack is the ideal environment to provide the focus, the challenge, and support to find the valuable learnings that lay latent in lost deals. The investment in Deal Hacks is recouped through increased win rates and margin. The investment in postmortems is a little more abstract but is realized by organizational wide learning from the event. Learning outcomes from postmortems should be communicated in a positive and de-personal-

ized format.

In phases one and two we targeted 50% of the sales population, and they went willingly through 'Deal Hacks.' In phase three we have enough social proof and experience to make the Deal Hack a core business process. Business as usual, you might say. By targeting the larger deals in phase three, we pull some of the late majority through but at this point the focus on driving the audience ends. By switching to a focus on deals in phase three, the majority of deals and revenue will be moving through the Deal Hacks, which is actually what we want. Whether or not the late majority and laggards go through (the remaining 50%) is academic. This is not just a learning and development program, and so we're not just concerned about processing salespeople through the program. We're more concerned about processing deals and revenue, which we have now achieved. When the majority of company revenue is flowing through Deal Hacks the machinery is in place and working.

# CHAPTER 17

# MEASURING AND REPORTING

*"If you can't measure it, you can't improve it."*

**Peter Drucker**

"Give me a place to stand, and I will move the earth!" wrote Archimedes in the third century BC. The greatest mathematician of the ancient world, and revered today as the father of mathematics, Archimedes was exaggerating to make a point. The point he was making concerned his observation that heavy objects can be more easily moved by a lever and a fulcrum. This had been known for centuries already, but Archimedes changed the game by developing the mathematics to explain it. Hearing this bold claim, King Hiero of Syracuse challenged Archimedes to make his claim into a practical demonstration. In response, Archimedes set about designing a system of pulleys and levers that could move the heaviest of warships in Hiero's naval fleet across land. To do this, Archimedes designed what we call today the 'Block and Tackle' system of pulleys. Legend has it that, using just one hand and seated some distance away, Archimedes turned the handle on his new system of pulleys, and moved the ship single handedly using his new invention.

Sometimes improving sales figures feels as hard as moving the earth. If it were easy, we'd not have the poor results we saw in Chapter 1, and we'd most likely not have the Sales Performance Paradox where there is a trend of increased inputs leading to decreased outputs. Using Archimedes 'Law of the Lever' as inspiration, what are the levers that you can use to more easily improve sales performance? I've asked this question many times of sales leaders over the years, and I always get very mixed response. Often I get the question, "What do you mean by a lever?" Which is a fair enough question. What I mean by a lever, is, *"Something that the sales leadership can pull on, to increase sales."*

I've not yet met a sales leadership team who can **collectively** and succinctly articulate the levers they should be using, when asked on demand. But as sales leaders we should be able to immediately articulate the levers that we are using to maximize sales performance in our sales organization. Not unsurprisingly, Deal Hacks are designed to clarify this and drive adoption of the levers that move sales numbers. We use four key levers that can impact on a deal:

1) Decision Makers
2) Decision Criteria
3) Decision Process
4) Deal Value

Using these levers on the deals in the Deal Hack, allows us to build measurable improvements in the individual deals. Moving the metrics in the individual deals across all of the sales teams rolls up into an organization wide sales performance reporting. That is how we move get the Archimedes 'Law of the Lever' effect and move the massive object that is the organizational sales number.

After the Deal Hacks have been run, the 'Deal Coach' creates a report to the sales manager of the team. This provides an overview of the deals 'Hacked', along with accountable actions for each deal. This allows the sales manager to coach their team on the deals concerned with the aim of improving those deals. As part of the report, a visual comparison of the health of the deals is created, comparing the 'Pre-Deal Hack' views of the team against the 'Post-Deal Hack' views of the 'Deal Coach'. Here's an example of this:

### Self Assessment by Sales Person pre-Deal Hack

| | Why Us? | | Why Now? | | |
| --- | --- | --- | --- | --- | --- |
| | Decision Makers | Decision Criteria | Value | Decision Process | Forecast |
| Deal 1 | Green | Amber | Amber | Amber | Q3 |
| Deal 2 | Green | Amber | Amber | Red | Q3 |
| Deal | Green | Green | Green | Green | Q3 |
| Deal 4 | Amber | Green | Amber | Amber | Q3 |

### Assessment by Deal Coach post-Deal Hack

| Deal Coach | Why Us? | | Why Now? | | |
| --- | --- | --- | --- | --- | --- |
| | Decision Makers | Decision Criteria | Value | Decision Process | Forecast Probability |
| Deal 1 | Red | Red | Red | Amber | Low |
| Deal 2 | Amber | Red | Red | Amber | Medium |
| Deal 3 | Green | | Green | Green | High |
| Deal 4 | Amber | Red | Red | Amber | Low |

The tables are an overview of the health of the opportunities based on red, amber and green criteria. Red means that the situation is not understood and we are not in control. Amber means that the situation is somewhat understood and so we are partially in control. Green means that the situation is completely understood and we are in complete control. The red does not mean that the opportunities are bad ones, it just means that there is some work to do to get in control of the situation, and the action plan is what will convert the red to amber and eventually green.

Forecast probability is the opinion of the Deal Coach, post Deal Hack, as to the probability of the deal closing within the forecasted time-period. 'High' means that there is a high likelihood, because we are in control and the deal is almost certain to close. 'Medium' means that there is a chance that the deal will close, but we are not in complete control and cannot accurately say. 'Low' means that it is unlikely that the deal will close because we are not yet in control of the deal.

I've never seen a deal where the 'Deal Coach' is more optimistic than the sales person. All of the deals covered in Deal Hacks find areas of improvement that had so far remained latent, despite manager coaching and deal reviews. From these areas of improvement we can start to identify trends in performance across the team. We've only got four deals in this report, but we can already see that 'Decision Criteria' and 'Value' are contenders for an intervention to improve the sales skills of this team. This data allows the sales manager to see how good the team members are at assessing their own sales performance and decision making in the deal. This can reveal insightful patterns in the performance capabilities that the team need to improve. This diagnostic has the potential to allow performance support interventions that can have an immediate impact on sales performance and results. The intervention could be learning, coaching or both, depending on the size of the gaps and the audience. But hopefully you can see that with more data from more Deal Hacks, a sales organization can easily diagnose and monitor the health of deals and sales capability accurately together and in real time.

Sales Leaders can get a roll up of all of the deals 'Hacked' across the whole sales organization, along with accountable actions for each deal by team to get them to green. This allows the sales leaders to coach the sales managers on individual deals if required. The visual comparison of the health of the deals against the reported health of the deals allows the sales leader to assess how good the teams are at evaluating their own performance. This can, in turn, reveal insightful patterns in the performance capabilities that the sales organization as a whole need to improve, which will have an immediate impact on sales results. There will be a prioritized list of competency areas for the sales organization to work on, to improve overall sales performance and decision making in opportunities.

You'll know when Deal Hacks are a success in your organization because you'll hear people referring to deals being 'hacked.' The language is in the water supply. The first time I overheard someone asking if their deal could be hacked, I smiled because I knew the concept was understood and taking root.

# BOOK SUMMARY

I n the first part of the book, I encouraged you to look for blind spots in your sales organization. If your salespeople are not achieving quota despite having more available resources and more support than ever before, this could be due to cognitive biases creating blind spots and a fixed mind-set that are preventing them adapting to the changing world around them. In Part Two, we learned that sales performance interventions fail, in part, because they are communicated as logical gains but are received as social threats. This drives a fixed mind-set which can shut down the ability to learn or adapt to change which brings a limitation to sales capability and has adverse effects on an organization's ability to grow. In Part Three, we saw how traditional approaches to sales transformation can unintentionally cause the very problems they are trying to solve. We need to find ways of challenging and supporting our sales teams that do not produce social brain thinking or threat responses, both of which can lead to cultures of entitlement or fear and reduce sales capability. In Part Four, we saw how Deal Hacks can provide balanced levels of challenge and support inside the workflow, which can produce higher levels of engagement and learning. They do this at the same time as helping deals to close, impacting directly and positively on sales results. In Part Five, we saw that we need to roll Deal Hacks out in a planned way that creates a pull effect aligning with the diffusion of innovation. We also saw how Deal Hack reports can enable sales leaders to see which deals need to be improved and the capability of the sales teams at executing the sales process.

I've chunked the journey into five parts to make it easier to understand and communicate. Optimizing sales forces is, however, never easy or straight forward. But with these five principals and the Deal Hack in your tool kit, you will now be in a better position to optimize your sales organization. Please contact me if you do implement Deal Hacks in your sales organization, it would be great to build a community of Deal Hack Coaches who can learn from, challenge and support one another.

# TOOLKIT

## Deal Tracker

| Deal | Worth | Decision Makers | Decision Criteria | Deal Value | Decision Process | Forecast Date |
|------|-------|-----------------|-------------------|------------|------------------|---------------|
|      |       |                 |                   |            |                  |               |
|      |       |                 |                   |            |                  |               |
|      |       |                 |                   |            |                  |               |
|      |       |                 |                   |            |                  |               |
|      |       |                 |                   |            |                  |               |
|      |       |                 |                   |            |                  |               |

# Three Whys?

| | Answer |
|---|---|
| **Why Anything?**<br>What pain do they have? | |
| **Why Us?**<br>Decision Criteria<br>Decision Makers | |
| **Why Now?**<br>Decision Process<br>Deal Value | |

Timeline

# Deal Risks

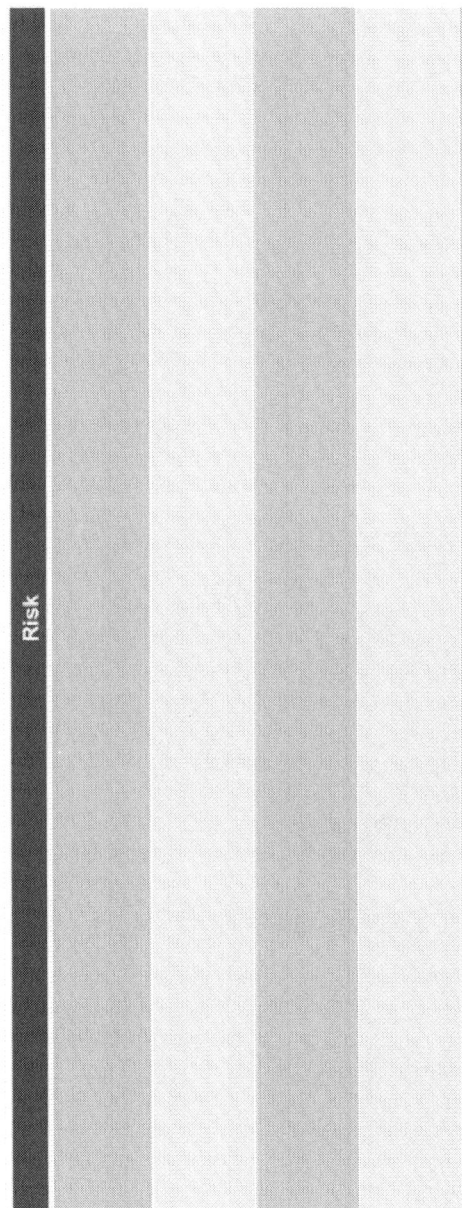

Risk

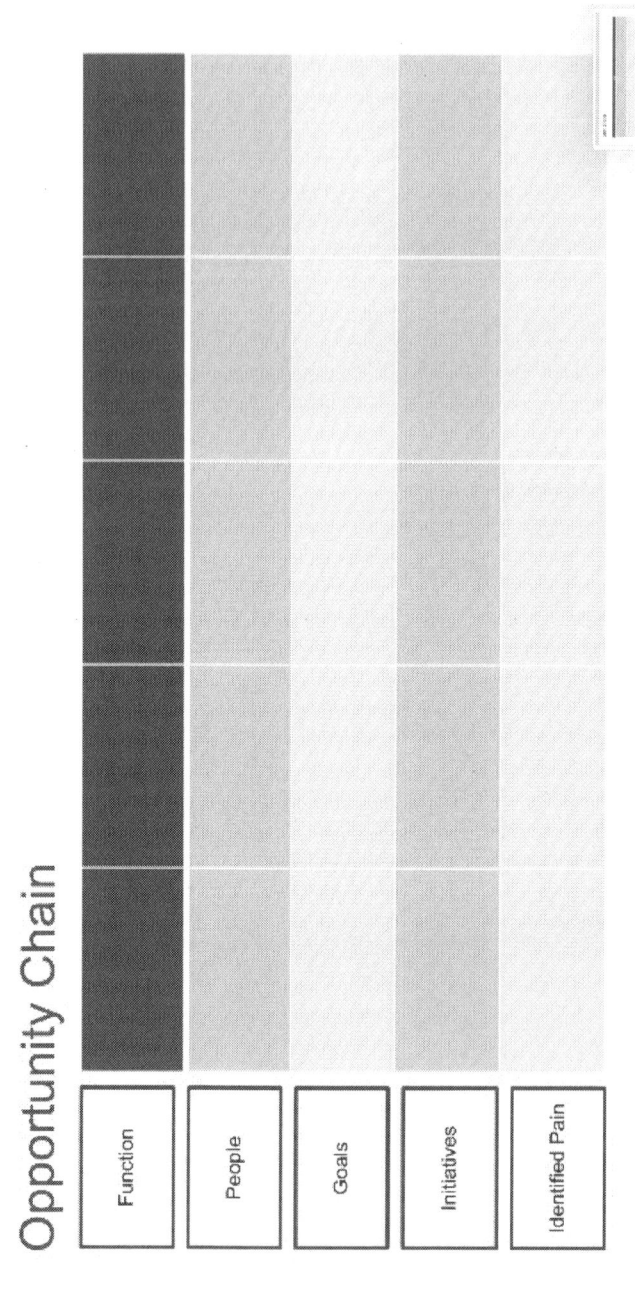

Opportunity Chain

Function

People

Goals

Initiatives

Identified Pain

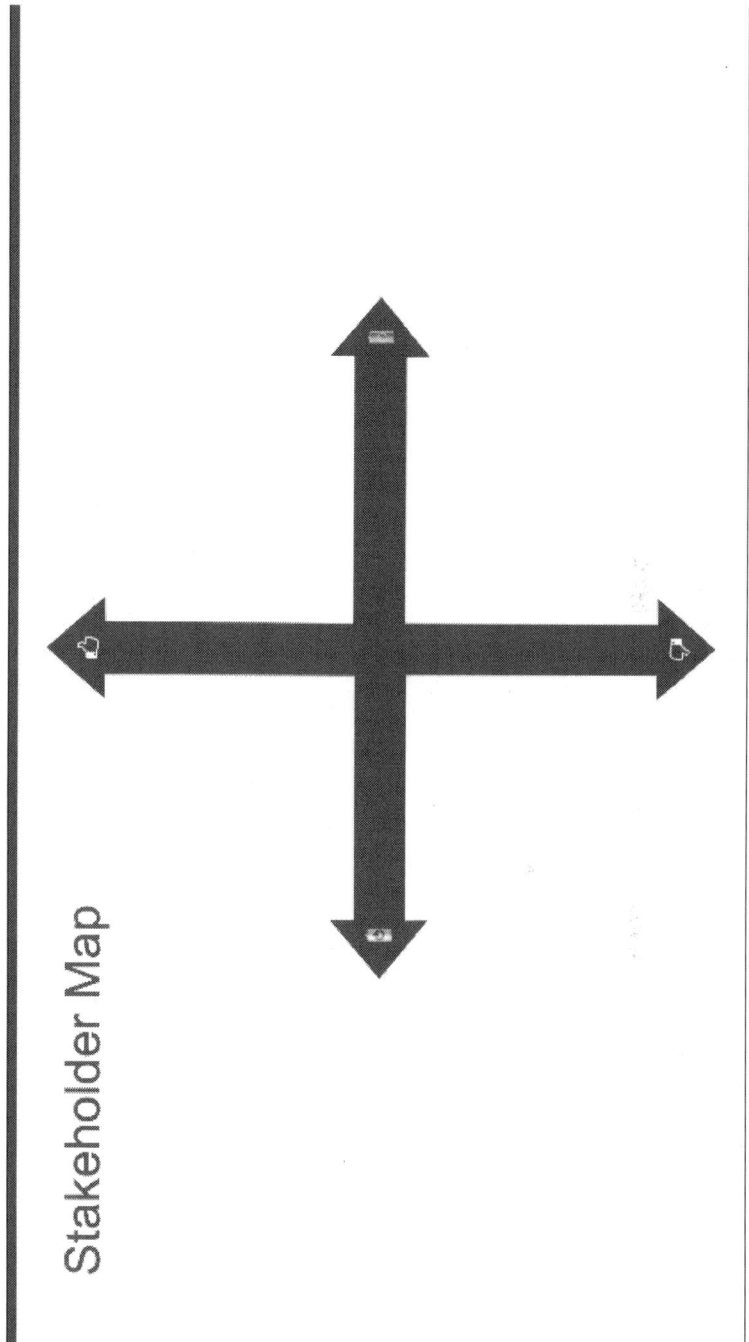

Stakeholder Map

# Competition and Decision Criteria

| Decision Criteria | Our Score | Comp 1 | Comp 2 |
|---|---|---|---|
| | | | |
| | | | |
| | | | |
| | | | |

## Actions

| Action | Who | Date | Coach |
|--------|-----|------|-------|
|        |     |      |       |
|        |     |      |       |
|        |     |      |       |
|        |     |      |       |
|        |     |      |       |

# INDEX

# D

# E

# F

# G

# H

# I

# J

# K

# L

# M

# N

# T

# V

# W

# Z

[1] Ralph Lorenz, Jacqueline Mitton. 2002. Lifting Titan's Veil: Exploring the Giant Moon of Saturn. Cambridge University Press. Pg. 182.

[2] Mary Kay. 2008. The Mary Kay Way: Timeless Principles from America's Greatest Entrepreneur. John Wiley and Sons. (p.XV).

[3]

Direct Selling News, May 31, 2016: DSN Global 100: The Top Direct Selling Companies in the World. http://directselling-news.com Retrieved 2017-01-28

[4] Mary Kay Company Quick Facts Mary Kay Company Quick Facts Retrieved 2017-01-28

[5] Steve W Martin. The Similarities and Differences Between Men and Women in Sales. www.stevewmartin.com. Retrieved 2018-5-18

[6] Dana Kanze, Laura Huang, Mark A. Conley, E. Tory Higgins. June 2017. https://hbr.org/2017/06/male-and-female-entrepreneurs-get-asked-different-questions-by-vcs-and-it-affects-how-much-funding-they-get

[7] Gladwell, Malcolm. 2008. Outliers: The Story of Success (p. 40). Penguin Books Ltd. Kindle Edition.
[8]
Gerald R. Williams, Larry C. Farmer, and Melissa Manwaring. 30 January 2008
Teaching Note New Technology Meets an Old Teaching Challenge. Negotiation Journal volume 24 number 1. Blackwell Publishing Inc. Pgs. 71-87

[9] Williams, G. R. 1983. Legal negotiation and settlement. St. Paul, MN: West Publishing Co.

[10] Ben Carter. 01 March 2014. BBC News http://www.bbc.co.uk/news/magazine-26384712

[11]" Jackie Brown 2010. Ask Me About Mary Kay: The True Story Behind the Bumper Sticker on the Pink Cadillac. Strategic Book Publishing. Pg. 5

[12] Accenture 2015: Powering Profitable Sales Growth. Five Imperatives from the 2014 Sales Optimization Study. Pgs. 5 and 19.

[13] Herb Greenberg, Harold Weinstein and Patrick Sweeney 2001. How to Hire & Develop Your Next Top Performer: the five qualities that make salespeople great. New York: McGraw-

Hill. Pg. 9.

[14] Jim Dickie August 2016. https://www.csoinsights.com/blog/overcoming-the-no-decision-sales-challenge-and-more. Retrieved 07.25.2017.

[15] Zaltman, Gerald. PhD. 2008. How customers think: essential insights into the mind of the market. Boston, MA: Harvard Business School Press, Pg. 3 Print.

[16]' Sales Culture Survey. November 2013. Australian Institute of Management VT. https://tredinternational.com.au Pg.9 Retrieved 07.25.2017

[17]  https://www.forbes.com/sites/louiscolumbus/2015/01/17/idc-predicts-cmos-will-drive-32-3b-in-marketing-technology-spending-by-2018/#49f89c191f78

[18] Accenture 2013. Top-Five Focus Areas for Improving Sales Effectiveness Initiatives
Trends and insights from the 2013 Sales Performance Optimization Study. Pgs. 7 and 11.

[19] Tony Gleeson. Nov. 2013. Sales Culture Survey. Australian Institute of Management. Pg. 21.

[20] Alicia Collins. August 2017. 7 Stats Sales Leaders Need to Know About Selling in 2017 https://blog.hubspot.com/sales/stats-about-selling Retrieved 19/8/2017

[21] Pink, D. (2013). To sell is human. 1st Ed. Edinburgh: Canongate, p.45.

[22] Why Buyers Don't Want To Meet Your Salespeople And What To Do About It
Introducing Forrester's Seller Archetypes To Win, Serve, And Retain Customers September 9, 2015

[23] Dixon, Matthew; Adamson, Brent; Spenner, Pat; Toman,

Nick. 2015. The Challenger Customer: Selling to the Hidden Influencer Who Can Multiply Your Results (p. 25). 07.25.2017 Penguin Books Ltd. Kindle Edition.

[24] Michael Chui, James Manyika, and Mehdi Miremadi. November 2015. Four fundamentals of workplace automation. http://www.mckinsey.com. Retrieved 2017-07-25

[25] David H. Autor, Frank Levy, Richard J. Murnane. Nov 2003. The Skill Content of Recent Technological Change: An Empirical Exploration. Quarterly Journal of Economics, 118(4)

[26] Heath, Chip; Dan Heath. 2007. Made to Stick (p. 194). Version 1. Random House UK. Kindle Edition.

[27] Frequent Exercise Rates Among Various Demographic Groups in June 2015. June 1-30 Gallup-Healthways Well-Being Index.

[28] Sales Culture Survey. November 2013. Australian Institute of Management VT. https://tredinternational.com.au Pg.17.

[29]      https://www.chicagobooth.edu/programs/exec-mba/academics/curriculum Retrieved 07.25.2017

[30] Friedman, Walter A. Birth of a salesman: the transformation of selling in America. Cambridge, MA: Harvard U Press, 2004. Print. Pg. 264.

[31] Financial Reporting Council. July 2016. Corporate Culture and the Role of Boards. Report of Observations.

[32] State of Sales. Insights and trends from over 3,100 global sales trailblazers. Sales force Research. Pg. 8.

[33] Peter Cheverton. 2008. Key Account Management Tools And Techniques For Achieving Profitable Key Supplier Status by 4th edition Pg. 50.

[34] Rackham, Neil, and De Vincentis John R. 1999. Rethinking the sales force: redefining selling to create and capture customer value. New York: McGraw-Hill. Pg. 22.

[35] Rackham, Neil, and De Vincentis John R. 1999. Rethinking the sales force: redefining selling to create and capture customer value. New York: McGraw-Hill. Pg. ix.

[36]' Sales Culture Survey. November 2013. Australian Institute of Management VT. https://tredinternational.com.au Pg.9 Retrieved 07.25.2017

[37] Rackham, Neil. Major account sales strategy. New York: McGraw-Hill, 1989. Print. Rackham, Neil, and De Vincentis John R. Rethinking the sales force: redefining selling to create and capture customer value. New York: McGraw-Hill, 1999. Pg. 5

[38] Rackham, Neil, and De Vincentis John R. 1999. Rethinking the sales force: redefining selling to create and capture customer value. New York: McGraw-Hill. Pg. 22.

[39] Phil Roberts. 2010: Service That Sells: The Art of Profitable Hospitality. Pg. 78.

[40] Adapted from Pittsburgh Post-Gazette, March 21 1996.

[41]

Kruger, J., & Dunning, D. (1999). Unskilled and unaware of it: How difficulties in recognizing one's own incompetence lead to inflated self-assessments. Journal of Personality and Social Psychology, 77(6), 1121-1134. doi:10.1037/0022-3514.77.6.1121

[42] Michael Palin. 16 Feb 2012. https://www.youtube.com/watch?v=x8Afv3U_ysc retrieved 28 July 2017.

[43]

J. E. Davidson and C. L. Downing. Contemporary Models of Intelligence. In R.J.Stanberg(Ed.) Handbook of Intelligence. New York: Cambridge University Press. 2000 Pg. 34-49

[44] Madhavan Ramanujam and Georg Tacke. 2016. Monetizing Innovation: How Smart Companies Design the Product Around the Price. Pg. 24-25. John Wiley and Sons.

[45] S. N. Chakravarty and R. Simon. Nov 5 1984. "Has the World Passed Kodak By?" Forbes Pg 188.

[46] Madhavan Ramanujam and Georg Tacke. 2016. Monetizing Innovation: How Smart Companies Design the Product Around the Price. Pg. 24-25. John Wiley and Sons.

[47] Karl Moore. March 2010. Transcript: Goodbye sales funnel, hello social media. https://www.theglobeandmail.com. Retrieved 08/08/2017

[48] Neil Rackham 1995. SPIN Selling. Pg. 175. Gower.

[49] Neil Rackham 1995. SPIN Selling. Pg. 175. Gower.

[50] Sharot, Tali. 2012. The Optimism Bias: Why we're wired to look on the bright side. Little, Brown Book Group. Location 106. Kindle Edition.

[51] Kruger, J. 1999. Lake Woebegone be gone! The "below-average effect" and the egocentric nature of comparative ability judgments. *Journal of Personality and Social Psychology, 77,* Pg. 221–232.

[52] Leonid Rosenbuilt and Frank Keil 2002. The Misunderstood limits of folk science: an illusion of explanatory depth.

[53] Linda Ng Fat and Elizabeth Fuller 2011. Chapter 6. Drinking Patterns. The Health and Social Care Information Centre. http://content.digital.nhs.uk. Pg. 4.

[54] Alan Smith. April 2016. Why You Should Love Statistics. https://www.ted.com

[55] Dweck, Carol. 2006. Mind-set - Updated Edition: Changing The Way You Think To Fulfill Your Potential. Little, Brown Book Group. Kindle Edition Pg. 72

[56] Sherrie Campbell. 30 Nov. 2017. 6 Ways to Develop a Growth Mind-set https://www.entrepreneur.com/article/305335 retrieved 08 June 2018

[57] Karl Moore. March 2010. Transcript: Goodbye sales funnel, hello social media. https://www.theglobeandmail.com. Retrieved 08/08/2017

[58] Georg F. Striedter. 2016. Neurobiology: A Functional Approach. Pg. 494.

[59] Jonathan St. B. T. Evans and Keith E. Stanovich. May 2013. Dual-Process Theories of Higher Cognition: Advancing the Debate

[60] Scarlett, Hilary. Neuroscience for Organizational Change: An Evidence-based Practical Guide to Managing Change (p. 4). Kogan Page. Kindle Edition.

[61] Alain Samson. 2015 The Behavioral Economics Guide 2015. Pg. 1.

[62] Barden, Phil. Decoded - the Science Behind Why We Buy-Hardcover – 1 Feb 2013 Pg. 30. John Wiley & Sons.

[63] Georg F. Striedter. 2016. Neurobiology: A Functional Approach. Pg. 494.

[64] Peters, Steve. 2012. The Chimp Paradox: The Acclaimed Mind Management Programme to Help You Achieve Success, Confidence and Happiness (Kindle Locations 238-239). Ebury Publishing. Kindle Edition.

[65] Sakai, K. & Passingham, R.E. 2003 Prefrontal interactions reflect future task operations. *Nat. Neurosci.* 6, Pgs. 75-81.

[66] Libet, B., Gleason, C.A., Wright, E.W. & Pearl, D.K. 1983. 'Time of conscious intention to act in relation to onset of cerebral activity (readiness-potential). The unconscious initiation of a freely voluntary act', *Brain* 106: 623-642.

[67] Haggard P. & Eimer M. 'On the relation between brain potentials and the awareness of voluntary movements', Experimental Brain Research (1999) 126: 128-133.

[68] Soon, C. S., Brass, M., Heinze, H.-J. & Haynes, J.-D. 2008. *Nature Neurosci.* doi: 10.1038/nn.2112.

[69] Kerri Smith. 2008. The brain makes decisions before you even know it. http://www.nature.com/news/2008/080411/full/news.2008.751.html Retrieved July 28, 2017.

[70] Peters, Steve. 2012. The Chimp Paradox: The Acclaimed Mind Management Programme to Help You Achieve Success, Confidence and Happiness (Kindle Location 117). Ebury Publishing. Kindle Edition.

[71] Manson, Mark. 2016. The Subtle Art of Not Giving a F*ck: A Counterintuitive Approach to Living a Good Life (p. 35). HarperCollins. Kindle Edition.

[72] Herculano-Houzel, Suzana. The Human Advantage: A New Understanding of How Our Brain Became Remarkable (MIT Press) (Kindle Location 343). The MIT Press. Kindle Edition.

[73] George Markowsky. June 08, 2015. https://www.britannica.com/topic/information-theory/Physiology. Retrieved July 28, 2017.

[74] Kahneman, Daniel. 2011. Thinking, Fast and Slow Pg. 37. Penguin Books Ltd. Kindle Edition.

[75] Edward H. Adelson, Professor of Vision Science at MIT in 1995. http://persci.mit.edu/gallery/checkershadow/description Retrieved 28/8/17

[76] Marilyn J. Cipolla. 2016. The Cerebral Circulation 2nd Ed. Morgan and Claypool Life Sciences. Pg. 1

[77] Suzana Herculano-Houzel. 2016. The Human Advantage: A New Understanding of How Our Brain Became Remarkable (MIT Press) (Kindle Location 356). The MIT Press. Kindle Edition.

[78] Kahneman, Daniel 2011. Thinking, Fast and Slow (p. 7). Penguin Books Ltd. Kindle Edition.

[79] Deloitte Access Economics: 2015. Economic benefits of better procurement practices.

[80] Tim Cummins: 2016. The 10 Critical Pitfalls of Modern Contract Management https://www2.iaccm.com/resources/?id=9150 Retrieved 20/8/2017

[81] Barack Obama Sept 2015: https://obamawhitehouse.archives.gov/the-press-office/2015/09/15/executive-order-using-behavioral-science-insights-better-serve-american Retrieved 28/8/2017

[82]ⁱⁱ Sunstein, Cass R; Thaler, Richard H. 2008. Nudge: Improving Decisions About Health, Wealth and Happiness (p. 10). Penguin Books Ltd. Kindle Edition.

[83] Walter Mischel. 2014. The Marshmallow Test. Understanding Self-Control And How To Master It. Pg. 5. Transworld Publishers.

[84] W. Mischel, Y. Shoda, and M. L. Rodriguez. Functioning in adolescence, "Delay of Gratification in Children," Science 244, no. 4907 (1989): 933-938).

[85] Walter Mischel. 2014. The Marshmallow Test. Understanding Self-Control And How To Master It. Page 5-6. Transworld Publishers.

[86] David Marcum, Steven B. Smith. 2007. Egonomics: What Makes Ego Our Greatest Asset (or Most Expensive Liability). Fireside. Pg. 224.

[87] Daniel Goleman, 2005. Emotional Intelligence: The 10th Anniversary Edition. New York: Bantam Books. Pg. 80– 83

[88] Simon, H. A. (1956). "Rational Choice and the Structure of the Environment". Psychological Review. 63 (2): Pgs. 129–138.

[89] Van Hiel, A.; Mervielde, I. 2003. "The Need for Closure and the Spontaneous Use of Complex and Simple Cognitive Structures". The Journal of Social Psychology. 143 (5): 559–68.

[90] Ron Ashkenas. April 16, 2013. Change management needs to change. http://blogs.hbr.org/ Retrieved July 28, 2017.

[91] Lieberman, Matthew D. 2013. Social: Why our brains are wired to connect (p. 58). OUP Oxford. Kindle Edition.

[92] Lieberman, Matthew D. 2013. Social: Why our brains are wired to connect (p. 68). OUP Oxford. Kindle Edition.

[93] Mathias Pessiglione and Mauricio R Delgado. 2015. The good, the bad and the brain: neural correlates of appetitive and aversive values underlying decision making. Current Opinion in Behavioral Sciences 5:78–84

[94] Leanne M. Williams et al. 2008. The Integrate Model Of Emotion, Thinking And Self-Regulation. Journal of integrative neuroscience, volume seven, number three (2008) Pg. 370 copyright Imperial College press.

[95] Bentham Jeremy. 1789. An Introduction to the Principals

and Morals of Legislation. Pg. 1

[96] Schutz W. 2015. Neuronal reward and decision signals: from theories to data. *Physiological Reviews.* **95** (3): 853–951.

[97] Padgett, David; Glaser, R. August 2003. How stress influences the immune response. Trends in Immunology. 24 (8): 444–448.

*[98]* Adam Smith. 1776. The Wealth Of Nations, Book I, Chapter II, pp. 26-7, para 12.

[99] Medina, John. Brain Rules (Updated and Expanded): 12 Principles for Surviving and Thriving at Work, Home, and School Pg. 12. Pear Press. Kindle Edition.

*[100]* Bainbridge, David. 2010. Teenagers: A Natural History (p. 83). Portobello Books Ltd. Kindle Edition

[101] Michael Corbalis. 2011. A very short tour of the mind Pg. 10. Duckworth Overlook

[102] Navarro, Joe; Karlins, Marvin. 2008. What Every BODY is Saying: An Ex-FBI Agent's Guide to Speed-Reading People. Pg. 26. HarperCollins. Kindle Edition.

[103] Brehm, Sharon S. 1981. Psychological reactance and the attractiveness of unobtainable objects: Sex differences in children's responses to an elimination of freedom. *Sex Roles, Volume 7, Number 9, 937–949*

[104]" Richard Leakey quoted In - Empathy Imperiled: Capitalism, Culture, and the Brain By Gary Olson.

*[105]* Cialdini, Robert. B. 2009. *Influence: Science and practice* 5<sup>th</sup> Ed. Pg. 31. Boston: Pearson Education, Inc.

*[106]"* Marmot, Michael. 2004. Status Syndrome: How Your Social Standing Directly Affects Your Health (Kindle Location

1313). Bloomsbury Publishing. Kindle Edition.

[107] Solnick and Hemenway. 1998. Is More Always Better? Journal of Economic Behavior & Organization. Nov. 1998

[108] Marmot, Michael. 2004. Status Syndrome: How Your Social Standing Directly Affects Your Health (Kindle Location 127). Bloomsbury Publishing. Kindle Edition.

[109] Clark, Andy (2015-10-02). Surfing Uncertainty: Prediction, Action, and the Embodied Mind (Kindle Location 199). Oxford University Press. Kindle Edition.

[110] Milton Schwebel 2003. Behavioral Science and Human Survival. Pg. 61

[111] Harsanyi J.C. 1980. A Bargaining Model for Social Status in Informal Groups and Formal Organizations. In: Essays on Ethics, Social Behavior, and Scientific Explanation. Theory and Decision Library (An International Series in the Philosophy and Methodology of the Social and Behavioral Sciences), vol. 12. Springer, Dordrecht

[112]' Marmot, Michael. 2004. Status Syndrome: How Your Social Standing Directly Affects Your Health (Kindle Location 35). Bloomsbury Publishing. Kindle Edition.

[113] Daniel Goleman. January 1998. Working With Emotional Intelligence. Appendix 1

[114] Ron Ashkenas. April 16, 2013. 'Change management needs to change' http://blogs.hbr.org Harvard Business Review.

[115] Jan Hills. July 2016. Minimize threat and maximize reward to accelerate change. http://www.hrzone.com. Retrieved 28 July 2017.

[116]' Kahneman, D. & Tversky, A. 1992. Advances in prospect theory: Cumulative representation of uncertainty. *Journal of*

*Risk and Uncertainty.* **5** (4): Pgs. 297–323.

[117] Canon, H, J. 1988. Nevitt Sanford: Gentle Prophet, Jeffersonian Rebel. Journal of Counseling and Development, 66(10), 451-457.

[118] Interview with Nevitt Sanford – Journal of Counseling and Development June 1988 – Vol. 66 Page 455

*[119]* Nevitt at Sanford 1966. Self and Society: social change and individual development pg. 44. Atherton Press New York.

[120] John D. Foubert 2014. Lessons Learned: How to Avoid the Biggest Mistakes Made by College Resident Assistants. Pg. 5. Second Edition. Routledge.

[121] Steve Glowinkowski. 2009. It's Behavior Stupid!: What Really Drives the Performance of Your Organization. Ecademy Press. Pg. 51

[122] David Fletcher and Mustafa Sarkar. 2016. Mental fortitude training: An evidence-based approach to developing psychological resilience for sustained success. Journal Of Sports Psychology In Action. Vol. 7. No. 3. Pg. 141.

[123]

Sanford, Nevitt. 1968. Where Colleges Fail: A Study Of The Student As A Person. Pg. 51. San Francisco. Jossey-Bass.

*[124]* John D. Foubert 2014. Lessons Learned: How to Avoid the Biggest Mistakes Made by College Resident Assistants. Pg. 5. Second Edition. Routledge.

[125] Sanford, Nevitt. 1962. The American College: A Psychological And Social Interpretation Of Higher Learning. New York. Wiley.

*[126]* Brown, Roediger & McDaniel, Belknap 2014. Make it stick: Pg. 2. Harvard University Press. Kindle Edition.

[127] Dweck, Carol. 2012. Mind-set - Updated Edition: Changing The Way You think To Fulfil Your Potential Pg. 219. Little, Brown Book Group. Kindle Edition.

[128] BARDWICK, Judith M. 1995. Danger in the Comfort Zone: From Boardroom to Mailroom -- How to Break the Entitlement Habit That's Killing American Business (Pg. 65). AMACOM. Kindle Edition.

[129] Csikszentmihalyi, Mihaly. 2002. Flow: The Psychology of Happiness. Pg. 6. Ebury Publishing. Kindle Edition.

[130] Roger Connors and Tom Smith. 2012. Change the Culture, Change the Game: The Breakthrough Strategy for Energizing Your Organization and Creating Accountability for Results. Portfolio. Pg. 92.

[131] Flamholtz, Eric G and Randle, Yvonne. 2011. "Corporate Culture: The Ultimate Strategic Advantage," Stanford University Press, Stanford California, pg. 9

[132] Ray Dalio. April 2017: How to build a company where the best ideas win.
https://www.ted.com/ Retrieved 14 September 2017.

[133] Mark Roberge. July 29. 2017. How to Interview a Sales Rep Candidate for Coachability. https://blog.hubspot.com/ Retrieved 28 July 2017.

[134] Jordan Belfort. Sept 2017. Way of the Wolf: Straight Line Selling: Master the art of persuasion, influence and success. (Paperback) by

[135] Belfort, Jordan. Way of the Wolf: Straight line selling: Master the art of persuasion, influence, and success (p. 2). Hodder & Stoughton. Kindle Edition.

[136] Charles Babbage. 1864. Passages from the Life of a Philoso-

pher. Pg. 67. Longman and Co.

[137] E. Scott. Reckard. December 2013. Wells Fargo's pressure-cooker sales culture comes at a cost. http://www.latimes.com/ Retrieved 28/7/2017

[138] Jim Collins. October 2001. GOOD TO GREAT. Fast Company. http://www.jimcollins.com/ Retrieved 28/7/17

[139] Jena McGregor. September 2-16. Wells Fargo's terrible, horrible, no-good, very bad week: https://www.washingtonpost.com/ Retrieved 28/7/17

[140]Consumer Financial Protection Bureau Fines Wells Fargo $100 Million for Widespread Illegal Practice of Secretly Opening Unauthorized Accounts. September 2016. https://www.consumerfinance.gov/ Retrieved 28/7/2017

[141] Jon Marino. September 2016. Wells Fargo CFO blames unauthorized accounts on under-performers. http://www.cnbc.com/ Retrieved 28/7/2017.

[142] Jena McGregor. September 2-16. Wells Fargo's terrible, horrible, no-good, very bad week: https://www.washingtonpost.com/ Retrieved 28/7/17

[143] Mark A. Peterson. 1993. Legislating Together: The White House and Capitol Hill from Eisenhower to Reagan. Harvard University Press. Pg. 4.

[144] John Emerich Edward Dalberg-Acton. 2012. 1972 Lord Acton: Essays On Freedom And Power. Pg. XV. Literary Licensing.

[145] Bardwick, Judith M. 1995. Danger in the Comfort Zone: From Boardroom to Mailroom -- How to Break the Entitlement Habit That's Killing American Business. Pg. 11. Kindle Edition.

[146] Ray Dalio. April 2017: How to build a company where the best ideas win. https://www.ted.com/ Retrieved 14 September 2017.

[147] Dr. Karminder Ghuman. 2010. Management: Concepts, Practice & Cases Pg. 356. Tata McGraw-Hill Education.

[148] Brenner, M. 1973. The next-in-line effect. *Journal of Verbal Learning and Verbal Behavior, 12*, 320-323.

[149] William Muir. July 2106. When the Strong Outbreed the Weak: An Interview with William Muir. https://evolution-institute.org/ Retrieved 14 September 2016.

[150] Margaret Heffernan. May 2015: Forget the pecking order at work. https://www.ted.com/ Retrieved 14 September 2017

[151] Cressey, D. R. 1953. Other People's Money. Montclair, NJ: Patterson Smith, pp.1-300

[152] Cialdini, Robert. Pre-Suasion: A Revolutionary Way to Influence and Persuade (p. 212). Random House. Kindle Edition.

[153] Cialdini, Robert. Pre-Suasion: A Revolutionary Way to Influence and Persuade (p. 217). Random House. Kindle Edition.

[154] Culture report 2016: Corporate Culture and the Role of Boards The Financial Reporting Council Limited.
[155]
Financial Reporting Council July 2016. Corporate Culture And The Role Of Boards. Report Of Observations Pg.24.

[156] Financial Reporting Council July 2016. Corporate Culture And The Role Of Boards. Report Of Observations Pg.39.

[157] Adapted from: The Obstacle Is The Way The Ancient Art Of Turning Adversity To Advantage by Ryan Holiday page 6.

[158] Adapted from: BARDWICK, Judith M. Danger in the Comfort Zone: From Boardroom to Mailroom -- How to Break the Entitlement Habit That's Killing American Business (Pg. 3). Kindle Edition.

[159] Manson, Mark. 2016. The Subtle Art of Not Giving a F*ck: A Counterintuitive Approach to Living a Good Life (pp. 45-46). HarperCollins. Kindle Edition.

[160] Mike Bosworth 2017. Architecting The Customer Experience. https://bankonpurpose.com/ Retrieved 28 July 2017.

[161] Heath, Chip; Dan Heath. 2007. Made to Stick Pg. 19. Random House UK. Kindle Edition.

[162] BARDWICK, Judith M.. Danger in the Comfort Zone: From Boardroom to Mailroom -- How to Break the Entitlement Habit That's Killing American Business Pg. 22. AMACOM. Kindle Edition.

[163] Grubbs, Joshua B.; Exline, Julie J Trait entitlement. Nov 2016. A cognitive-personality source of vulnerability to psychological distress. Psychological Bulletin, Vol. 142(11), Nov 2016

[164] Grubbs, Joshua B. and Exline, Julie J. August 8 2016. Trait Entitlement: A Cognitive-Personality Source of Vulnerability to Psychological Distress. Psychological Bulletin. http://neurosciencenews.com Retrieved 28/7/2017

[165] Susan S Raines (2013) Conflict Management for Managers. 1st Ed. Jossey-Bass A Wiley Imprint. Pg. 136.

[166] Manson, Mark. 2016. The Subtle Art of Not Giving a F*ck: A Counterintuitive Approach to Living a Good Life (p. 46). HarperCollins. Kindle Edition.

[167] Patterson, Kerry; Patterson, Kerry; Grenny, Joseph; Grenny,

Joseph; McMillan, Ron; McMillan, Ron; Switzler, Al; Switzler, Al; Maxfield, David; Maxfield, David. 2013. Crucial Accountability: Tools for Resolving Violated Expectations, Broken Commitments, and Bad Behavior, Second Edition (Business Books) Location 251 -282. McGraw-Hill Education. Kindle Edition.

[168] Milgram 1974. The Perils of Obedience. Essay.

[169] Patterson, Kerry; Patterson, Kerry; Grenny, Joseph; Grenny, Joseph; McMillan, Ron; McMillan, Ron; Switzler, Al; Switzler, Al; Maxfield, David; Maxfield, David. 2013. Crucial Accountability: Tools for Resolving Violated Expectations, Broken Commitments, and Bad Behavior, Second Edition (Business Books) Location 251 -282. McGraw-Hill Education. Kindle Edition.

[170] John Blakey and Ian Day. 2012. Challenging Coaching. Going beyond traditional coaching to face the FACTS. Nicholas Brealey Publishing. Pg.1.

[171] Ray Dalio. April 2017: How to build a company where the best ideas win. https://www.ted.com/ Retrieved 14 September 2017.

[172] Robert J. Kelly November 2015. Research Report Supporting Sales Coaching. Sales Management Association. Pg. 6.

[173] Martin J. Gannon. 2004. Understanding Global Cultures: Metaphorical Journeys Through 28 Nations, Clusters of Nations and Continents 3rd Ed. Pg. 142. SAGE Publications.

[174] Brown, Roediger & McDaniel, Belknap 2014. Make it stick: Pg. 5. Harvard University Press. Kindle Edition.

[175] Brown, Peter C. 2014. Make It Stick. Pg. 17. Harvard University Press. Kindle Edition.

[176] BARDWICK, Judith M. 1995. Danger in the Comfort Zone: From Boardroom to Mailroom -- How to Break the Entitle-

ment Habit That's Killing American Business. Pg. 32. AMA-COM. Kindle Edition.

[177] Adapted from Conrad Gottfredson. 2011. Innovative Performance optimization. Strategies and Practices for Learning in the Workflow. Pages 37-38 McGraw Hill

[178] Encyclopedia of Human Memory [3 volumes] edited by Annette Kujawski Taylor Ph.D. Pg. 1131

[179] 2017 Workplace learning report: How modern L&D pros are tackling top challenges. Pg. 37 https://learning.linkedin.com Retrieved 28/7/2017

[180] Donald L. Kirkpatrick and James D. Kirkpatrick 2009. Evaluating Training Programs: The Four Levels. Pg. 26. Accessible Publishing Systems PTY, Ltd.

[181] Ley, T., Lindstaedt, S. N., & Albert, D. 2005. Supporting Competency Development in Informal Workplace Learning. In K. Althoff, A. Dengel, R. Bergmann, M. Nick & T. Roth-Berghofer (Eds.), *Lecture Notes in Artificial Intelligence - Professional Knowledge Management: Third Biennial Conference, WM 2005, Kaiserslautern, Germany, April 10-13, 2005, Revised Selected Papers* (Vol. 3782 / 2005, pg. 190). Springer-Verlag GmbH.

[182] Ken Robinson. 2010. https://www.ted.com/ Retrieved 03 October 2017.

[183] Rackham, Neil, and De Vincentis John R. 1999. Rethinking the sales force: redefining selling to create and capture customer value. New York: McGraw-Hill. Pg. 22.

[184] John Blakey and Ian Day. 2012. Challenging Coaching. Going beyond traditional coaching to face the FACTS. Nicholas Brealey Publishing. Pg.1.

[185] Kotler, P. 2000. Marketing Management, (Millennium Edition) Prentice Hall. Pg. 9

[186] Feynman, Richard P. Some remarks on science, pseudoscience, and learning how to not fool yourself. Caltech's 1974 commencement address. 1974. http://calteches.library.caltech.edu/51/2/CargoCult.htm Retrieved 27/08/2017

[187] Subroto Bagchi. June 1, 2008. The High Performance Entrepreneur. Pg. 133. Penguin Portfolio.

[188] Alan. Briskin, Sheryl Erickson, John Ott and Tom Callanan. 2009. The Power of Collective Wisdom: And the Trap of Collective Folly. Pg. 2. Berrett-Koehler Publishers Inc. San Francisco.

[189] Duane F. Shell, David W. Brooks, Guy Trainin, Kathleen M. Wilson, Douglas F. Kauffman, Lynne M. Herr. Dec. 2009. The Unified Learning Model: How Motivational, Cognitive, and Neurobiological Sciences Inform Best Teaching Practices. Pg. 27.

[190] Dennis S. Charney, Pamela B. Sklar. 2018. Charney & Nestler's Neurobiology of Mental Illness. Pg. 139. Oxford University Press.

[191] Merrill D. Bowan, 2008. Integrating Vision With The Other Senses. Int Vis Other Senses - w-Illustrations 6/10/2012. http://simplybrainy.com/ Retrieved 28 July 2017.

[192] Herculano-Houzel, Suzana. The Human Advantage: A New Understanding of How Our Brain Became Remarkable (MIT Press) (Kindle Locations 1146-1148). The MIT Press. Kindle Edition)

[193] (Medina, John. Brain Rules (Updated and Expanded): 12 Principles for Surviving and Thriving at Work, Home, and School Pg. 194. Pear Press. Kindle Edition.)

[194] Royal Collections Trust: sent to Queen Victoria by Flor-

ence Nightingale, 11 October 1858. https://www.royalcollection.org.uk/collection/1075240/notes-on-matters-affecting-the-health-efficiency-and-hospital-administration-of    Retrieved 27/08/2018

[195]   https://www.hubspot.com/marketing-statistics    Retrieved July 28, 2017.

[196]' Defetyer, M. A.; Russo, R.; McPartlin, P. L. 2009. The picture superiority effect in recognition memory: a developmental study using the response signal procedure. *Cognitive Development*. 24: 265–273.

[197] (Medina, John. Brain Rules (Updated and Expanded): 12 Principles for Surviving and Thriving at Work, Home, and School Pg. 192. Pear Press. Kindle Edition.)

[198] https://www.nationalmedals.org/laureates/harry-coover retrieved 24 August 2018

[199] David Atlee Phillips. 1977. The Night Watch: 25 Years of Peculiar Service. Pg. 109. New York, Atheneum.

[200] Robert Dallek, 2003. *An Unfinished Life: John F. Kennedy, 1917-1963*. Boston: Little, Brown and Company. Pgs. 363-375

[201] Irving L Janis. July 1982. Group Think 2nd Revised Edition. Pg. vii. Houghton Mifflin (Academic)

[202] Irving L Janis. 1971. Psychology Today Magazine. Pg. 84. Ziff-David Publishing.

[203] Irving L Janis. July 1982. Group Think 2nd Revised Edition. Pg. 9. Houghton Mifflin (Academic)

[204] Ray Dalio. April 2017: How to build a company where the best ideas win.
https://www.ted.com/ Retrieved 14 September 2017.

[205] Ray Dalio. April 2017: How to build a company where the best ideas win. https://www.ted.com/ Retrieved 14 September 2017.

[206] Brent Adamson. April 2017. https://hbr.org/2017/03/the-new-sales-imperative Retrieved 14 September 2017.

[207] Kotter, John (1996). *Leading Change*. Harvard Business School Press.

[208] Peter Cheverton. 2008. Key Account Management Tools And Techniques For Achieving Profitable Key Supplier Status by 4th edition Pg. 76.

[209] Brent Adamson. April 2017. https://hbr.org/2017/03/the-new-sales-imperative Retrieved 14 September 2017.

[210] Anderson, S.R. Bryson, J.M. and Crosby, B.C. 1999. Leadership for the Common Good Fieldbook. St. Paul, MN: University of Minnesota Extension Service.

[211] Len Scott. R. Gerald Hughes. 2015. *The Cuban Missile Crisis: A Critical Reappraisal*. Pg. 17. Taylor & Francis.

[212] William A. Sherden 1988. The Fortune Sellers: The Big Business of Buying and Selling Predictions. Pg. 1. John Wiley and Sons

[213] ibid Pg. 2

[214] Peter Cheverton. 2008. Key Account Management - Tools And Techniques For Achieving Profitable Key Supplier Status. 4th edition. Pg. 38. Kogan Page.

[215] Shefner-Rogers, C. L. (2006). Everett Rogers' personal journey: Iowa to Iowa. In A. Singhal, & J. W. Dearing (Eds.), Communication of innovations: A journey with Ev Rogers. Thousand Oaks, CA: Sage. Pg. 113

[216] Valente, T.; Rogers, E. 1995. The Origins and Development of the Diffusion of Innovations Paradigm as an Example of Scientific Growth. Science Communication. 16: 245–246.

[217] Singhal, A. 2016. Contributions of Everett M. Rogers to development communication and social change. *Journal of Development Communication*, 27(1): 57-68

[218] (*Rogers, Everett (16 August 2003). Diffusion of Innovations, 5th Edition. Simon and Schuster. Location 232*)

[219] Arvind Singhal, Ph.D. April 24, 2002. Introducing Professor Everett M Rogers 47th Annual Research Lecturer University of New Mexico, Albuquerque www.arvindsinghal.com Retrieved 28/7/2017

[220] Ken Blanchard. 2007. http://www.kenblanchard.com/img/pub/ignite_volume1_2007.pdf Retrieved 28/7/2017.

[221] Robert K. Merton 1996. On Social Structure and Science. The University of Chicago Press. PGs 175 – 182

[222] Everett M Rogers. 1983. Diffusions of Innovation Pg. 247. Macmillan Publishing.

[223] Charles Babbage. 1864. Passages from the Life of a Philosopher. Pg. 67. Longman and Co.

[224] Joeri Van Den Bergh, Mattias Behrer. 2013. How Cool Brands Stay Hot: Branding to Generation Y. Pg. 81. Kogan Page.

45736230R00172

Printed in Poland
by Amazon Fulfillment
Poland Sp. z o.o., Wrocław